SEA *of* DREAMERS

SEA *of* DREAMERS

Travels with Famous Ocean Explorers

PHIL TRUPP

FULCRUM PUBLISHING
GOLDEN, COLORADO

To Zachary Lee and Amy Elizabeth Price
and Julian Louis Trupp—for the wonders of new life.

Copyright © 1998 Phil Trupp
Book design by Bill Spahr
Front cover image copyright © 1998 Image Club Graphics, Inc.
Digital composite by Bill Spahr
Back cover image copyright © 1998 Woods Hole Oceanographic Institution

Library of Congress Cataloging-in-Publication Data

Trupp, Philip Z. (Philip Zbar)
    Sea of dreamers : travels with famous ocean explorers / Phil Trupp.
        p.   cm.
    Includes bibliographical references and index.
    ISBN 1-55591-290-7
    1. Underwater exploration.   2. Oceanographers—Biography.   I. Title.
GC65.T78   1998
551.46'0092'2—dc21
[b]   98–23241
                                                                              CIP

Printed in the United States of America

0 9 8 7 6 5 4 3 2 1

Fulcrum Publishing
350 Indiana Street, Suite 350
Golden, Colorado 80401-5093
(800) 992-2908 • (303) 277-1623
website: www.fulcrum-books.com
e-mail: fulcrum@fulcrum-books.com

CONTENTS

ACKNOWLEDGMENTS

Sea of Dreamers owes much to many talented people. The author is especially grateful to Bob and Charlotte Baron, Sam Scinta, Daniel Forrest-Bank, and Bill Spahr of Fulcrum Publishing, without whom this book would not be. Copyeditor Sharon DeJohn contributed a keen sense of story.

Among the scientists who gave me new ways of seeing, I am indebted to the late Ned Ostenso, former acting chief scientist of the National Oceanic and Atmospheric Administration. Ned helped guide the book from its inception and was unselfish in lending his time to even the smallest details.

Barbara Moore, head of NOAA's National Undersea Research Program, critiqued the manuscript and provided much inspiration. She was a beacon who pointed me in new directions and kept me on course.

Dr. Cindy Lee Van Dover, whose intellect and vision have forever altered my view of the sea, graciously gave insights that animate this work. She is a true original whose special gift of words will surely help bridge the gap between science and the rest of us.

The author is also grateful to Dr. Charles Hollister of Woods Hole Oceanographic Institution and the staff of WHOI. Dr. Hollister weighed in bravely on charged political ground and took a stand when others hesitated to speak.

Finally, I am moved by the support of my family, and especially Sandy, who is no stranger to the struggle of book building. Her wisdom lights these pages, and for this I offer gratitude and love.

PREFACE

The people you will meet in these pages are visionaries. Over the past half-century they have explored on and under the world's oceans, travelers in a hidden universe who have transformed our vision of the Earth. They may soon startle us with news of life thriving in the oceans of distant planets.

Here you will find their discoveries: sunken mountain ranges, alien life-forms, traces of lost civilizations, sunken ships and bars of gold, the eerie glow of drowned volcanoes.

Like their achievements, these explorers are anything but ordinary. They are in turn cantankerous, unrelentingly compulsive, brilliant, seductive. None are alike. Yet if they paused in their explorations to rally to a single idea, they might join with George Bernard Shaw in asserting that it is not only good for us to be shocked occasionally, but necessary to our understanding of the universe that we be shocked often. This they are eager to do.

They offer many wonders, glimpses of the unknown, and something more: a passion for truth, the universal quest that has taken them from the world's oceans to the peaks of mind and spirit.

In the end, they offer us their hearts. They show us that to search is to love and to love is to be revealed, unafraid in a realm where all is possible and dreams become reality.

Chapter One

"BOTTOMOGRAPHY"

When once it has been seen,
it will remain the most vivid memory in life.
—William Beebe

I

AS A CHILD I RECALL STANDING ON THE SHORELINE of an Atlantic beach and thinking it was like being at the edge of a world more mysterious than the dark side of the moon, more powerful than imagination—a world that shaped the grand concoction of the universe. And from the Atlantic I would return to my home overlooking the inner harbor of Baltimore, to our balcony above the wide, oily skin of the harbor. I watched, fascinated, as the big ships moved over the surface, silently retreating from a world at war. To me they were wanderers from that mystical ocean I always carried around inside my head.

At night I turned to the sky, using my wobbly tin telescope. The unknown both above and below drew me, sea and sky intimately joined, but I always returned to the shore of the Atlantic to ponder what was out there hidden beneath the gray mass rolling away to the horizon. Someday I would know the truth. I would touch the unseen, put it in to words, and make it live in others' minds and imaginations. Two decades later, I would begin to realize my ambition.

I became actively involved with the "ocean world" in the early 1970s as a journalist, diver, and explorer, a combination that provided "wings" with which to roam the planet. Over a period of two decades, I traveled from the oil rigs and shipwrecks of the North Atlantic to the warm coral reefs of the Caribbean and Latin America. By 1978, I was leading the first team of American divers into the waters around Castro's Cuba. The following year, I headed the first team of journalists to live and work on the sea bottom in America's only underwater habitat,

Hydro-Lab I. From there I went on to the Pacific, the Indian Ocean, the Java Sea, and the Coral Sea. But it was in Hydro-Lab, living the life of a "man-fish," that my perceptions truly changed. It occurred to me that my true obsession was with the outlines of the submarine universe. I wanted to see and to understand the size and shape of the floor of the sea, this virtually unexplored planet within a planet.

Hydro-Lab was located at the head of Salt River Submarine Canyon, off the north coast of St. Croix in the U.S. Virgin Islands. The canyon itself was a deep V-shaped gash leading into the open Caribbean Sea. Isolated from the world above, I fell in love with the submarine geology. I loved the majesty of it and was awed by the power of the limestone cliffs covered with living coral. Here was a place preserved in time, a place young, wild, almost prehistoric.

Day and night we would venture out into our sunken "Grand Canyon," leaving our little yellow cylindrical habitat far behind. Because our bodies were saturated with nitrogen we could dive very deep for a very long time, defying the ordinary laws of physics. We were, in every sense, citizens of the deep. The world "up there," the world of sun and sky, was now deadly territory. If we rose to the surface without an arduous sixteen hours of decompression, the nitrogen would bubble out into our blood like uncorked champagne. Locked in the deep, we sensed our vulnerability in the vastness of our surroundings.

The canyon was in every way otherworldly. I would swim down the sloping bottom to the precipice, where the cliff face dropped a mile straight down into the abyss. Weightless as a space traveler, I would hover above the void, staring through a column of thick, clear liquid. The water changed color from emerald to cobalt to black. Hundreds of feet below, the slanting rays of the sun were swallowed in the darkness, the black diamond of the deep sparkling at the bottom of the world.

I would sometimes venture out at night, alone, against all the rules. I heard the sounds of sand hissing along the bottom, and the click-click snapping of shrimp; there were strange random noises, grunts and whistles, which to this day I cannot identify. In the perfect darkness I felt the walls of the canyon looming on either side, imagined the face of the cliff at the foot of the canyon, how the bottom vanished into deeper territory and spread out from there. I have never felt more alone or more challenged. More than anything I wanted to know the shape of this terra incognita. I invented a word for it: "bottomography": the art (and occasional science) of describing the geography of the world's seas and oceans much as a geologist sees the shape, form, and meaning of the Earth's high and dry territories.

It was in Hydro-Lab that I discovered Maurice Ewing, a man who shared this obsessive desire to "see" what the basement of the planet looked like. Ewing had an obsessive vision of a new underwater world waiting to be explored. My introduction to Ewing occurred through the pages of a biography I had brought with me into Hydro-Lab, *The Floor of the Sea* (Little, Brown, 1974), by former *New Yorker* staff writer William Wertenbaker. Although I never met Ewing, I shared his singular vision, and I did have one advantage: I was living on the bottom while Ewing, a geologist, had to view it via crude instruments while steaming over the surface.

I turned the pages, spellbound, imagining the voyage he launched in 1966: port of embarkation, Dakar, on the west coast of Africa north of Sudan; destination, Hudson Canyon, New York. It was a 3,000-mile-wide swath of mystery. Soundings had been made, but mostly these were rough sketches, vague maps with many of the major features missing.

Ewing's passion was almost exclusively confined to rough-and-tumble fieldwork. A rumpled, Nemo-driven geophysicist, he could be brusque and impatient, his intensity traced line-by-line over a rugged face. His big hands suggested the life of a third mate at the bitter end of a career at sea. And in many ways this white-haired professor, who held down the Higgins Professorship of Geology at Columbia University and later founded America's leading geophysical think tank, the Lamont-Doherty Geophysical Laboratory, was a volatile mix of ancient mariner and scientific loose cannon. He could not be pigeonholed, couldn't be pinned down to place or time. He was a teacher and an explorer of world-class stature, yet he enjoyed it when his students called him by his incongruously ordinary nickname, "Doc."

If I shared his passion to "see" the ocean bottom, I also identified with his wanderlust. Waiting wasn't his style. He was fond of flying off to obscure ports-of-call, hopping onto any available ship (never mind if it was a rust bucket) and making his way across the surface of the sea—any sea—flinging dynamite over the rail to gauge the ratio of depth by measuring how long it took for the echo of the explosion to bounce off the bottom and register on his sounding devices.

The late Ned A. Ostenso, former head of the National Sea Grant College Program, was a close friend of Ewing (and at one time my science advisor). "He was a powerful and very forceful figure," Ostenso recalled. "An absolute workaholic who expected everyone to emulate his habits, which wasn't easy." This was quite a statement from an exacting man who was once acting chief scientist of the National Oceanic and Atmospheric Administration.

Scholars credit Ewing with "institutionalizing" ocean data, gathering massive amounts of it, and producing wonderful, dedicated students. He could be hardheaded and not-so-tactfully tough-minded. Yet he was open, however grudgingly, to new and even radical ideas. For instance, when the concept of sea floor spreading emerged in the early 1960s, he was skeptical. To him, the notion of continents adrift on huge subsea "tectonic plates" was "simpleminded." To counter the theory, he published a paper on sedimentation concluding that sea floor spreading wasn't possible. Ostenso confronted him and prepared a rebuttal, which he submitted to Ewing as a professional courtesy.

"Oh, he was furious," Ostenso told me. "How did I have the gall to contradict him? That sort of thing."

Ostenso's paper was published. It was followed by others that backed the spreading theory, which was cutting-edge science at the time. Ewing continued to argue against it; it just didn't make sense to him because it was too "easy." Yet several years and many voyages later, he became a convert and used Ostenso's data to make his points.

"He was always big enough to change his mind," Ostenso said.

In my more romantic Hydro-Lab moods, I imagined my kinship with Ewing, living with big seas and making them my laboratory, shouldering my way through what Kipling called the "roaring sapphire thereunder." I admired his determination, as evident in "the Ewing look": small blue eyes behind silver-rimmed spectacles; a mane of white hair blown across a stolid, weathered face; big hands rough from years of hauling tackle and lines and hanging on tight when the seas rose up to snatch away his sounders. Until his death from a stroke in May 1974, a few days before his sixty-eighth birthday, he consistently pushed himself. He was sturdy and tough enough to shape a new vision of what the world was really like, despite the frightening rebuffs of angry seas.

Ewing insisted that the bottom of the world, nearly three-quarters of the planet, held the clues to larger mysteries of existence and the unseen. He was amazingly gentle in stating his ideas but noticeably frantic (some said "desperate") in his search for raw data. When he attended conferences at which distinguished oceanographers com-

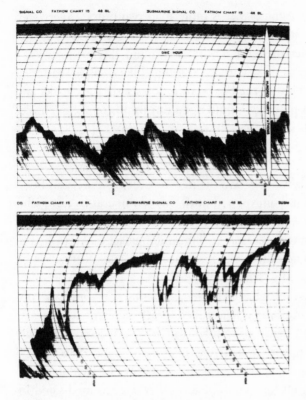

Graphic images recorded in 1932 off the coast of Massachusetts showing a fairly irregular sea bottom. Earlier soundings used lead lines or explosive devices. *Photo courtesy National Oceanic and Atmospheric Administration.*

plained about the unreliable ways of the early depth-sounders, Ewing often infuriated them by suggesting that they ought to learn how to handle ordinary tools.

Ewing carried the evidence of his persistence with him into what was then a very genteel scientific arena. He walked with a limp, the result of being swept overboard during a winter gale in 1954, and he could be as moody as the sea that had damaged his body. He was stooped and tired-looking, and he kept very late hours. He seldom slept for long stretches at a time; it was his style to grab a few minutes of sleep here and there in his frenetic schedule.

Charles Drake, a prominent geophysical researcher, tells a story of his student days, when Ewing joined his research vessel at Nassau, Grand Bahama. He says "Doc" appeared utterly exhausted, so the younger Drake volunteered for the first watch, allowing Ewing to catch some sleep before standing the second. But Drake allowed him to sleep through it. A few hours before dawn, Ewing exploded onto the deck, enraged. "Don't ever do that again!" he roared. It was his ethic never to delegate his share of the unavoidable grunt work.

Three-quarters of the planet is more than two miles underwater, and "Doc" thought it absolute folly to believe that the remaining one-quarter of Earth's features, the world of sun and sky, held the only significant expressions of scientific meaning. Like a clever writer of science fiction, he plotted the big picture, foreseeing the shocks and thrills and twists of plot that would open our minds to the dynamics of the oceanic landscape.

II

Ewing's real-world laboratory was the new territory of the ocean floor, virtually unknown and unexplored until this century. Even now, after the halcyon days of research between 1950 and 1980, it is still virtually unknown, a field in which yesterday's immutable fact is overturned in a day or a week. In no other field of science is the rate of discovery so rapid, so normal—and so frustrating.

Roaming freely through Salt River Submarine Canyon, I was obsessed by the big questions: What unseen forces shape the continents? How are mountain ranges built? What causes islands to spring to life and suddenly disappear? Which central forces cause earthquakes? Strange to recall that at the beginning of the century we lived in a kind of geologic dark age. Our curiosity, such as it was, seemed sated by Jules Verne. We had no idea that twentieth-century reality would leap so far ahead of fiction and give us a vision so astonishing, revolutionary, ever changing.

Fifty years ago, ocean science was so insular that everyone knew everyone else in the field. Today there are international conferences focusing on every aspect of the seas. A few years ago, it could be said that at least half of our geophysical knowledge of the oceans was collected by Ewing and his sea-going assistants. Today the little community of outsiders has become a scientific industry, now temporarily becalmed by the prevailing apathy in public policy. When the time is right, there will be a revival, perhaps an explosion, of Ewingesque hunger for the big questions.

Ewing's historic 1966 mission off the African coast aboard his research vessel, *Vema*, involved theory, technology, and the payoff of hard work. *Vema*'s low-tech echo sounder traced eerie black lines across a rolling ribbon of paper. To the determined explorer of the unseen, this machine was a kind of lie detector; it would reveal the truth in black and white, truth being the only thing that counts in the sea.

At the time of the *Vema* mission, only a handful of civilian topographic maps of the North Atlantic existed, and these focused almost entirely on the contours of the Atlantic west of Bermuda. Mainstream scientists swore that the method of charting the sea floor was so primitive it couldn't even be called a science, and they weren't far wrong.

But *Vema,* steaming at full speed, was about to reveal a landscape so striking, so primal, that our vision of the planet would be forever altered. At night, while my fellow Hydro-Lab aquanauts slept, I poured over these tracings, imagining myself hiking over this amazing unseen world.

A few miles off the coast of Africa the picture of the Atlantic began to take shape. Imagine watching the black lines moving across the rolling paper coil and witnessing the following images: The continental slope falls into the deep over a series of volcanic peaks that rise nearly to the surface. The peaks are sharp as talons, prehistoric and wonderfully preserved in the airless environment of the deep. Suddenly we are looking through a window of time. This is Earth as it was before the dawn of life; it is rugged, unforgiving, the mountains rising out of the ancient sediments, reaching for the sky and falling back along steep, razorlike scarps. And beneath these mountains loom the shadows of even sharper peaks, buried under eons of sediment; they shimmer with possibilities. How old are these buried mountains? Were they ever exposed to the atmosphere? How did the more prominent mountains described on *Vema's* profiler emerge from the deep sea and overwhelm the older ones?

In the unsheltered Atlantic, the mountain ranges abruptly give way to a gradual slope of featureless bottom. This is an emptiness unknown on the Earth's surface, a void that stretches toward the Cape Verde Islands and commands hundreds of thousands of square miles. Subsequent soundings will show features unseen by *Vema.* For the *Vema* crew, the sounder only hints at a buried skeleton of old mountains vanished long before any living creature could see or touch them.

Again the bottomography changes. At about 14,000 feet a needlelike spike is traced on the profiler. It is a near-vertical cliff cresting at a peak several thousand feet above the sea floor. On the far side the angle is equally sharp, and there are deep layers of sediment ponded at the base. Another rise begins, shooting past a second line of cliffs, and dropping thousands of feet to the base of what appears to be a dead volcanic mountain, a guyot or "sea mount." The top of the volcano is gently rounded; it had once jutted above sea level where the eroding action of wind and waves flattened the peak. This is the massive geologic platform of the Cape Verde Islands.

West of the islands the bottomography dives into deeper water and rises again on a range of prehistoric cliffs and valleys; it is only a glimmer, a subtle suggestion of the spectacular features that lie ahead.

The island chain recedes and the sounder outlines a rough basement and layers of sediment. No one has ever seen these features. To those watching the black line traces, it must have been very much like discovering a new galaxy, the shape of which could hardly be imagined.

I carried these images in my head during my daily Hydro-Lab excursions. The geology of the cliffs came alive, as if whispering of the past and future. Carefully, lovingly, I wandered over Ewing's black-and-white revelations.

About 600 miles off the African coast a new range of contours rises out of the shadows. The sounder reveals row upon row of foothills shaped like triangular shark's teeth and split by deep gorges and valleys. These craggy peaks are the foothills of the planet's largest mountain range, the Mid-Ocean Ridge, which splits the Atlantic in two. From Cape Horn northward, the Ridge snakes between Africa and Europe and on to Iceland, where a massive plateau rises to interrupt the flowing, fractured features. North of Iceland the mountains rise again before diving beneath the polar ice cap. The Ridge continues for more than 34,000 miles, through the Arctic Ocean, spilling into the vault of the Pacific and the Indian Ocean.

A small "sounding boat" using a lead line to measure subsurface features. *Photo courtesy National Oceanic and Atmospheric Administration.*

I imagined flying above the sea, all the water drained away, looking down on the scale of a mountain range that challenges our concepts of mass. It spreads east and west across more than 600 miles of Atlantic Ocean bottom, nearly one-third of the oceanic basin. A Rift Valley—a jagged gash thousands of feet deep—splits the mountain range down the middle. This Rift Valley is large enough to swallow many of the world's terrestial mountains.

This meandering monolith is crisscrossed by deep horizontal faults, any one of which would conceal countless Grand Canyons. Who would have imagined that such geology existed? No science-fiction writer could have invented it. The Ridge soars to peaks above 10,000 feet. Here and there the mountain peaks break the surface of the sea, forming the Azores and Iceland, then plunge back into the darkness.

*****

Line by line, over many voyages, Ewing brought us the shape of the world's seas and oceans. But his view of the Atlantic as an elongated, sinuous cavity extending north and south nearly 7,000 miles is locked in my imagination. The Mid-Ocean Ridge is so formidable that it blocks the flow of cold Arctic water. Since *Vema* we have discovered the Atlantic's astounding deeps, such as the Puerto Rico Trench, which drops more than 27,000 feet below the abyssal plain. And while this may seem very deep, subsequent excursions into the world's largest ocean, the Pacific, have revealed trenches that plunge seven miles into nowhere. We have discovered the Pacific "Ring of Fire," the multitude of live subsea volcanoes, trenches, and fracture zones that rock Asia, Japan, and the West Coast of the Americas.

The Atlantic is a great arena of volcanism. Thanks to Ewing we can now see to the north the Great Meteor Sea Mount, a volcano thought to be long extinct. It is sixty-eight miles in diameter and 13,000 feet high, its summit the size of Rhode Island. In the mid-1960s, Ewing could only speculate on the history of this and other "dead" volcanoes strung along the Atlantic sea floor.

All along the Mid-Ocean Ridge are earthquake zones. Little was known in 1966 of what would follow: the revolutionary theory of "plate tectonics," the continents floating on a sea of magma, the plates expanding, colliding, and reshaping the face of the planet.

Ewing's voyages have brought us a long way from the beginning of the century, when all was mystery and conjecture. Each mile traced by *Vema* stripped away the darkness.

III

Ewing's legacy looms large. A few years after his death, plans were made to inspect the Mid-Ocean Ridge close up, using the most sophisticated submersibles available. They would dive to depths of 10,000 feet below the Atlantic surface, an undersea adventure then equal to landing on the moon. French and American scientists planned the French-American Mid-Ocean Undersea Study, known simply as FAMOUS.

The project got under way in 1971, with the French making use of the submersible *Archimede* and the United States working with *Alvin*. There were problems with both. *Archimede* had the proper depth capability but was large and hard to maneuver. *Alvin*, the interior of which is often described as a "Swiss watch," bottomed out at just under 6,000 feet.

A year later, *Alvin* was outfitted with a new titanium hull that allowed dives to nearly 12,000 feet. The French called on a streamlined submersible, *Cyana*, known as the "diving saucer."

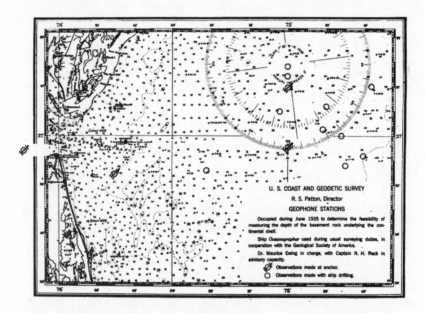

The first sonic map recorded by Maurice Ewing in 1935. Ewing used explosives to measure and plot segments of the bottom. *Photo courtesy National Oceanic and Atmospheric Administration.*

Modern digital images of submerged volcanoes off the coast of Hawaii. The mountains rise 6,000–9,000 feet from the sea floor. *Photo courtesy National Oceanic and Atmospheric Administration.*

The explorations centered on a sixty-square-mile area south of the Azores Islands, west of Gibraltar. It was a site already well known and documented. Automatic cameras were lowered and came back with pictures of lava frozen in the deep. Seismographs recorded continuous small tremors in the Rift Valley.

When *Archimede* made its initial dive in 1973, it scraped a rock wall nearly 300 feet high and struggled in a swifter-than-anticipated current. The submersible completed seven dives into the valley and proved it was possible to maneuver, collect samples, and make photographs.

A year later, *Alvin* and *Cyana* joined *Archimede* for the culmination of FAMOUS. They dove beyond 8,000 feet, recording huge lava formations and leaving little doubt that Earth's interior is being re-shaped from the Rift Valley, generating ever-newer sea floors as the plates move about.

The landscape confirmed Ewing's earlier visions of a rugged pre-historic terrain, torn by fracture zones. Clearly the sea floor was spreading, re-creating itself almost continuously. The scientists found a wide spectrum of minerals along the spreading zones, including manganese oxide, a source of nickel and cobalt. There were lead, zinc, gold, and silver, a constantly renewable source of riches. A story in *Time* magazine exclaimed, "The sea floor, mankind's newest frontier, may well turn out to be a major source of raw material for tomorrow's world."

"Bottomography" still resonates. As a child I had been lured by visions of the ocean floor, but had only science fiction as a guide. The surface blocked my passion for the imagined mysterious landscape. But life in Hydro-Lab and Ewing's vision changed my world. Now the hidden planet was open to me. I wondered how I would shape my place in it.

Chapter Two

"LIFE UNDER PRESSURE"

That which is far off and exceeding deep,
Who can find it out?

—Ecclesiastes

I

THIS QUESTION, AMONG OTHERS, WAS ON MY MIND when I was invited to visit an obscure island in the Bahamas owned by a man who invented Hydro-Lab and the mini-submarines that flash across the screen in James Bond movies.

Lee Stocking Island is tucked away in the Exuma chain of the southeastern Bahamas. Its owner is a true genius, one of those quietly important people who advise presidents, juggle diversified empires, and surprise the world with their originality. But in his heart of hearts, my host was a man in love with the sea and excited in a hardheaded way by its possibilities. In short, he was a poetic believer in discovery, adventure, and industry.

John H. Perry, Jr., then chairman of Perry Oceanographics, the parent company of Perry Submarine Builders, Perry Ocean Engineering, and Perry Ocean Services, was a powerful force in the realm of exploration. At the time of my visit to Lee Stocking, he was devoted to the development of solar/hydrogen energy systems, biological research, and the use of mini-subs and robots. His empire combined the hopeful with a hard-core profit motive.

With Perry's personal pilot, Charlie Weeks, I headed out of West Palm Beach aboard the company's twin-engine plane. Perry was waiting for us at Lee Stocking. The Straits of Florida rolled below, the sea golden in the sun with the white filmy water breaking over the shoals. Farther out, where the volcanic Bahama Banks rise up out of a mile-deep canyon of water, a mist—the gossamer "Bermuda Curtain"—clouded the face of the sea.

I recalled the time our crew got lost flying out here. We had just penetrated the haze when our compasses began disagreeing with one another. Radio bands were a hiss of white noise. We dropped below the clouds searching for land, but the sea was starkly empty and streaked with whitecaps. Forty-five minutes overdue, and very low on fuel, I thought: *We're running out of time. We're going to ditch.* I wondered who among us would make it.

We were lucky. A tiny spit of sand appeared on the horizon a long way away. When we finally closed in we could see it was almost pure bush, yet it was the most welcome sight on Earth. There was an empty, sun-stunned airstrip. The runway was baked to dust and chocked by foliage. The moment we touched down the radio cleared up and the compasses quit disagreeing.

I recalled the incident to Charlie Weeks. He was one of the few pilots who would soberly acknowledge the existence of odd events in the "Bermuda Triangle."

"Novices get lost out here," he said. "If you aren't instrument-trained you'll fly in circles." But what about our compasses, the loss of radio contact?

"Weather," he replied. "Warm water, cold air. Makes for strange happenings."

Weeks had met Perry in 1943, when both were serving as Army Air Corps pilots ferrying aircraft in the European theater during World War II. After the war, Perry hired Weeks to take charge of the company's airplanes and to manage its real estate holdings. The real estate share of the Perry empire was not inconsiderable; his father had discovered Palm Beach before anybody had ever heard of the place, and the younger Perry had continued in the acquisitive mode. I asked Charlie if he could sum up his boss in a word.

"Innovative," Weeks replied.

Perry greeted us on the white runway that cut across the eastern flank of the island. He was a medium-sized man, who appeared small in his floppy blue shorts, a worn polo shirt, and an impeccable Bahamian-style sombrero that shaded his face. I had expected someone taller, more physically commanding, but when he shook my hand his persona changed. Perry didn't apply one of those power-grips, those painful and infuriating bone-crushers meted out by ordinary men struggling with their masculinity. He generated an amazing intensity and plugged directly into my circuits—one explorer greeting another in the middle of nowhere.

"You're sleeping on the boat," he announced unceremoniously in a kind of sharp, sergeant-major voice. It was a voice strangely insistent, very clear and deliberate, as if each syllable had been weighed in advance. All business, no downtime.

"Weather's knocking around," Perry went on as Charlie Weeks and I piled into his little green golf cart for the ride to the main buildings. "Don't mean to be pushy," he said. But he made it clear that if I wanted to spend time with him in his personal undersea habitat, Hydro-Lab II, it was now or never.

Weeks jumped out at the main building and we drove on toward the dive locker. Perry explained the plan. He would launch one of his mini-subs, the *Ocean Hunter,* and run out around the eastern point of the island where Hydro-Lab II lay thirty feet below the surface on its ballast slab, near the undersea drop-off. He had placed it on the seabed in the early 1970s to be used as a movable scientific tool, but it was often used for a little rest and relaxation.

As Perry spoke it struck me that here was the truly self-contained man, a substantial personality without pretension, and he had achieved great things. It was impressive that he'd purchased the undeveloped Lee Stocking Island with three partners for a mere $100,000.

"When I came here in the late 1950s," he recalled, "it was like moving into another century. I thought: *'This is what Fletcher Christian and his boys found at Pitcairn.'*"

Over the years he carved an on-the-edge scientific laboratory out of rough, scrubby bush, quite an accomplishment even for a man who had achieved wealth and stature. Yet there was no condescension, no pomposity. He treated me as if we had known each other forever. It's the sea, I thought, the great leveler; it diminishes the egos of those who come to grips with it and turns us into eager children of wonder.

The dive locker was a painted outbuilding, a slave to the sun and wind. It was stocked with worn aqualungs, regulators, black rubber fins, masks, faded wetsuits, and mounds of dented lead weights. Obviously this was no boutique setup. The air inside was close, fetid, neopreney, strangely secondhand: the standard grunge of working dive lockers the world over.

On one wall Perry had mounted a human skeleton. A sign in big black letters dangled from its neck: I MADE TWO MISTAKES: I STAYED DOWN TOO LONG AND CAME UP TOO FAST!—a picturesque reminder of the tyrannical laws of life under pressure. When he saw me looking at it, he chuckled, "Gets the point across."

We donned wetsuits, hauled our gear over the dock, and climbed aboard the yacht/sub-tender. Tied to the stern was the streamlined two-seater submersible that wowed moviegoers in the James Bond film, *The Spy Who Loved Me*. The little submarine bobbed in our wake in clear water; it was trim and futuristic, with a missilelike bow and an acrylic upper body that allowed nearly 180 degrees of vision.

By now it was close to mid-afternoon. The sun was closing on the horizon and the sea had taken on a reddish tint. Gray and black clouds streaked the sky and the wind was rising. Light swells shouldered against our hull. Farther out we could see long whitecaps cresting and disappearing along the reef in the agitated sea.

Perry went forward to speak with his boat handlers. They were young men, handpicked and proven at sea. They shared his mission and much of the heavy lifting. Rank had been suspended as an awkward impediment to the larger mission of Lee Stocking, but they always addressed him as "Mister Perry."

At the time of my visit, Perry held a unique position in the oceans community. The voyage of the submersible *Alvin* to the grave of the *Titanic* was a spectacular success. Perry had predicted it years earlier. The discovery and exploration demonstrated the excellent use of scientific submersibles. Perry, a preeminent manufacturer of undersea vehicles, had been more successful than his giant competitors, such as General Electric, General Motors, and General Dynamics. The major companies had produced impressive undersea boats, but they were complex and very expensive. Perry built workhorses, simple machines designed for specific jobs at half the price.

He had arrived at ocean engineering in the formative years between 1950 and 1969, which saw the emergence of the Navy's ten-year plan to expand the oceanographic capabilities of academic institutions. The Soviet Union's launch of *Sputnik I* in 1957 was the platform on which scientific and military policy was reshaped. Congress had formed a special subcommittee on oceanography, and in 1961 President John F. Kennedy responded, pledging his administration to "concerted attention to our whole national effort in the basic and applied research of oceanography." A year later, Rachel Carson's *Silent Spring* (Houghton Mifflin, 1962), a book Perry saw as an ultimate truth, jolted us into awareness of environmental issues. He correctly saw all this as fertile ground for his ambitions in science and bio-engineering.

The political climate of the 1970s was receptive to generous federal involvement in the oceanic and atmospheric sciences. The Earth Science Administration was formed, and South Carolina Senator Earnest Hollings introduced a bill to create a Department of Environment and the Oceans. A seemingly endless stream of legislation created a federal presence in coastal zone management, mammal protection, marine sanctuaries, deepwater ports, fishery conservation, deep seabed mineral resources, ocean thermal energy, and promotion of American fisheries.

Perry had been a part of this buildup. He had served on federally appointed panels, was the confidant of presidents, and moved through Washington as an insider. As his contacts and power grew, so did his confidence. He made things happen, a legacy he'd adopted from an ambitious father and the industrial superhero who'd given him his first job at age eight. Henry Ford opened a Model-T dealership in Hastings, New York, Perry recalled. "Everything was in good shape, except for one thing. They were serving lemonade but there was nobody around to do it. So Ford says to me, 'Hey, young fellow. Want a job?' I was the lemonade boy. It was heaven!"

Despite Perry's influence in Washington, by the time I had arrived at Lee Stocking the political climate had chilled. The oceans were on hold. Perry was frustrated and impatient. The escalating body of ocean activity was under frontal assault. The dismantling begun under President Reagan convinced Perry that the halcyon days were over. Now it was up to private capital to prove the ocean's worth. It was a challenge he relished.

II

We edged out of the lee of the island. The escort boat began to roll. Perry kept an eye on *Ocean Hunter* bobbing in our wake. The little sub seemed very small and vulnerable.

"She's a wet sub. If she goes under we just go back and get her," Perry explained.

Hydro-Lab is visited by a Perry Cubmarine. *Photo courtesy National Oceanic and Atmospheric Administration.*

I had never been a passenger in a "wet sub." My experience was with commercial "dry subs," familiar submersible airspaces used to inspect oil pipelines, gather biological samples, and do all manner of chores on the bottom. Dry subs use ballast tanks to take them under. Wet subs, on the other hand, are designed to fill up entirely with seawater. Passengers breathe air through aqualungs. Thrusters take the place of ballast tanks and control buoyancy. It is elegantly simple. Like a shark, as long as the sub moves forward it won't sink.

Unfortunately, I had reason to be slightly uneasy about locking myself into what amounted to a sinking ship. I had spent a few years working with the Kitteridge *K-250,* a one-seat underwater blue-collar dry machine. Our little sub was cantankerous at best. To our horror, she sank one day while under tow in foul weather. I was in charge of bringing her back to the surface. Heading out to Perry's habitat I recalled that sinking. The little yellow *K-250* wallowing as water poured beneath the seal of her acrylic dome. We crowded the fantail of our work boat, helpless as our investment vanished beneath the surface with one last pathetic sigh. There were squalls all around and entering the water was hazardous. I jumped in anyway and followed the towline to the bottom. There she was, the little sub bouncing over the white sand flats. I remembered opening the dome, scrambling inside the bucking hull, and locking down. I turned on the emergency air to purge the water. I prayed the boat would rise. When it finally broached the surface, it rolled uncontrollably on the heaving sea. I looked around.

Now our work boat was swamping, and Coast Guard helicopters buzzed overhead. I had no way of knowing the Coast Guard thought we were dopers or locals retrieving "green groupers" tossed overboard from the latest busted Panamanian freighter.

Perry sensed my hesitancy and kept up a running narrative. He spoke of his alternative energy program, his determination to develop a practical hydrogen fuel cell, and about his larval lobster experiments. Lobsters had never been successfully raised in an artificial environment, yet Perry was supremely confident; he would eventually succeed, it was a matter of faith. One day, he said, Lee Stocking would be a nexus of scientific adventure, a place where researchers from around the world would find new ways to exploit the sea. If the lobster experiment worked, a remarkably cheap source of protein would be available to starving peoples.

"We'll feed the world," Perry said. "Won't be easy, but we'll make it happen."

As we rounded the island and neared the Hydro-Lab II site, the boat slowed and we slipped over the stern into the warm, clear water. We tugged on the towline and the *Ocean Hunter* floated alongside. The sub had a bullet-shaped hull and space for aqualungs and regulators. Up front was a joystick/peddle arrangement to work the diving planes; a pair of stubby "wings" positioned the sub when it was under way.

I climbed into the rear seat and adjusted my mask. Perry slid neatly behind the controls, his mask pushed up high on his forehead. My heart was pounding. I thought: *You've been wanting to do this for years, and now you're here and you'd better focus hard, concentrate on each and every detail and stow the jumpiness!* Perry pulled his mask down and stared at me over his shoulder, silently checking me out. I had the feeling he could read my mind, trace the wavy bands of nerves the way Ewing's bottom sounders traced the sea floor. Strapped into this little boat that would soon fill with water, I steadied up and focused on the extraordinary position I was in. It was proof once again that one gets what one wants, the trick being to make sure you know what it is you really want!

"All set?" Perry called over the dull wash of the beamy sea. I jammed the regulator into my mouth and gave him the okay signal: thumb and forefinger joined to make a little circle. "Here we go," he said, locking the acrylic covering along the lower portion of the hull.

I looked around. Another diver appeared. He swam to the bow and freed the towline. *Ocean Hunter* drifted away in the current. The diver gave us the okay signal and Perry signaled back. We were ready for the plunge.

The sound of our breathing was clear and brittle. Waves danced around us, painting designs on the acrylic surface. It felt as if *Ocean Hunter* was impatient to get down to the place where she felt most at home—on the bottom.

Perry reached forward and opened the sea cocks. In less than a minute the sub filled with seawater. We sank slowly into the liquid inner space. I looked toward the surface. Foam swept across the fragmented face of the sea. Except for our bubbles expanding as they drifted up to the vanished sky, there was no hint of where we had come from.

The sub's propulsion unit kicked in. There was a sudden surge of power as we "flew" over the bottom, making two or three knots, good speed for a submersible. The shadow of *Ocean Hunter* undulated like a dancer over a field of coral heads and sea fans. Basket sponges, some big enough to cradle the entire sub, loomed off the bottom bold and rotund as happy sea gods. And fish, more fish than seawater it seemed, raced ahead of us in our bow wake. We joined a school of oceanic jacks, whose big round eyes looked like black pearls set in living silver.

I melted into the surroundings as I had given myself to the canyon at St. Croix. We sailed high above the fringing reef. The adjacent sand flats spread out into the fog of invisibility. The bottom dropped away at a steep angle.

Perry cut the power and the little submarine feathered onto the bottom. Ten yards away, Hydro-Lab II commanded a field of ochre sand, eel grass, and wavy soft corals. *This is real,* I thought. *I am in the company of a man so enchanted by the sea that he has built his own subaqueous castle—the stuff of fantasy made real.*

Hydro-Lab II was at once quirky and wonderful. If I hadn't known better I might have guessed it was a prefab outbuilding or a bizarre aquarium accidently dropped overboard from a passing barge. Instead of a sleek cylindrical hull with a large round viewing port, like Hydro-Lab I, Perry's personal underwater space was a small rectangular structure propped on high steel I beams. Its peaked roof and ordinary-looking windows gave it a homey appearance. With seven feet of headroom, it was a cozy sanctuary for three divers, and it had the advantage of being portable.

Perry raised the sub's acrylic top. We unfastened our seat straps. I looked at Perry, who motioned toward the habitat. The scuba tanks would remain inside the sub. I took one last deep gulp of air from my regulator, floated out of my seat, and with a few fin-kicks glided to the slab beneath the raised floor of the habitat.

There was a "moon pool" entrance. Perry pointed upward, the signal that we should enter. I exhaled and floated straight up, my head inside the habitat, the rest of me still encased in the sea. I removed my mask. We hoisted ourselves through the moon pool, and thirty feet below the surface we shook hands again as if we'd met for the very first time.

"Welcome," Perry grinned.

We'd been through the hurried formalities on land but this was entirely different; a new land, a new code of conduct. We were transformed in some inexplicable way. Perry was more relaxed and easy in his manner. This was his personal castle beneath the sea. Inside Hydro-Lab II he was free, unfettered. Yet the ways of the world "up there" weren't completely abandoned. Even if he appeared transformed, an essential part of him remained connected to the surface; it was a part that appeared slightly aloof, even in this ethereal setting, an independent area of the brain that allowed him to remain grounded even though the "ground" was going about its business on the surface.

There were a pair of damp rattan chairs placed against the perspiring steel walls. I sat on one of them while Perry stretched out on a cot. He said he came here whenever he could. His favorite thing was to relax and listen to symphonic music played on his tape deck. Among other things, he had studied music at Yale and had never lost his fondness for it. In the undersea environment sound waves flow faster than in air and are omnidirectional. The Mozart playing in the background filled the airspace entirely; we were submerged in music.

"You know," he said, "a habitat is a technical achievement. And it's also psychological."

Indeed it is. Time loses its meaning. One naps without dreams or memory. There are no long periods of sleep. It's easy to be up before dawn, strolling through an endlessly new environment, meeting creatures you'd never dreamed of. New patterns take shape. Stay on the bottom long enough and individual creatures become recognizable, not just as angelfish or barracuda, but as characters whose quirks are familiar as those of your neighbors.

Another intriguing aspect of life under pressure is the constriction of vocal chords. Hydrostatic pressure produces a squeaky "helium voice," scientific jargon for sounding like Mickey Mouse. Once, during rough weather in St. Croix, I jostled my fellow Hydro-Lab aquanauts out of their bunks and asked them to secure their diving gear in the lockout tunnel. The moment I gave the hurried order we all burst into laughter. Mickey was exercising his generalship!

Despite the change in his voice, Perry never seemed to lose his command. Listening to him tell his story was like taking a short course in twentieth-century marine technology, blended with scientific speculation. He was also a study in Yankee persistence, a man who had taken over his father's burgeoning newspaper empire, cleverly enlarging and diversifying it with the same toughness he'd displayed as a member of the Yale boxing team. His fascination with submarines began when he flew sub patrol along the Atlantic coast during the war.

"Funny," he said. "I just got interested in how they worked."

He told about how in the early 1950s he would skin-dive and spearfish off the beach. One day while he was swimming to shore in the Bahamas with a string of speared fish, a shark picked up the blood scent and followed him in. He was unaware of being tailed until friends on shore shouted and waved. He turned to see an eight-foot-long shark skimming along in his wake, preparing to move in on the fish, Perry, or both.

"I turned around and tried to shoot the damned thing. Instead I shot myself in the hand. Now the water was full of my own blood. So I figured I'd better build my own sub and go after him."

Just how he intended to go after sharks with a submarine was never quite clear. Yet that incident excited a profound chain reaction in a man who was an incorrigible "tinkerer" in an age when the best minds spoke of splitting the atom. Construction began on a plywood and fiberglass hull in the backyard of his Palm Beach home.

"It was a dismal failure," he said. "A cross between a kayak and a blimp. I couldn't get it to go down. You build a boat that's *supposed* to sink and it won't. Well, I learn quickly. I hauled it to the dump and started over."

Like many people who set out to understand the sea, he became obsessive. He worked weekends and nights, juggling the family empire and his sub-building hobby.

His next version of a submarine worked, after a fashion. He had learned about internal pressure hulls and external flooding methods.

The little boat ran on battery power, and when it was finished he hauled it to the Florida inland waterway. It submerged to about twenty feet. On the way up, however, he rammed the bow of a fishing boat. He threw open the hatch and called to the fisherman.

"You okay?"

"No problem," came the reply.

But later that evening Perry received an unexpected telephone call from the Coast Guard. They told him the fishing boat sank and they had to haul it in. They sent him a bill for eighty-three dollars. He sent it to his insurance company, which canceled all his insurance—house, car, everything.

Perry is one of those people who push harder when circumstances are pushing him. He hired an engineer to work out stress figures on a "real" pressure hull. He was convinced there was money to be made in commercial submarines. By the late 1950s, he was in touch with the Woods Hole Oceanographic Institution and a man whose name was later immortalized on the world's most famous sub, *Alvin*.

"Al Vine was at Woods Hole," Perry told me. "He was very intrigued by the possibilities. I had a commercial sub for hire, and in 1959 Al paid a charter fee to use the boat for whale-watching off Cape Cod."

But the whale-watching wasn't much of a success. The weather turned nasty and the whales headed in the opposite direction. No matter. The possibility of using the sub intrigued the press. The "Today" show called and suddenly Perry was a media darling.

Nationwide visibility helped him promote the concept of the practical submarine workhorse: easy to lease, up to any job. Encouraged, he went to the Navy with a new design capable of working at 600 feet. The Navy engineers studied it and tossed it back at him. "Keep working and let us discover you," they said.

"I was insulted," Perry confessed. Though he wouldn't admit it at the time, the little jab inspired him to push harder.

A few years later, in 1966, tragedy led to a big break. An Air Force bomber had crashed in the sea off Palomares, Spain, dumping a live hydrogen bomb onto the sea bottom. The same Navy people who had brushed him off were now on the phone hoping Perry had a small submersible capable of bomb hunting. By this time he'd built his fourth sub, the *PC-4*, with a depth range of 600 feet. The little boat was flown to the site of the crash and soon found the wreckage of the plane, which in turn led directly to the errant bomb. This time the entire world was aware that a small, odd-looking undersea boat had helped avert a potential nuclear disaster.

Again Perry became a media darling. He appeared on the television shows "To Tell the Truth" and "I've Got a Secret," promoting his appearances by touring Manhattan in a mini-sub on a flatbed truck.

"That settled it," Perry said. "I decided to go into ocean engineering."

By 1970, Perry Oceanographics was in business and Perry was in touch with Edwin Link, inventor of the commercial flight simulator. Perry wanted to build a "lockout" submarine, a vessel that would ferry divers to a given site and allow them to swim out of a pressurized tunnel to work on the bottom. The result was *Deep Diver,* one of the most useful—and successful—undersea vehicles ever built.

In 1967, President Lyndon B. Johnson had appointed Perry to the biggest federal marine think tank ever assembled. The Marine Science Commission (later known as the Stratton Commission) set about designing what amounted to a "wet NASA." The idea seemed perfect at the time. The space program was blossoming, "technology transfer" was a popular buzz term, and Cousteau, the romantic "Pasha," was gaining a wide popular audience.

Dreams of a "wet NASA." In this artist's rendition, divers explore the sea supported by a mother ship and housed in a sophisticated habitat. *Photo courtesy National Oceanic and Atmospheric Administration.*

Cousteau had built Continental Shelf Station-I (Conshelf-I), a boilerlike habitat anchored forty feet off the island of Pomegues, near Marseilles. One of his longtime divers, Albert Falco, called it *Diogenes,* after the truth-seeking Greek philosopher who lived in a tub. Meanwhile, Navy Commander George F. Bond worked up detailed plans for a series of similar habitats and Link established a Florida-based research center, Harbor Branch Foundation. Link was testing submersibles to work with teams living beneath the sea. Yet for all of America's know-how and energy, it was the Pasha's nonstop popularizing that excited the world.

Perry was less romantic. His submarines were pragmatic inventions that made a fine profit. His competitors, giant companies such as General Electric, General Dynamics, Reynolds Aluminum, and Rockwell International, were turning out big, sophisticated Nemo machines that leased at $15,000 a day. Perry stuck to his knitting, building smaller, work-specific vessels operating at practical depths of 400 to 600 feet. Submarines such as Reynolds's *Aluminaut* were capable of much greater depths and carried large crews. Ironically, the large corporations seemed motivated more by Cousteau's visionary proclamations than by the mundane demands of stockholders who were seeking profits.

But bigger didn't equal better. Perry's competitors had miscalculated. They were still thinking "wet NASA" at a time when federal funds were being siphoned off to support the Vietnam War.

Cousteau, too, seemed to miss the point. He continued to be intoxicated by the hyperbolic "maybes" of ocean exploration. It was only a matter of time, he believed, before the seas would be lit by underwater habitats strung along the continental shelf. He spoke of whole cities beneath the waves, submerged Atlantises.

Perry remained steadfastly pragmatic. He had grown up in a world of finance and industry; entrepreneurship was a time-honored pursuit. Economic reality and the profit motive were the twin sisters of his success, and he produced more commercial submarines than anyone in the world.

His work with the cabinet-level commission chaired by Julius Stratton, president emeritus of the Massachusetts Institute of Technology, helped produce five volumes, *Our Nation and the Sea.* It had the appeal of Cousteau's adventurousness, a blend of science and romance, and an ambitious proposal to create a "law of the sea." But Perry's own vision was more focused than the conclusions spelled out in the Stratton Commission report.

"Look at the ocean out there," he said, motioning toward one of the big square ports of Hydro-Lab II. "It's not worth anything unless you can *do* something with it."

Despite the public appeal of exploration, Perry was convinced of the need to balance science, technology, risk taking, and profit. His dedication had been spelled out in what had to be the ultimate profit-sharing venture, "National Dividend Plan." Its premise was that the government should cut taxes on business and capital gains, and suspend growth for three to five years, enough time to bring the federal budget into balance. Savings would be placed in escrow accounts, out of which registered voters would receive a quarterly payout: a "dividend." The plan would make virtually every American a "shareholder" in the Gross Domestic Product. Politicians would be voted in or out based on their performance as it affected the dividend. It was a reflection of Perry's belief that nothing good happens unless there's a payoff. Presidents from Johnson to Carter had reviewed the plan and had passed it off as impractical. This did not sit well with the forceful, never-flinching pragmatist. Inside Hydro-Lab II, in the incongruous surround of the sea, he ruminated over details of the plan, dropped names of congressmen who believed in it. Why not give it a try? Who had a better track record in challenging endeavors? It was all true. But for some reason his National Dividend Plan did not resonate for me at five fathoms.

"When I got in this business," Perry said, "I had eight multibillion dollar companies competing with me. They built these huge machines and wanted to lease them at tens of thousands of dollars a day. Hell!— I could produce something for less working at the edge of the continental shelf, where most of the action is. And my subs leased for twelve *hundred* a day!"

Perry's biggest submersible was built for the Brazilian government. This ambitious "Cubmarine" (Perry's trademark name) was capable of supporting a crew of five at depths of 2,000 feet. It was a business coup and a scientific success, a happy anomaly.

Those were heady days for Perry. He was making big bucks where big bucks were hard to come by. He had successfully transferred his adventurous aviator personality into a whole new realm. In the 1930s, when his father was building a newspaper empire, the young Perry was dispatched with his biplane to negotiate contracts and scope out new opportunities. A flying businessman was cutting-edge stuff in those days. Now he had shifted his edge to another order of magnitude. John H. Perry, Jr., was making a fortune in an area that most people thought of as pure fantasy.

At one point Perry had seventeen submersibles working the North Sea oil fields. The lease rates were profitable, even if the jobs were mundane. Perry Cubmarines were busy laying pipelines, digging undersea trenches. Off Greenland a Cubmarine was used to tie a line around a wrecked helicopter. (A Perry vehicle was also used to locate a lost submarine near Talamora, in the Azores.) One job called for a Cubmarine to inspect the inside of a pipeline 1,000 feet underground. The pipeline carried water from the French Alps to Marseilles. There wasn't sufficient space for the vehicle to turn around, so it was forced to *back out* over several miles.

At one point Perry was approached by several U.S. intelligence agencies. The assignment: Build a 105-foot-long vessel for spy purposes.

"Spy purposes?" I asked.

He laughed, his voice high and echoing inside the Lab. Behind him a long, silvery barracuda passed by the window.

"I'll tell you the truth," he said. "That damned project was so hush-hush. To this day I have no idea what it was about."

The very idea seemed to violate Perry's own pragmatic need to know.

His success with submarines evolved into robotics and the engineering of designs for unmanned remote-controlled vehicles (ROVs). It was another breakthrough. His ROVs could dive to 20,000 feet and were used to retrieve the nose cones of Army missiles. And robots could stay under practically forever, at costs well below manned operations. Perry was at the top of his game. Combined with the Cubmarine operations and the new ROVs, Perry Oceanographics at its peak sustained a payroll of 150 employees.

We sat silently for a time, taking in the peace and remoteness of the surrounding hydrosphere. The walls of Hydro-Lab II seemed to melt away. Perry's words blurred.

Immersion provides a magical tissue. Moods and emotions are transmitted in oddly disjointed ways. Thinking becomes a matter of piecing together fragments. It is calming, and I recalled the same sense of peace I had experienced during my mission in Hydro-Lab I. In my diary I had written the following: "I am not conscious of time, only light and shade. ... People in isolation tend to wake up earlier each day, and if they are comfortable are given to feelings of euphoria."

I was wrapped in the same comfortable, womblike feelings, but after a while I sensed that Perry was growing agitated. Even in the light-headedness of his underwater castle, he made sure to get his points across. He began pacing, talking rapidly in the high-pitched undersea voice that generally reduces the most serious subjects to the level of trivia. Not so with Perry. His energy transcended the laws of pressure and depth. Having constructed four habitats, he concluded they were the most expensive housing units ever built. By comparison, the pyramids of ancient Egypt were bargain-basement items.

"You can't imagine the enormous expense of holding this thing down," he said. "These walls are one-inch-thick steel. Got two tons of lead under there. So take a guess. How much did it cost?"

I made some wild guess based on what I knew about Hydro-Lab I. I was way off.

"A thousand dollars a foot," he said. "You see, unless there's a profit motive there's no point even thinking about living in the sea. Cousteau had this thing about whole colonies. Why would anyone want to do that?"

Cousteau had later turned less than enthusiastic about his much-touted "city beneath the sea." Unlike Perry, he had downplayed the costs and concluded that the sea was "too demanding" an environment for habitation.

Perry told me he had taken a financial hit on Hydro-Lab I when it was stationed off Freeport, Grand Bahama, in the 1950s. Forty scientific investigations had been carried out over five years at a lease rate of $500 a day.

"A break-even deal at best," he sighed.

Hydro-Lab I had been built under Navy contract at Perry's new facility in Riviera Beach. Link was involved in the negotiations. George Bond was attached as the Navy's diving guru. The project, extremely sophisticated in its day, appealed to Perry's unstoppable urge to tinker.

"There were a lot of what-ifs," he said. "A terrific challenge."

Link believed the eight-by-sixteen-foot structure should be tethered to the bottom by guy wires. Perry insisted it be anchored to a ballast slab. Link's view prevailed.

"We built it and put it in place off Riviera Beach," Perry explained. "It was okay for a while. Then a storm hit. The thing reacted like a blimp ripped off its moorings. We had to chase it downstream for miles!"

After that, Hydro-Lab I grew "feet."

Perry didn't think twice when the National Oceanic and Atmospheric Administration came along and offered to buy it.

"I practically gave it away."

III

NOAA took possession of Hydro-Lab I, spent $1.5 million sprucing it up, and moved it to Fairleigh Dickinson University's West Indies Lab at St. Croix. But soon came the money crunch. Congress wondered if there was enough scientific work to justify the Lab's existence; it cost about $3,500 a day to support a crew of four in what Dr. William Shane, the hyperbaric physician at Fairleigh Dickinson, described as a "pup tent in the woods." With three bunks, primitive radio gear, a sink with instant boiling water, a handheld shower head, and no bathroom (dwellers did their "physiological house cleaning" with the fish), living in Hydro-Lab I amounted to simple, effective barbarism.

The entire "wet NASA" bubble, which had expanded at the speed of light in the 1960s, was imploding in the lavish, debt-happy 1980s. More than sixty underwater habitats had been built worldwide, their sophistication growing exponentially. The *Ageir* habitat could support a half-dozen scientists for two weeks at depths down to 580 feet; *La Chalupa,* stationed off Puerto Rico, carried a crew of five at 100 feet for two weeks; and *Sealab-II,* off La Jolla, housed a crew of ten for up to a month. But by the end of the decade more submersibles and habitats were rusting in garages than in salt water.

"Anybody could see it was over," Perry said. "It was fun while it lasted."

The boy who'd served lemonade in Hastings at Henry Ford's Model-T showroom had lived through the changes of the times. Observing him in the confines of Hydro-Lab II, he reminded me of the Balinese saying, "We have no art. We do everything as well as we can." Perry had seen many peaks and bailed out before the slide into the troughs. He'd run the most successful civilian diving equipment company in the world. When his sensors picked up the tremors he sold it off, first to Byrd Company of Norway and then to Martin-Marietta.

Still upright in his personal castle, Perry was emphatic, viewing undersea research in his personal terms. "I'm against these programs,

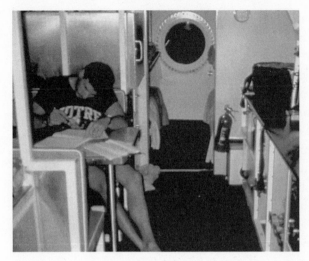

A researcher at work inside NOAA's new Aquarius habitat of Conch Reef in the Florida Keys. *Photo courtesy National Oceanic and Atmospheric Administration/ University of North Carolina– Wilmington.*

especially if it's run by bureaucrats. At least NASA used private industry. If nothing else we gained a strategic military platform in space."

But what about all the wealth on the seabed, especially manganese nodules, common to all the oceans? The possibilities seemed enormous. As much as one-quarter of the seabed is covered by nodules in addition to huge amounts of copper, nickel, and cobalt. The distribution of these minerals had been plotted in 1973 as part of the International Decade of Ocean Exploration. Why not take advantage of it?

"Yes, the wealth is there," Perry replied. However, the cost of getting it to market far exceeded potential profit. It was the same old story.

"You've got to understand," he emphasized, "it's easier getting to the moon than going down thirty feet. In the ocean, as opposed to space, you've got almost no visibility. You're dealing with huge hydrostatic pressure. There's the corrosive effects of the environment. I can't stress it enough. It's only when private money is involved that things get done."

He was right. No matter. The day I departed Lee Stocking Island I had the feeling that Perry, despite his pragmatism, had more than a touch of the romantic in him. After all, who crosses paths with Hollywood, swears by the First Amendment, buys his own island, and checks into his own underwater hotel without some small glow of romance?

Soon after my visit to Lee Stocking, Hydro-Lab I was removed from Salt River Submarine Canyon and placed in storage. It has since been relocated to the Florida Keys, where its mission appears to be somewhat less than its makers' initial vision. Later, a storm knocked Hydro-Lab II onto its side. It lay there on the seabed, symbolic of an era drawing to a close.

Yet Perry has once again restructured his vision. The outpost at Lee Stocking has been renamed the Caribbean Reef Research Center, the centerpiece of the Perry Foundation. Emphasis has shifted from submersibles and habitats. The island is now a center of activity known as "Project: 3rd Millennium: A World Hydrogen Community," focusing on what Perry believes will be a competitive, emission-free energy system capable of being scaled up for global use.

The center also explores low-cost aquatic food production, "rational" habitat conservation and enhancement, and the ecological requirements of important species living in coastal areas.

Perhaps sensing his mortality, Perry has published an unsentimental (at times savage) autobiography, *Never Say Impossible: The Life and Times of an American Entrepreneur.* The title is a delayed response to remarks made during a long-ago lecture given at Yale by Alexander P. de Seversky, then the world's foremost authority on aeronautics. Perry vividly recalls Seversky's insistence that airplane speeds would never exceed Mach 1, 685 miles per hour. These days, his trips to Europe aboard the Concorde routinely fly at Mach 2.

IV

Perry's vision has survived the research blitz initiated by the supply siders; it continues even as the romance of Cousteau has faded. The promise of a payoff may seem more distant, and it may be that future exploration of the sea depends on a wild card—another *Sputnik,* another *Silent Spring.* Perhaps human survival is the true wild card for the next millennium.

Any new ocean initiative, like others in the past, must explode with a "bumper sticker bang" and Machiavellian logic. I can hear Perry's voice declaring: *Find a reason, find a motive, look for profit, and you'll find the future.*

*****

I saw Perry again in the winter of 1966. We met in the bar at the Ritz Carlton in Washington, D.C. Though I hadn't seen him in years, he was instantly recognizable, still the unmistakable presence with wide shoulders and the big hands of his boxing days at college, the hands of someone who works them hard, gets them beat up bullying steel hulls. He seemed to be bursting out of his blazer, and I noticed his ubiquitous white socks and Topsiders. His eyes were mercurial as those of a boy who has combined passion with a secret. He smiled— no small gesture given the fact that only a few minutes earlier he'd broken a tooth snacking on mixed nuts.

"Sit, sit," he announced. "Still enjoy your red wine?" He was flanked by his wife, Elena, and his stepdaughter, Rene. Perry said the women had been scouting NOAA and other outposts in the bureaucratic maze seeking interest in the Caribbean Research Center and his work in fuel cell development. Apparently it had been a day of frustration.

"What they don't get," Perry said, "is that you need power. Hell, you can't do a thing without power."

He glanced at Elena and Rene seeking a sign of affirmation. Elena politely asked about the book I was writing and Perry's place in it, but he seemed not to be listening. He'd been on a separate mission meeting with various congressmen to push his National Dividend Plan. Yes, there was Lee Stocking and the Perry Foundation, but at eighty he was less interested in flinging himself into the sea; instead, he wished to reshape the economy.

"I don't believe in balancing budgets," he told me. "I believe in surplus. I explained this to you before." And he went on to explain it again, how each voter would receive a "dividend" from the surplus created by cuts in corporate and other taxes.

The cigarette smoke swirling through the bar didn't agree with him, and he complained about it and reminded me he had sold his family's tobacco farm soon after the surgeon general issued a 1960s report on smoking and health.

"Wouldn't have anything to do with it after that."

Elena said as soon as she could find a local dentist to fix Perry's broken tooth ("Do you know anyone good—I mean really good?" she whispered) they were leaving Washington by boat from the mouth of the Chesapeake Bay. From there they would enter the intercoastal waterway and sail to South Carolina. Winter in the Atlantic is no place for sport boaters; the intercoastal was the most prudent route.

Perry let out a guffaw. "Oh, sure. Sailing the intercoastal." I had a feeling this was not his idea of high adventure.

I leaned across the table and gripped his hand. I suddenly missed him, missed his intellect, his get-it-done-now ways, his sometimes baffling energy.

"John," I said, feeling a surge of warmth, "it's too bad you don't live here."

He smiled, revealing the broken tooth. "Well, hell!" he said. "I'll get you back down to the shop."

"Stay in touch," I said, rising to go.

"Oh, sure. We'll get you back to the island."

"Okay," I said. "Next summer it's the *Shark Hunter.*"

"Yeah," he grinned. "Sure thing."

I sensed—I *knew*—we would not see each other again.

Chapter Three

LIFE OUT OF THE SHADOWS

We had to search huge areas
before encountering any monsters at all.
—Hans Hass

I

WHENEVER MY FAMILY AND I TALKED ABOUT IT people would smile in that patronizing way that is a silent signal, a kind of code look that says, *You must be out of your mind!*

Our belief in the existence of a "living fossil," a prehistoric shark known as Carcharodon *megoladon,* might have been self-induced fantasy. Yet we had reason to believe otherwise. As David Attenborough noted in his *Life on Earth* (Little, Brown, 1979), most of the world's surface is covered by water, so most of the world belongs to the fish. By our calculations, Attenborough's odds were on our side.

We had discussed the possibilities with experts at the Motte Marine Laboratory on the Gulf Coast of Florida. With calm good humor and slightly patronizing patience they reminded us that living fossils had indeed been discovered in this century. There was the capture in 1938 of a live coelacanth off the coast of South Africa, a fish thought to be extinct millions of years ago. In 1952, a mollusk known as *neopilina,* considered extinct for more than 350 million years, was discovered in an ocean trench two miles deep. And in the late 1970s, there were strange blurry photographs of an eighty-foot-long reptilian-looking creature snagged in a trawling net in the Sea of Japan. The photographs were more tantalizing than edifying. The long snaky "thing" tangled in the net was badly decomposed, and it so sickened the Japanese fishermen with its stench that they tossed the carcass overboard in a great hurry. So much for scientific investigation.

More credible was the discovery of an ancient frill shark by Norwegian researchers in waters more than one-half mile deep. But as for the monster we were seeking, the Carcharodon *megoladon* (C*m*), a super-shark the size of a locomotive—no—C*m* was as dead and gone as Tyranosaurus rex, faded into extinction millions of years ago during the final era of the giant reptiles. C*m*, we were informed, was a freak of nature, a "mistake" too big to survive its own fearsome appetites. We had to wonder. If the common horseshoe crab could survive for millions of years unchanged, why not C*m?* The sea, after all, is big enough to accommodate big appetites.

Those who are obsessed by the sea aren't easily discouraged. We were confident history and allegory were on our side. For centuries many of the most enduring visions of the sea encompassed its various "monsters." Graphic renderings of huge octopi and Loch Ness–like creatures ambushing sailors trailed back into the fog of time. There was the testimony of the Phoenicians, who believed the more distant the sea, the more horrific were its creatures. Himlico of Carthage, sailing along the coast of Europe in 500 B.C., wrote: "The monsters of the sea move continually hither and thither, and wild beasts swim among the sluggish and slowly creeping ships." Anyone who has spent a long time at sea knows Himlico may have been exaggerating, but not that much.

Were these long-ago descriptions the dreams of fabulists? Less than 1 percent of the sea has been explored; therefore, nothing can be ruled out.

There are hundreds of sea diaries produced by reliable sources. Of particular interest are the diaries of the Reverend Hans Egede. In 1734, he awed his congregants with stories of "very terrible" animals rising out of the waves to snatch sailors from the decks of their ships. His tales have been dismissed as allegorical accounts designed to reel in the sinners. But it is hard to dismiss his description of a creature bearing an eerie resemblance to the twenty-five-foot Tylosaurus, a classic "sea dragon" of the Cretaceous period. This T-rex of the deep was a world-ranging species with crocodile jaws and spines along its back. Even in its decomposed state, the mangled snakelike animal tangled in that Japanese trawling net bore a striking resemblance to this description. Reverend Egede did not have the benefit of paleontology and its imagery, which developed more than a century after his death. The Tylosaurus-like creature he described in such detail must have come from someone's experience.

Our hunt for C*m* was also favored by the numbers. Some 1,413,000 types of plants and animals had been named and documented. Two centuries earlier, Carolus Linnaeus described a mere 4,236. By the beginning of the twentieth century, the number had grown to more than one-half million. Given the ever-escalating rate of discovery, we were encouraged to speculate that one might go backward in time to rediscover species written off and assumed to be extinct. And while it is true that the numbers belong mostly to life on dry land, one has to consider that little of the sea has ever been explored, so it is impossible to know how the numbers will change as we dig deeper into the unknown.

II

Our quest for the ancestor of today's great white shark (Carcharodon *carcharias*), the villain of Peter Benchley's classic thriller, *Jaws,* began in the mid-1970s. Our jumping-off point was the fossil-rich sands of Venice, Florida, a sleepy little town on the Gulf Coast between Sarasota and Naples.

Beginning in 1975, our family made annual pilgrimages to Venice. We came armed with scuba gear and a variety of field tools. It was a wonderful place to explore, since Venice proudly calls itself the "sharks' tooth capital of the world." Its beaches are laden with all manner of ancient remains, everything from tiny trilobites to antler horns, mammoth tusks, and the curved fangs of saber-toothed tigers. The most prolific fossils, however, are shark teeth, an evolutionary spectrum from the earliest tileosts to the C*m*, which we believed still roamed unseen in the depths of the Gulf of Mexico.

We didn't expect to stumble on an actual C*m*. Our focus was on the discovery of clues, indications of its existence. After all, you don't just bump into a hundred-foot-long sea-going monster in the shallow meadows of the seas near Venice. The area we were working was no deeper than sixty feet. The bottomography presented a gradual slope from the shore out to the Seven Mile Ledges, a series of limestone outcroppings running north and south along the entire Gulf Coast. The area was too shallow to accommodate very large creatures. Our theory was that C*m*, if still active, would cruise the deeper regions in the company of the whales and other large prey. Only when the open ocean menu was lean would C*m* forage the hunting grounds of Venice's near-shore waters.

We began our search with a geological survey. About 30,000 years ago the shoreline of the Gulf Coast extended seven to ten miles farther out to sea. Human remains have been discovered along the submerged outcroppings. The so-called ledges that parallel the modern shoreline along a north-south track were ancient gathering places for humans and other mammals. If we were to uncover evidence of a living C*m*, it would be on the seaward side of the ledges in deeper water.

The most convincing evidence (aside from an actual encounter) would be the recovery of an unfossilized C*m* tooth. Each species of shark has a distinctive, one-of-a-kind set of teeth set in parallel rows along its jaws. These are in perpetual renewal, so that sharks are almost always equipped with a full complement of teeth.

A shark's jaws are amazingly efficient. The predator seizes its prey, the lower jaw pinning the victim in place with the force of 240 pounds per square inch. The shark thrashes its head and body from side to side; the teeth literally saw its prey into eatable chunks. The great white, at forty feet and three tons, can gulp down forty pounds of flesh in a single bite. Its ferocity has earned it the genteel French nickname *requin*, requiem for the dead. If a great white can inflict such carnage, what might be expected from its infinitely larger ancestor?

Prehistoric dental records would answer many of our questions. Sharks possess no bony skeletons. When they die just about every part of their body decays, yet their teeth last practically forever. The size and shape of a shark's teeth are its foolproof "fingerprints." For instance, the tiger shark has serrated teeth partially rounded on one side with a long spiky "fang" jutting radically out from the other. Draw a semicircle and add a sharp right- or left-leaning triangle (depending on which quadrant of the jaws the teeth come from), and you have the unmistakable calling card of a tiger shark. When humans are attacked, the shape and size of the bite wounds, along with the teeth often found imbedded in the body, tell surgeons exactly which species is responsible.

The massive teeth of C*m* are especially distinctive. They are beautiful instruments of death. Shaped to a near-perfect triangle, they are on average the size of a large man's hand and weigh anywhere from a half-pound up to four or five pounds. The edges are deeply serrated and sharp as a scalpel. I have seen fossil-hunters bleed after carelessly grabbing a million-year-old C*m* tooth. It is easy enough to imagine our prehistoric ancestors collecting these amazingly efficient teeth at the water's edge and using them as tools. A newer C*m* tooth could easily slice through a palm tree; its smaller teeth might be fashioned into spearheads of great stopping power.

Given the escalating discovery of "living fossils," why not a living C*m*? After all, myth and fact remain intertwined. In the 1980s, the late Dr. Harold Edgerton, a professor at the Massachusetts Institute of Technology and inventor of the stroboscopic light that first illuminated the bottom of the sea, was obsessively tracking "Nessie" the Loch Ness Monster, in the fiords of Scotland. There are tens of thousands of organisms at the bottom of the sea that have yet to be discovered.

So much is unknown. Consider a story published June 10, 1996, in *The Washington Post,* "In Inky Depths, Pursuing a Tentacled Giant." This story describes the prototype of countless "sea monsters," a giant squid known as *architeuthis,* Greek for "chief squid." No one had ever seen this creature in the wild and the *Post* story informed readers that architeuthis "can grow to almost twice the length of a city bus and can weigh more than a ton. It has eyeballs the size of a human head ... set in a blood-colored, torpedo-shaped body. It has thousands of suckers lining its eight arms—each as thick as a weight lifter's thigh—and a pair of tentacles [like] bungee cords which it uses to draw smaller animals into its slashing beak. And this predator is jet-propelled."

Dead and dying giant squid have occasionally washed ashore. It was only in the late 1800s, however, that parts of their massive carcasses were examined in scientific laboratories. According to Clyde Roper of the Smithsonian Institution's Museum of Natural History, "We know more about long-extinct dinosaurs than we do about the giant squid." Roper is mounting a $3.5 million expedition with scientists from New Zealand and four other countries. They plan to search the waters of the South Pacific using the submersible *Johnson Sea-Link* and (hopefully) observe the ways of *architeuthis* in its realm 4,000 feet below the surface. A secondary goal, presuming Roper can find proper funding, is to study a peculiar food fish, a haddocklike novelty known as the orange roughy, and the roughy's "missing juveniles." Amazingly, the "juveniles" being served up as seafood are more than a century old. So if we can accept the "chief squid" and ancient juvenile roughys, why not the all-time king of the deep, the voracious, huge-toothed C*m*?

III

Our little team of explorers (my wife, Sandy, and our children, Rebecca and John) began routinely combing the fossil deposits on the beaches of Venice and Casey Key at the high tide lines. We did our initial searching soon after sunrise, when low tide exposed an otherwise submerged ribbon of sand. We shifted through bony fragments and countless sharks' teeth, the mortuary of a lost world. I imagined what the bottom might look like if the water were drained away and we could see the panorama all the way out to the limestone ledges. Perhaps it resembled an area at the bottom of the North Pacific where, for reasons unknown, the remains of sharks' teeth and the intricate ear bones of whales litter a vast plain of mud.

But the basement of the Gulf is very different. I envisioned an eerie prehistoric tableau: the reliquiae of giant reptiles buried in thick layers deep beneath the surface, blackened remnants of the more recent mammals, their bones scarred by saber-toothed cats and stacked like cordwood. And all along the ledges, where humans and animals comingled thousands of years ago, would be the palpable chaos of coexistence, life and death wrapped in an ageless silence. Beyond the fringing ledges, in the bowl of the ancient sea, Cm might still roam in perhaps a frantic quest to sustain its bulk.

"Too big to survive ... ." This phrase repeated itself inside my head as we continued our searching. Why had nature created such a monster? What purpose animated a species that required an unsustainable daily diet? In creating Cm had nature committed a gross miscalculation? And if Cm was a mistake, what might be deduced from the evolution of *Homo erectus,* so physically puny by comparison, yet infinitely (and more ingeniously) destructive?

Our beachcombing turned up many intriguing finds. We filled our collection bags with bone fragments, fossilized semicircular canals that once served as gyroscopes for dolphins, and as always there were hundreds of sharks' teeth. It was exciting but equally frustrating to discover fossil Cm fragments; it was a bit like finding broken gemstones, their true value perversely deconstructed. We stooped in the hot sun, fingering what amounted to badly weathered suggestions of the prize we were after. We donned masks and snorkels and rooted beneath the black fingerlike jetties of stone that reached out from the shoreline.

All manner of fossils washed into the crevices beneath these jetties. In the rhythmic rise and fall of the surf, working in a blinding curtain of silt, we groped and dug and probed. The sand slipped through our fingers as we deposited our finds into collection bags. An hour spent struggling in the surf was exhausting. We'd crawl back onto the beach, huddle in a circle of shade cast by the palms, and pick through the anonymous fossils. Day after day, the same routine—but no C*m* and no suggestion that we were closing on the prize.

This pattern continued for four years. Later we stepped up our scuba diving, swimming off the beach to run search patterns over the sand flats. We never encountered a shark, odd in a place that for years regularly sent bathers screaming out of the water whenever the predators supposedly were nearby. These "shark spottings" were made by local heli-patrols that sounded their alerts through bullhorns: "Sharks in the water! Repeat—Sharks!" I suspected they were actually spotting pods of dolphins, which when viewed from the air bear a striking resemblance.

One morning we were diving off Sarasota between the Siesta and Longboat Keys, an area where Dr. Eugenie Clark, the University of Maryland professor known as "The Shark Lady," had reported an attack by a tiger shark on a twelve-year-old boy. When we surfaced we were informed rather laconically by our captain that the waters were swarming with tigers (*Galeocerdo cuvieri*). Tigers are gently described by Australian sharkophile Ben Cropp as "robust ... teeth triangular and sharply serrated ... a voracious scavenger known to attack man. ..."

"Big suckers," the captain drawled a little too cheerfully. Asked why he neglected to alert us through our transponder or by tapping out a warning signal, he gave us the usual roll-eyed look we'd come to expect from the local skippers.

"Hell," he chuckled. "Wouldn'a done no good no how."

It was an annoying but essentially accurate assessment. I remembered it several years later while working briefly with Sea World's Shark Institute at Marathon, in the Florida Keys. The Institute captured, caged, and studied very large sharks, which were kept in a murky enclosure about fifty yards long and half as wide. A wooden catwalk spanned the length of this "shark pen." To cross the pen one had to mount two steps to gain the wooden catwalk; at the far end were two more steps, which (inexplicably) dead-ended at a cinder-block wall.

Given the fact that large sharks were swimming only a few feet below, crossing the catwalk on the first leg was challenging enough; turning around and returning from the dead end made a lot of us sweat. The span was narrow and had no railings.

One evening, the director of the Institute hosted a party for a group of VIPs. A "trip" (his word) across the catwalk was planned as the high point of the evening. We'd sipped white wine at the reception, and as the sun dropped below the horizon the director turned on the floodlights above the shark pen. Dark torpedo shapes swarmed near the surface, attracted to the lights.

"Time to walk the 'plank,'" the director announced.

As I look back on it, it is hard to recall a more terrified group of party goers. We wondered if in point of fact we were sufficiently skilled to place one foot confidently in front of the other. What happens if you slip? was the unspoken question on everyone's mind. And as we s-l-o-o-o-o-w-l-y traversed the impossibly narrow "plank" above the pen, a big bull shark, massive as Melville's worst obsession, churned up beside us, rolled onto its side, and stared coldly with its black vacuity of an eye.

Thump! The shark nudged one of the pilings. The catwalk trembled. Again. *Crunch!* And we realized in a perspiring rush that we frail human creatures had become tantalizing chum caught in the glaring floodlights. If we slipped, "it wouldn'a done no good no how."

It seldom occurred to my family during our searches that we'd be attacked. The odds were on our side. David H. Baldridge, a researcher who'd spent years documenting shark attacks, reported that a peak had been reached in 1959: a mere fifty-six attacks worldwide. In fact, encounters have been declining steadily, with reported fatalities averaging about one a year. We were operating mostly in isolation on a daily basis, far from crowds of bathers. Baldridge has reported that about 65 percent of attacks happened on weekends, supporting the contention that shark attack is more likely to occur when there are greater numbers of people in the water.

To our little party, isolation equaled safety.

IV

A strange thing happened during one of our expeditions along a crescent of beach at the southern tip of Venice known as Casperson's. We'd been collecting samples in relatively deep water, scouring the bottom, filling our net bags with jumbled finds, hauling them to shore, and returning to the sandy fields we'd been mining. It was nearly noon. A glare of sun denuded all color from the wide stretch of sand. We were cataloging our finds when my son, John, shouted and pointed excitedly toward the sea. Just offshore a long curved figure sliced through the breakers. Whatever it was jutted at least six feet above the surface. Intense sunlight reflected off the surface of the sea has a way of blotting out minutiae. The lack of detail was frustrating, but we clearly saw a snakelike creature moving parallel to the shore. A distinct knobby shape protruded from the peak of this puzzling figure. The knob appeared to be about the size of a human head. We were amazed as this thing cut a wake, turned sharply, and made for deeper water. In less than a minute it had appeared and vanished below the surface of the Gulf.

I spent the rest of the afternoon in our library of *squalophilia*. My first guess was that we'd seen an unusually large thresher shark (*Alopias vulpinus*) perhaps cruising through a school of bait fish. The thresher is instantly recognizable by its beautiful tail, often longer than its body, which it uses to "thresh" the water and frighten the schools of fish upon which it feeds. The relatively small thresher is considered safe and unlikely to attack humans. If what we saw was the tail of a thresher, its body would have to be about fourteen feet long and it would weigh a thousand pounds.

But the more I learned about the size, shape, and usual habitat of this shark, the less likely it appeared that the thing slicing through the sea off Casperson's was indeed a thresher. To begin with, *Alopias vulpinus* was not a creature common to the Gulf of Mexico. Further, the object had a rotund girth, a kind of snakelike roundness, while a thresher's caudal fin is tall, narrow, and thin. As for the knob at the top of the tail, it was too pronounced to be compared to the elegant little notch characteristic of the thresher. Finally, the knob faced in the wrong direction. I realized with a certain uneasiness that what we'd seen had slipped inexorably into the stew pot of the "impossible."

I resisted the slippage. Once over the edge it was hard to turn back. Imagination would cloud all our work. Before reaching any conclusions, no matter how tentative, I wanted to survey creatures unknown at the start of the century (at least unknown in their present form) and that were indigenous to the Gulf of Mexico and north-flowing Gulf Stream. The thing we spied that day at Casperson's was bizarre and very real. I wondered if long-ago observers had reported anything like it. No matter how strange their sightings might have been, at least I'd have something to relate to, some clue that might help identify what we had seen.

Pre-twentieth-century sailors plied the Gulf Stream with suspicious eyes. There were horror stories about the Sargasso Sea, a deep central mass of warm water in the North Atlantic. This area was thought to be a dense desert of sargassum weed so thick it created a graveyard for any ship venturing into it. Yet Columbus made it through in 1492, the galleons of the conquistadors turned eastward through the Sea on their return to Spain, and the Danish ship *Dana* performed a biological survey amidst the bladdery weed. No colony of ghost ships has ever been spotted in this alleged limbo of the lost. What has been documented in this century, however, are two unusual creatures coasting through the warm Gulf Stream flow, two possibilities for sea-monsterdom. Could one of these be what we saw at Casperson's?

The first are tropical eels of various species. T. F. Gaskell, in his fascinating book *The Gulf Stream,* says there may be eels 100 feet long slithering through the Stream. He notes that unusually large juvenile eels (elvers) have been spotted. Since an elver of three inches can be expected to grow to five feet or more, a five-footer may mature at twenty times its juvenile size.

Another maybe-monster is the oarfish, sometimes called the ribbonfish. The giant of this species has a red dorsal running the length of its body from head to tail. The forward end has long red spines, which can be elevated to a tall crest. This would take care of at least some of the tales of sea serpents with bright red hair in the Gulf Stream.

These creatures bore no resemblance to what we had witnessed. I found myself pondering the shapes of the sea-going plesiosaurs of the Jurassic period. These were flesh-eating marine reptiles with paddle-shaped fins and long, brontosaurus-like necks. But Jurassic deposits were not common to the eastern United States. We were exploring Cretaceous seas, working a seabed thick with Cretaceous leavings. Over time our paleontological snooping fixed on the later plesiosaurs with broad, relatively short turtlelike bodies and long necks and tails. One fossil species was forty feet long, with a neck measuring eighteen feet. Such an animal would not have been uncommon in the Gulf.

Was it a plesiosaur we had seen, some bygone relic thought to have been extinct for millions of years? Did our encounter lend credence to the ancient sailors who had reported similar sightings in the Atlantic? And what of the strange "apparitions" reported by the conquistadors hauling their Mayan spoils through the Gulf of Mexico and northward along the Florida Keys?

It seemed odd. At the start of the twentieth century, science had unilaterally banished all living fossils to the sillier machinations of science fiction. It was perfectly acceptable for Jules Verne to exploit the imagination, but modern science had made it heretical to entertain the notion that sea monsters existed beyond the pages of a book. We were somehow disciplined to discount the "fanciful" images handed down over time by sober and scholarly observers. I recalled the following quote from Olaus Magnus, Archbishop of Uppsala, in 1555: "All fishermen of Norway are agreed there is a Sea Serpent (two hundred feet) long and (twenty feet) thick that lives in caves and rocks near Bergen. … He puts up his head on high like a pillar." Was the Archbishop a fabulist? I found similar references in *Natural History of Norway* (1752); Philip H. Grosse's *Romance of Natural History* (1860); and *The Case for the Sea Serpent* by R. T. Gould, published in 1930.

It was a dilemma. As a skeptical writer at the end of the twentieth century with deep respect for science and learning, I found it difficult to dismiss the Archbishop and the others.

One of the people who has helped give substance to the supposedly impossible was a retired aeronautical engineer named Tim Dinsdale. A man steeped in the scientific method, Dinsdale wrote an incredibly detailed book, *Monster Hunt,* published in 1972. In it he listed a number of saltwater sightings of the so-called Loch Ness Monster. I was fortunate to have met him at a convention of the Atlantic Alliance for Maritime Heritage Conversation, of which I was a co-founder.

Dinsdale was an encyclopedia of the inexplicable. In addition to evidence of a half-dozen sightings of "Nessie" in the Sea of the Hebrides, off the west coast of Scotland, he showed me a sketch by an American, Brian McCleary, which bore the following caption: "March 24th, 1962: About 15 ft. protruding from water. … Oval green eyes, and visible nostrils. Head … more like snake than fish, or any other marine animal. …" McCleary's sighting was made off Pensacola, Florida.

Dinsdale, a bright, modest man with a little goatee and a calm, unaffected manner, struck me as the sort of person who has seen something rare and has become possessed by it. Perhaps because of this, or in spite of it, everything he said seemed understated. He told me of a press conference he held in London in 1970 to report on sonar contacts made at Loch Ness and Urquhart Bay.

"Unfortunately," he said, "there was little scientific coverage." The news appeared with the usual errors and dramatizations, though some reports were serious.

He told me he needed something definitive, something that can't be ignored: close-up photography or a video of Nessie in a natural habitat.

A few years later Dinsdale's definitive experiment was carried out by none other than Dr. Harold Edgerton, the famous "Papa Flash" who had invented stroboscopic photography. One of the most prolific and ingenious scholar/inventors at MIT, "Papa" stunned the scientific community with his views on Nessie and his patient commitment to study Loch Ness.

I interviewed Edgerton in Boston. He bore traits similar to many of the scientific pioneers I'd known: direct, plain spoken, self-effacing, choosing to define himself by the practical results of his work. Over lunch at his condominium in Cambridge with his wife, Esther, I could see across the Charles River to the Perpetual Life Insurance building, on top of which a constantly flashing strobe light honored Papa's revolutionary invention.

"I helped install it," he said. "I like that kind of work, you know."

He handed me a series of black-and-white photographs of the first atomic bomb tests at Alamogordo, New Mexico. I will never forget them. His strobe had captured the birth of the explosion. Instead of the usual blinding flash of light, the photograph revealed what appeared to an almost incomprehensibly hideous face punctuated by dozens of glowing oblong "eyes," its weight seemingly carried on four fiery legs. In another photo the face had expanded, still dark and impenetrable, but with more "eyes," and the legs towered like black lightning. Not even a millionth of a second had passed between the two photographs.

I was used to seeing pictures of atomic mushroom clouds and nuclear firestorms, but these images were beyond anything I had ever imagined.

"It looks almost alive," I said.

"Well, maybe so," Edgerton replied.

Earlier he had allowed me to thumb through original photographs that had awed the world, timeless instants of wonder: a drop of milk forming a perfect crown, a bullet passing through a lightbulb, a stop-motion series of a cat tumbling through space and landing on all fours, the frozen motion of a hummingbird's wings.

Fantastic images, yet they paled upon seeing those first images of the beginning of the atomic age. The bomb transcended reality, vaporized the existential. Were these visions of the beginning and possible end of the universe? I was disturbed and frustrated, and to this day I can't properly describe what I saw. It was as if a forbidden image had entered my consciousness, where it remains, immutable and bewildering.

Given the magnitude of what Edgerton had accomplished—among other things, he was known as the "man who lit the sea"— my question to him about the possible existence of a Loch Ness Monster was merely a throwaway, a test of his skepticism. I had no idea that this pragmatic scientist who had given us a whole new way of seeing would take the question seriously.

"My experiment was to install side-scan sonar in the loch and hook it up to a van," he told me. "It was a boring thing to sit in that van. One day, two days, three days waiting for something to happen."

But wasn't the whole idea of Nessie slightly outrageous? I posed the question despite our own puzzling sighting in the Gulf, and because the interviewing of geniuses forces one to shrink the perimeters of poetic license.

"Well, they scoffed at plate tectonics," Edgerton shot back. "After tedious days and nights at Loch Ness, we got two contacts. Real good ones. A great big thing came swimming in then went away. I'd say it was about two hundred meters away. I can tell you surely there are things out in that loch that are alive and moving, and they don't come within range of your cameras."

But why didn't they close in?

"Well, that's *the* puzzle," Edgerton sighed.

Sonar images were generated, though they were more suggestive than confirming. Edgerton pushed two prints across the table, hazy images resembling the petals of a giant tulip. I studied them as Edgerton sipped potato-leek soup from a gold-leafed ceramic bowl. Given proper scale, the images bore a strange resemblance to the flippers of a plesio-saur. I wondered: *How much of this is pure fancy, a mind game, like seeing faces in the clouds of a summer afternoon? How much is pure wishful thinking?*

"You don't consider this conclusive?" I pressed.

"I'll bet there's *something* in that loch," he replied firmly. "Why? Because I know there's something that gives you a big sonar echo two hundred meters away." Perhaps the loch was filled with Nessies, he continued. "To have a viable colony you need at least twenty animals to perpetuate it. But I'm no biologist. We need more and more experimentation."

By the time I left his condo, Papa had conveyed the impression that examining the past isn't a matter of looking over one's shoulder at a series of well-defined, receding objects. Rather, it is like staring down into a deep pool of water. Sometimes an object floats to the surface; sometimes nothing. The hard part is patience.

V

My family returned to Florida and again went looking for C*m*. I have a feeling that most breakthroughs—the Eureka factor—operate on Ernest Hemingway's simple equation for talent: *ten percent inspiration, ninety percent perspiration.* We apparently had gained our prescribed level of perspiration when luck took a turn for the better.

The first break came on an usually calm day in August. I was snorkeling in about eight feet of water off the beach at Venice with my daughter, Rebecca. There was practically no wind and the surface of the sea was glassy, the water temperature too warm to be thought of as refreshing. The sandy bottom was a patchwork of shadows and glaring sunlight. We both spotted it at the same time—a large triangular tooth. Down we went. I grabbed it, instantly feeling its deep serrations. No treasure hunter hauling up gold doubloons could have been more excited.

"Wow!" Rebecca cried.

Again we glanced below the surface. Another big tooth lay directly beneath us. Rebecca dove and returned in amazement. Two wonderful specimens within the space of a minute. Fossil-hounds may search forever and not win such prizes.

The finds were significant. In a photo-essay on page one of the *Sarasota Herald-Tribune*'s Metro section, Rebecca was featured holding one of the big fossil C*m* teeth.

And what a tooth it was; it was nearly as big as her face, a five-pound killing instrument in near-mint condition. Serious collectors enviously called it an "investment-grade" recovery. Its surface was gray and virtually unscathed. The boss (the portion that anchored into the jaw) was thick and smooth. Calculating the tooth to be an average size for this particular C*m,* our math worked out impressively. We had uncovered traces of a true monster, a shark between sixty and sixty-five feet long. Using the comparative figures of author/collector Gerard R. Case and others, we dated the finds to the Miocene period, which ended fifteen million years ago. Case, in his very useful handbook, *Fossil Sharks: A Pictorial Review,* described the C*m*s of the period as being from 60 to 100 feet long, and pointed out that if a shark of this size existed today "bathers along the seashore would probably not go near the water at all!"

Our next big break was a mixed blessing. Not long after the C*m* finds off Venice beach, I was diving the seaward side of the Seven Mile Ledges, where depths ranged from 40 to about 100 feet. These ledges are striking because they look so much like artifacts. The limestone walls, uniformly eight to ten feet high, run in straight lines with occasional hard right-angle turns, as if the primitive peoples who lived out here 30,000 years ago had carefully built protective cover against the marauding saber-toothed cats and other predators that gathered at the water's edge. I could almost sense a human presence. Prowling the ledges was a little like entering a room after a party had ended. An almost palpable aura of habitation hung like a ghost in the depths.

It was a windy, gray morning. The occasional rays of sunlight brought a dull color to the overcast sky, but no color spilled into the sea. Because of the wind it was difficult to set the anchor firmly into the ledges. The long, frayed sisal line and the battered length of outgoing chain hissed and clattered against the bow as the boat fell sideways into the troughs and lifted like a toy onto the crests.

The seabed was a virtual sandstorm. As wind sends objects flying in all directions through the air, so an angry sea disturbs the subsurface world, flinging silt and sand through the water column. On a calm day underwater visibility might be 60 to 100 feet. However, on this morning clarity was reduced to perhaps ten feet, and a stiff current was running.

I knelt on the sand and held tightly to the ledge. I breathed slowly and waited for my buddy, a member of the local sport diving club. I knew he must be nearby in the cloud of silt, but where? I checked my air gauge. I might stay in this spot running out of air and never see him.

I faced a critical decision, to wait until he appeared or take off alone. I clearly understood the first rule of diving, *never dive alone.* But after a rough ride out to sea and a bruising effort to get into the water, I wasn't about to abort. I waited five more minutes. My buddy, apparently invisible in the gloom, failed to appear. I was on my own.

I swam along the limestone ledge, pulling myself forward, hand-over-hand, my face pressed close to the sand. The ledges were a repository of fossils washed in from the Gulf. The eons of vanished life came tumbling in, lodging in the grottoes and crevices. The beaches and shoreward sands were certainly prolific, but the mother lode was out here.

It is a rare privilege to encounter this alien world and to experience its mystery. Here is the unseen graveyard of creatures that ruled the planet for millions of years, creatures whose existence still challenges us with their diversity. And if their lives awaken our keenest perceptions, their disappearance is a riddle.

As I picked through the chaos of fossil material I had the sensation of touching the unseen. A cosmic door had opened onto a long passageway and each fragment had a story to tell, a story of evolution told in a language only vaguely intelligible.

Peering into the gloom of the grottoes along the ledges, I thought of the vast numbers of organisms inhabiting the Earth's web of submarine caves. Virtually every serious penetration finds yet another "living fossil," tiny organisms roaming beneath the continents through fissures and canyons in the continental slopes. A few years ago, the remains of a 10,000-year-old dugong was discovered in a water-filled cavern beneath the Yucatan.

Is there a great subterranean sea with sunless shores stretching across an eternal night? And if so, what forms of life may be found there? Did life on Earth begin in those depths?

Suddenly I saw it! I grabbed an outcropping and hung on, my body flapping like a pennant in the current. Just out of reach, perhaps five feet away, was a white glistening triangle, a white luminescence in the darkened water.

I stared in disbelief. It was a shark's tooth easily as big as the C*m* we'd recovered off Venice beach. Even in the cloudy, silt-laden water I could make out the huge boss, the clean, razorlike serrations at the edges. But it was the color that amazed me. It was snowy white. White is not the color of the past. White is new life.

Was it possible? Could this be the thing we had searched for all these years?

The bottom was a confusion of sand swirling through the piles of blackened bones, changing the shape and contours of the landscape second-by-second. There was no choice. I fixed hard on the glistening white triangle, because in the sea an object lost from sight is an object lost for good. Sand was moving over the triangle, obscuring it. I let go and lunged toward the whiteness. Just as I was about to touch it, it disappeared.

I swam in circles, rapidly consuming my air supply, struggling in the current. I swam and I swam and after a while I felt the sting of salt against my eyes.

It was gone. There was a moment of fury. Where was my buddy? If only he had been there. A witness; that's all I needed—simple confirmation. Now I had neither the white triangle nor a witness.

The fury faded and a kind of dull angst numbed my brain. I rose to the angry surface of the Gulf. My buddy waited in the stern of the boat. "Hey, sorry I lost you down there," he said in a voice he might have used if a tree on his property had crashed through the roof of my house.

I removed my air tank and lead weights. They slammed hard against the dive platform and threatened to fall back into the sea. Was I okay? my buddy asked. I nodded. My voice deserted me. All I could think of was the white triangle and worlds within worlds that might never be seen.

A month later I headed out to the Caribbean island of St. Eustatius in search of a sunken city.

Chapter Four

PYRAMIDS AT THE BOTTOM
OF THE SEA

The question is, will we come to plunder or to appreciate?
This is a debate that grows louder, not quieter.
—Robert Ballard

I

I LANDED AT ST. MAARTEN IN THE DUTCH CARIBBEAN and made arrangements to explore the wreck of a British man-of-war, HMS *Proselyte*,
which sank in 1801 on a reef known as Small Bank. Whatever booty
she may have carried had long ago been salvaged. As a journalist, I was
more focused on documenting the site as a splash of color for a larger
story about the Antillean island chain.

What I was really looking for was the sunken city I'd been hearing
about. I had very few leads, mostly rumors. Yet it was thrilling to imagine
a city beneath the sea, a Caribbean "Atlantis."

But first the *Proselyte*.

As we churned offshore heading to the wreck site it seemed significant
that only a few decades ago we had no convenient way to undertake a
search for even this relatively accessible shipwreck. Twentieth-century
technology changed everything. We had discovered many ways to probe
the seas, and the elegant freedom of scuba allowed one to walk into a
sporting goods outlet, plunk down a few hundred dollars, and come
away prepared for "Nemoism." And on the high end of technology we
had at our disposal real-life nautili, a fleet of scientific submersibles
and robot vehicles to trace the footprints of history advancing across
the floor of the world's oceans.

The sea is the historic pathway of civilization. The legacies of those
who traveled it are locked in the pyramids of the deep. The secrets are

waiting to be found, to be touched. And touching these lost treasures is like touching the stars.

"She be down a long time," my island guide remarked as we neared the wreck site. "Still plenty to see if you be looking."

First traces of the vessel appeared just beneath the surface, where the seabed formed a small declivity. *Proselyte* bore no likeness to the Hollywood version of a shipwreck; no intact hull resting upright on the bottom, tattered sails flapping in the currents. Most real-life ship-wrecks live up to the wreck part, looking as if bombs have exploded inside their hulls. A sinking ship doesn't feather its way down; it breaks up and slams into the bottom at a mile a minute.

My guide made a sweeping gesture indicating that the once-proud warrior was scattered in all directions. She had apparently run up on the reef, breached her hull, and tumbled down the face of the reef into the full fury of a storm. Most of her hull was buried beneath the sediments. The first recognizable artifacts were two big anchors, their flukes and metal stocks encrusted with coral. Nearby lay a field of less recognizable wreckage: a jumble of ballast stones, iron fittings, twisted spikes that once secured the hull planking.

We gently fanned the powdery white sand to remove the overburden that covered like a dusting of snow what remained of the ship. Within minutes we found a shard of porcelain. After more than two centuries it shone bright with fine blue details, and I could make out a hint of a royal seal. An exciting moment. I held this tiny hint of the past as if it were a living thing. It was only a shard, yet the sensation was a little like cradling an impossibly small creature in the palm of my hand, feeling its warmth and its fragility. We uncovered a shattered ceramic plate. Some vanished sailor, probably an officer, had taken his meals from it. I wondered who he might have been, wondered if he survived the sinking.

My guide motioned to a break in the reef where the bottom formed a mini-cliff. We drifted slowly downward. As the deeper seabed came into focus I saw another scattering of ballast stones and artifacts. There was a stack of planking, a wooden boneyard now decorated by red and pink corals. Blackened barrel hoops stood upright on the sand. A school of mullets formed a rainbow ribbon as they swam through the openings.

Gently, gently I fanned. Fragmented bottles appeared, thick green-black glass with patches of white marine growth. My guide picked up a bottleneck with a hush of white coral encircling its mouth; he pretended to take a belt. Grog, the generic name for anything alcoholic served aboard ship. A sailor received it happily and consumed his ration when (presumably) he wasn't on watch. How did it taste? I imagined a viscous, bitter liquid, a syrupy residue distilled from the cane in these parts. It probably went down badly but glowed inside with the relieving warmth.

My guide cupped his hands and pointed at the bottom, indicating that the larger remains of the hull lay buried below the sand. I imagined a twisted skeleton, a capsule frozen in time, waiting for the day when perhaps others would come to rescue it and return it to the world of sun and sky. It was altogether captivating and the hour or so we spent underwater raced by.

After we came up, our little boat with its coffeepot engine headed toward Phillipsburg. Images of the *Proselyte,* a ghost of a ship that once sailed the oceans in defense of Her Majesty's empire, flashed through my imagination. Perhaps she had anchored near the town, taking on supplies and cargo. I imagined her crew enjoying the freedom of shore leave.

"Be lots more down dah," my guide shouted over the growl of the engine. "Island be surrounded by ships from all ovah. Some carry treasure. I have been told this but I have never seen any."

"What kinds of treasure?"

"Galleons. Got more gold den all de banks in des parts."

That evening we sat at the beach bar drinking rum. The night sky was clear and the stars reflected on the dark water.

"You be goin' to 'Stacia?" my guide asked.

St. Eustatius ('Stacia as she is known in the Windward Islands) was at the time merely another anonymous spit of land in the Antillean chain. Once a wealthy Dutch mercantile center and military garrison, it was now a backwater, one of many volcanic peaks with a population small enough to be counted in a single afternoon. But 'Stacia had an ironic connection with the United States. In her halcyon days the little island was the first to recognize and salute the Revolutionary American Navy when it sailed through the Windwards. There had been a diplomatic exchange at Gallows Bay and congratulatory cannon fire from Fort Oranje. This incident stung British pride after their defeat and expulsion by the American colonists. In 1781, they sent an avenging fleet to the island, stormed ashore, and sacked the old city of Oranjestad. The British frigates launched a wicked barrage, destroying 'Stacia's seawall. The Caribbean rushed in to drown Oranjestad.

"Whole city underwater," my guide said. "What be left of her."
"Still there?"
"Yes, truly. Maybe you see it."
I was captivated. I had read much of sunken cities such as Port Royal, which in 1692 sank into the harbor at Kingston, Jamaica, following an offshore earthquake. Port Royal was infamous in an era of infamy, the headquarters of just about every pirate gang in the Caribbean. Yet one cataclysmic moment "the wickedest city in the world" trembled and plunged below the waves, taking with it a glittering storehouse of pirate loot. I had long dreamed of exploring Port Royal, and a few years later I would make a concerted (though unsuccessful) attempt to do so. I would learn a bitter lesson in Jamaica. The drowned patrimony of Port Royal was not an open attraction, and hostile suspicion tainted anyone who wished to examine it.

"We have been robbed by your scholars!" I was scolded by a surly Jamaican archaeologist. He glared at me as if I were a criminal who should bear the humiliation of a collective guilt.

But for the moment at St. Maarten, wrapped in my naiveté, I was captivated by the lost city of Oranjestad, a mere puddle-jumping plane trip away from where we sat sipping rum at the beach bar. I didn't fix on treasure; gold and silver loot, captivating as it may be, never held much fascination for me—it was corrupt blood money. Instead, the shimmering ghost of the sunken city itself held my imagination. I was captivated by the lure of actually seeing a drowned civilization, a hint of Atlantis. It would be the thrill of thrills.

Unfortunately, I didn't visit 'Stacia that year. Other expeditions took precedence. Yet like the mystique of an unrequited love the passion for Oranjestad lingered.

Finally, in the summer of 1979, I landed at 'Stacia's dusty Franklin Delano Roosevelt Airport. Curious name for such an offbeat outpost. No one seemed to know how the famous FDR came to be associated with such an obscure island. I was the only passenger to disembark, and if I didn't know better I would have guessed that the island, simmering in the white glare of the sun, was deserted. The little tin shack of a terminal was empty. There was a walkway leading to a chain-link fence. Beyond the fence the island road was a web of cracks and decay. Salt-tough island grass sprouted snakelike through the ruined concrete. Some find romance in this sort of emptiness; I find desolation. The tiny Short-330 that brought me here seemed to belong to another era.

Yet the backwardness of the scene was symbolic of the lost city I longed to see.

The sunken city of Oranjestad, what was left of it, lay close to the surf. Over the centuries it had been battered into a rubbly ruin. But slowly, as I grew accustomed to its bizarre shapes and patterns, the ruin began to take on a distinct logic. Low walls glowing with coral formed rectangular surrounds. The buildings had crumbled to dim outlines. Sand filled each passageway. Here and there a partial wall with a vacant window stood open to an empty sea. The bottom was dark and peppered with ceramic shards, fragmented clay pipes, thick shattered glass. Along one wall, standing at right angles to the beach, a large cannon mount loomed like some wounded, round-shouldered soldier. Where a cannon had once faced seaward there was now an oversized notch; the cannon itself lay at an oblique angle in the sand, its breech slanting mournfully skyward.

The ruin of Oranjestad was no Atlantis, but it was captivating. I was exploring the remains of a civilization built by humans and destroyed by humans. Beneath this rubble lay all the essentials of a lost culture. I was in no way equipped to dig through the remains; others had tried, some successfully, others not so successfully. It is a rule of the new art and science of twentieth-century marine archaeology that the sea does not give up her secrets without a fight. No ship dies an easy death, and this sunken relic of a city had been no less violently destroyed. Among these broken walls and cobbles people once carried on the necessary activities of daily life. Only ghosts remained. The city had been reduced to a habitat for tropical fishes, its human voices banished forever.

Father offshore in about sixty feet of water the clean sand sloped away into the darker depths. Bottles and ceramic shards were scattered randomly. It reminded me of a landfill, an undersea dump. And here I learned another lesson: Much archaeology involves carefully digging through such "dumps," using tweezers if necessary to make sense of castaway refuse.

Fanning the sand, I came upon fragments of wood and iron and ceramic pottery. Then came a surprise—a tiny silver spoon. I held it in my palm, spellbound. I wondered if it had been part of a condiment tray, or perhaps it belonged to a child. It was slightly bent and tarnished with a thick patina of oxide. The black coating dissolved into an inky cloud as I rubbed its surface.

So this was the detritus of old Oranjestad two centuries after the British plunder. Piece by piece it had migrated from shore, fleeing its makers into deep water. Many tons of artifacts were still out of sight. The tides and currents would inexorably pull them into the deeper vault of the sea. In another century most of it would be lost. Lost if the archaeologists forgot about its existence or found more important sites. Lost if its story was relegated to myth. This it seemed was the greatest danger, the trivializing, the reduction to myth of what was once alive and vital. Like Atlantis, we are inclined to make do with storytelling. At some point along the way the words become transformed and have little to do with the object they presume to describe. This is the point of no return, the ultimate loss.

My guide touched my shoulder. I had forgotten he was there. It was time to go. When we reached the shore I carried a sense of having lived another life in another time, when big sailing ships clustered in the harbor and precious metals were exchanged for the exotic spices of the Indies. People built and lost fortunes here. Now all these fortunes belonged to the sea.

"You be so quiet," my guide remarked. "What you thinkin'?"

"Time," I replied. "Time and history."

"Ah," he said. "That be what it is all about."

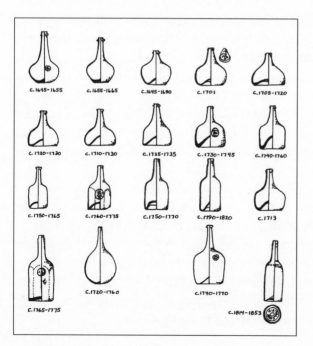

Artist's rendition of ancient bottles recovered from various Caribbean sites. *Drawing by Kathryn Williams.*

II

The *Proselyte* and Oranjestad never let go of me. I had explored a great many shipwrecks, mostly vessels sunk during the latter half of the century. Many of them, especially those off the mid-Atlantic coast of the United States, were victims of German U-boats and hardly qualified as historic. While these modern vessels were in a far better state of preservation than the *Proselyte,* they couldn't compete in enchantment. Oranjestad was especially compelling. Those shattered walls lingered, dreamlike.

On a later expedition through the Bahamas I examined the so-called "Road to Atlantis" off the northeast coast of Bimini. It was an exciting prospect. My guide, entrepreneur and daredevil explorer Neal Watson, was skeptical of "sensitives," UFOers, and Devil's Trianglers.

"I've seen stuff like this before," he said as we motored into the Atlantic.

But then everyone had opinions. True believers swore the "road" was an ancient artifact, a connection to an actual Atlantis. This connection had been "verified" by some of the world's notable psychics, the first being the legendary Edgar Casey. It was Casey who in the late 1940s claimed to have conjured the vision of the road while in a trance.

What I found was a series of rectangular stones measuring about four by eight feet, lying side-by-side over a distance of about 300 yards. They were submerged beneath ten to fifteen feet of water. Straight lines seldom occur in nature, and so many of them together struck me as evocative and a little baffling. Yet such formations are common to island environments; geologists call them "building blocks." I had seen others in shallow water from the Caribbean to the Pacific to the Indian Ocean. I had to agree with Watson. If Atlantis did exist we wouldn't find it in Bimini.

I was becoming engrossed in the cultural aspects of the sea. I explored every historic place I could find. But it was the wreck of the RMS *Rhone,* the royal British mail packet, that captured my heart.

The *Rhone* is a famous old shipwreck. A few years ago she was used by Hollywood as the set for the underwater thriller *The Deep.* For some reason this commercialization offended me. I was turned off by the idea of using this historic vessel as a stage prop and was relieved when the British government declared it to be a protected site.

The story of the *Rhone* parallels that of many lost ships. In the end her fate was measured in minutes and inches. One of the finest ships of her time, with broad decks, a powerful engine, and auxiliary sail, she carried mail and passengers in classic high style. In 1867, she lay at anchor at a bunkering station near Peter Island, in the British Virgin Islands, when a hurricane loomed on the horizon.

As the storm swelled into the sky the *Rhone* headed for open water. No luck. She missed her shelter at Salt Island by a mere thirty feet. Wind drove her straight into Black Rock Point. After the initial blow she slid down the rock face and cascaded backwards into the sea. Wind and waves pounded her for days.

Who could have guessed that her tragedy would lead to such fame? But then ships, like people, are often better known after death, and the quality of their death confers special meaning to their lives.

The *Rhone* was important to my growing involvement with nautical archaeology, and a very strange thing happened to me at the wreck site, a profound encounter, which to this day leaves me baffled. My initial encounter, with the ship occurred as we dove in the shadow of Black Rock Point. We couldn't miss the wreck. The moment we entered the water it almost reached up and pulled us in.

For a wooden ship going on her second century she was in magnificent condition. Her eighteen-foot screw was awesome, her coral-encrusted portholes still in place. We wandered through the sunlit compartments where ceramics remained (miraculously) in their cupboards. Her long companionways seemed to echo with the voices of lost sailors. The big engine block had been transformed into a kind of iron sculpture decorated by spiky orange fire coral. The sea makes art of her captives and clearly the *Rhone* counts among her masterpieces.

We passed over the boilers, water pumps, plates, and grating. The midsection revealed a winch and a row of open-ended wrenches standing in a row like sentinels. We entered a compartment near the bow. In the gloom stood an open sea chest, its interior lined with yellow corals. A spray of tropicals flashed in the shadows.

Close-by the hull lay a mast with an intact crow's nest. It sprawled across the sand like an arm crooked at the elbow. The crow's nest was bursting with sea life.

There was one last area we wanted to probe. An edition of the Port of Spain *Gazette* published soon after the sinking tells of a nineteenth-century helmet diver named Murphy who encountered an "enormous jewfish" (a giant member of the grouper family) in the ship's saloon. We found the saloon and poked inside. The 300-pound fish was still there, eyes round and red, gray-black scales big as half-dollars, its jaws slack and large enough to swallow any one of us. The fish backed away. Cautious and sagacious, he was the indomitable survivor.

But the truly remarkable thing happened as we headed to the surface. My normal diving mode is to cross my arms over my chest as I swim. This gives my body a bit more hydrodynamic shape and helps keep me warm. I was in this position when I felt something hard in my left hand. A few seconds later I broke the surface and looked. In my palm lay a round brass object carved in the shape of a wreath.

I was stunned. What was this thing? How did it get into my hand? I clutched it tightly and swam back to our work boat, *Dulcinea.* Carefully I handed the object to our first mate, Carol Craig. She stared at it in wonder.

"Where?" she asked.

I shook my head. "I don't know. It was just there."

She examined the indistinct numerals stamped on the oval of brass at the center of the wreath. There was a square slot in this numbered, undecorated portion.

"It's a belt buckle," Carol announced. "Look here." She demonstrated how webbing might be attached and the end of a belt slotted through the opening. "It's an old design," she said. "You see it in women's things."

A belt buckle out of nowhere lands mysteriously in my hand. I thought: Check the nineteenth-century British marine registry for its number and I'll find the owner and return the buckle to his or her relatives.

The idea seemed so reasonable at the time. But what of the historic nature of the site and the law protecting it? Was it right or legal to keep this artifact no matter how well intentioned I might be?

"Maybe I should toss it back," I suggested.

Carol shook her hear. "You do and it'll be gone forever. Resurrect the lost soul who owned it."

From that moment on I was joined at the heart to nautical archaeology. A fateful moment. A wonderful moment. But I had no idea I was enlisting in a war among institutions, governments, idealists, and scammers. I was an innocent, dripping wet, with a rare bit of history clutched in my hand. Thousands of miles away gunfights had broken out over similar artifacts in the Florida Keys. Lives and reputations were being shredded. Unknowingly, I was about to leap into the trenches of a war over the pyramids of the deep.

III

Sunken treasure: an irony within a riddle wrapped in a blood sport. Almost immediately it was clear that in the manner of pirates and privateers of old the object of all the fuss was personal gain. Loot in all its permutations. It drove the greedy, and disguised in high-sounding language it drove the idealists.

The spoilers had drawn battle lines. On one side were the academics, the trained nautical archaeologists who desired nothing less than absolute dominion over "drowned patrimony." Monetary gain didn't interest them, at least not directly; it was history they were after. But history translated into the coin of prestige, publication, tenure. When an academician finds a sunken treasure the payoff is a job for life.

On the other side were the treasure hunters, those who wanted the freedom to roam the seas, find ancient shipwrecks, and essentially "mine" them, often destroying them in the process. If a wreck proved profitable they'd reinvest and go after others, selling off the "goodies" to pay for the search. The academics considered them looters, destroyers of history. As one marine archaeologist put it: "Imagine selling off the Sphinx stone-by-stone so you can plunder other treasures." The mantra of the academics was and is: Thou shall not sell the goodies!

Caught in the middle were legions of amateurs who worked both sides of the line. And looming over everyone were the state and federal governments who wanted most if not all bankable treasures placed in their vaults for "posterity."

All sides were engaged in a very public brawl (debate is too polite a word) over who should get what and who should make the rules.

Soon after my investigation of the *Rhone* I received a call from the Smithsonian Institution. The editors of *Smithsonian* magazine asked if I would research and write an article on the "treasure wars" by interviewing the combatants and coming back with a definitive story. My editor, Timothy Foote, put the major question this way: *Who really owns treasure?*

This is fairly obscure stuff, I told myself in the beginning. But I was wrong. Sunken treasure and nautical archaeology have entered

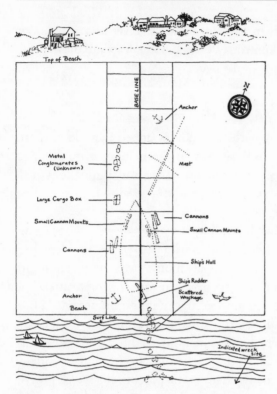

This map shows a vessel wrecked near shore and buried in the sand. Virtually every beach hides some lost marine artifact. *Drawing by Kathryn Williams.*

the realm of pop culture. I would eventually rise with the tide, write a book on the subject, and become pleasantly deluged by major publications requesting variations on the *Smithsonian* article. Like the treasure hunters, I was hooked. And treasure, I soon discovered, is a full-time obsession. For several years I became an "authority," a "talking head" on radio and television shows, flying around the country to make appearances and give lectures. It was a heady experience but also a dangerous one. Few subjects excite more passion than the lure of lost booty. After one heated radio show in Miami I had to be escorted back to my car by an armed security guard.

Marine archaeology was born late in our own century and its primary roots are in the United States. This is important to understanding the spirit that characterizes the field. It is also important to gain a sense of just how much raw material is out there, the truly mind-boggling proportions of the historic trove on a worldwide scale.

The trail of treasure leads back to the earliest times. Long before our prehistoric ancestors learned to live together in primitive villages 30,000 years ago, they were venturing across rivers and lakes in crude vessels. And having made it safely from one shore to another, they took bolder steps: They confronted the seas. From the beginning they have inadvertently deposited their belongings beneath the waters.

What is treasure? This is an important question with more than one answer. To the marine archaeologist it is a historic artifact; it represents an encapsuled civilization, perhaps many civilizations. To an archaeologist a bottle or a belt buckle is perhaps more relevant than gold.

To treasure hunters that same ship is profit. Even though they may be at pains to salvage a wreck using established archaeological techniques, the bottom line is drawn. The "goodies" come first.

I was fortunate to have known the late Peter Throckmorton, the self-taught conceptual godfather of undersea archaeology. He was one of those irresistible intellectuals who believed fate was a matter of belief. If one believed strongly enough, if the vision was supercharged with energy, then the possibilities were endless. His intensity was electric, often surprising; it hummed in his compact, muscular body. Perpetually restless, he possessed a kind of Jack Kerouac *On the Road* wanderlust; he was a demi-beatnik with a copy of *The Journal of Albion Moonlight* in one pocket and Rimbaud's *The Drunken Boat* in another. An iconoclast of the 1950s, he hated "suits" (a word he used derisively) and had a special fondness for fine, soothing beverages.

In the late 1950s and early 1960s, Throckmorton and his friend Arthur C. Clarke, the famous creator of *2001: A Space Odyssey,* pieced together the puzzle of a Mogul silver wreck off the southeast coast of Sri Lanka at a site known as the Great Basses Reef, in the Indian Ocean. At the height of this particularly precarious "dig" Clarke was partially paralyzed and Throckmorton nearly killed by the vicious surge of the sea. Yet in the worst possible conditions, Throckmorton had managed to develop the art of site mapping. His was a rough prototype, but it deftly illustrated the importance of an on-paper approach, the schematic of the often incomprehensible chaos of an archaeological site. He also managed to find a solid wall of silver coins embedded in the reef.

In what became a typical outcome of treasure hunting fever, neither Throckmorton nor Clarke struck it rich. The coins they found were commonplace among collectors. The market was awash in 1702 rupees and the cost of excavating them would have far exceeded their bullion value.

In Clarke's fascinating book *The Treasure of the Great Reef* (Ballentine, 1974), the usually unemotional author says of the Great

Basses dig: "It was one of the unforgettable moments of a lifetime. "He knew he was staring at something few men have ever seen—honest-to-goodness treasure. The impact on his life, he added, was a little like "finding a flying saucer in one's backyard."

Clarke moved on. But Throckmorton, the tough, unrelenting intellectual, was hooked. He couldn't stay out of the water. In 1960, he lured to Turkey a University of Pennsylvania team, which later excavated a Bronze Age merchant ship in deep water off the Aegean island of Yassi Ada. It was an excavation that became the icon for all future underwater digs.

Until Yassi Ada, land-based archaeologists were convinced that useful work in the sea was impossible. The concept of mucking around in the deep seemed preposterous, a waste of time. A popular academic sport at the time was to scoff at the sea-going "lunatic fringe," which included Throckmorton and the soon-to-be preeminent underwater guru, Dr. George F. Bass.

Yet the techniques pioneered at Yassi Ada were on an order of magnitude of improvement over the Great Basses dig. Archaeology changed forever. Unlike the eroded and pilfered land sites of terrestial archaeology, Throckmorton demonstrated that sunken ships are a frozen moment in time, wonderfully preserved in the anaerobic environment of the sea. A ship entombed in the sand and sediments could last relatively unscathed for centuries. It was a precious time capsule, an undisturbed reflection of the era and culture from which it came—a true pyramid of the deep.

Throckmorton's articles for *National Geographic*, "Thirty-three Centuries Under the Sea" (May 1960) and "Oldest Known Shipwreck Yields Bronze Age Cargo" (May 1962), exploded like a firestorm. Traditional archaeologists found themselves in the awkward position of the ancient astronomers who had insisted that Earth was at the center of the universe.

Years later, just before his death, I spoke to Throckmorton about the Great Basses dig and the future of nautical archaeology. A kind of antihero who never backed away from controversy, he had been at serious odds with a determined group of his colleagues. The struggle had drained him. He was in a sense becalmed, a spirit seeking a favorable wind that simply refused to fill his sails. Bass and others had leaped ahead of him, and this pained him a great deal. Perhaps he felt used, ripped-off. Some suggested he was suffering terminal burnout, though there was sometimes a hint of malice in this suggestion. He had become a professor of nautical archaeology at NOVA University in Florida and was working to establish a field school for graduate students in the Caribbean. It was an uphill engagement. Bass had moved on to Texas A&M and was establishing the driving engine of today's subsea search for history, the Institute of Nautical Archaeology (INA).

Apparently Throckmorton had been factored out of the INA equation, and he didn't wish to discuss it in detail. But on the subject of the Great Basses and his other major digs he was open and generous.

"You couldn't place a reasonable value on the silver," he said of the Great Basses. "We couldn't figure out how much was down there."

Apparently the Dutch East India Company's records of the ship's manifest had been destroyed.

"It would have cost us thirty or forty thousand dollars to work the wreck for a few weeks before the monsoon set in. It was a very expensive gamble," he explained. "We took it as far as we could. The wreck was a mess. Working conditions were just awful. We had to crawl around on the wreck site. Aside from a few cultural items, all we could find was money. I got sick of the money. It doesn't give you much history."

This was 1986, much time had passed, and he felt easy enough to talk about the greed that may beset any treasure dig. Treasure was a word he used like "suits."

"There were moments when we believed we were going to be millionaires. You know how it is. Treasure brings out the worst in everybody, especially government. If you want to get rich go into commercial salvage. I have a wreck right now I'd like to get at that's full of copper ingots. That's business. History is another matter. I don't feel I have the right to own historical objects. History belongs to everybody."

He was critical of treasure hunters such as Mel Fisher, who after sixteen years of searching found the 1622 treasure-laden Galleon *Nuestra Señora de Atocha* near Florida's Marquesas Keys. Part of the recovered cargo, the "primary cultural deposit," consisted of forty-seven tons of silver bars stacked like cordwood on the ocean bottom. Fisher, a former chicken farmer from Gary, Indiana, continued to escalate the market value of the mother lode from an initial $400 million in 1985 to $1 billion-plus a few years later. As of this writing, he is still attempting to dispose of artifacts at auctions in Atlantic City, Las Vegas, and elsewhere. The glow of his treasure seems to have dimmed.

Yet Fisher had a kind of magic. His single-mindedness was as vivid as the huge gold coin he dangled from his neck. A creature of Jobian faith, he understood that belief combined with fantasy is the chemistry of reality. I had interviewed him often, the first time in 1978 aboard his floating office/museum, a faux Spanish galleon called the *Golden Doubloon,* moored at the gas docks in Key West. He hadn't found the *Atocha* but had pulled in a number of "traces": silver and gold coins and a fair collection of artifacts. His critics claimed none of it belonged to the missing galleon, that Fisher was conning would-be investors. He ignored the criticism.

"We're going to open an exhibit at the Queens Museum in New York," he enthused while crushing out yet another cigarette in an ashtray overflowing with butts. "Wait till you see it. You won't believe your eyes."

That he discovered the *Atocha* in 1985 was remarkable, though it served to sharpen outrage over his salvage practices and drove him into the trenches with Florida state and federal bureaucrats who tried unsuccessfully to strip him of his finds. But what really struck me about Fisher was his phenomenal luck. During one of his forays to Las Vegas in search of investors, I followed him through a casino as he sniffed out the slot machines. When he found one that seemed promising, he picked an anonymous desert rat off the floor and asked if he'd drop coins into the machine as Fisher pulled the handle.

"Why not do it yourself?" I wondered.

"Won't work that way," Fisher replied.

Fisher instructed the stranger to reach around with his right arm so that it passed under his left, take hold of the slot's long, silver handle, and turn his back on the machine. Within one-half hour Fisher walked away with $1,000 worth of winnings. A year later I again found him at the Las Vegas Hilton. Security guards surrounded him as he entered the elevator I was on. He was carrying $5,000 in slot winnings. "Just lucky, I guess," Fisher grinned.

He was suddenly famous and infamous. He claimed to be doing "real" archaeology at the *Atocha* site but no one believed him.

Throckmorton said the work was "superficial." There was no real conservator on board. "It was just goodies, goodies, goodies," he complained. "To me conservators are the unsung heroes. If you don't have good conservators, you're doing nebbish archaeology."

Throckmorton was equally blunt in his appraisal of academics. They had let him down, abandoned him, some would say they had plagiarized his ideas. It is a cloud still hanging over the academic community, though few will admit it. Throckmorton's name seldom surfaces.

"They're stuffy," Throckmorton told me. "They have their own little world and they become creatures of it. They're pedantic. They seem to want to be bureaucrats. They don't want to get out there and get wet and do the work."

But the science has advanced. Archaeologists armed with the highest of high-tech instruments have begun to make an inventory. Important discoveries have been made, the wreck of the *Titanic* being a spectacular example.

IV

Finding the *Titanic* was the child of hi-tech methods, though infinitely more historic finds have emerged by sheer accident. For instance, in December 1984, the Texas A&M team, successors of Throckmorton, fully excavated a Bronze Age ship off the coast of Turkey. The vessel is one of the oldest to be surveyed by scientific methods, yet she was discovered by an ordinary Turkish sponge diver who offhandedly mentioned to Throckmorton that he'd seen an object resembling "a biscuit with ears." Throckmorton asked the sponger to draw a picture. The result was a sketch that looked very much like a copper ingot, a type known to have been produced in ancient Cyprus. It was stunning. Here was evidence of a ship that sailed before the Greeks waged the Trojan War, that hauled copper across the Mediterranean when Tutankhamen ruled Egypt.

The excavation has thus far produced one of our richest historical troves. A golden goblet has been recovered, along with jewelry in the shape of a bird of prey. Amber and faience beads were uncovered nearby about seventy-five yards off Cape Ula Burnum, near the village of Kas. Also found were elephant tusks and hippopotamus teeth, both highly prized by the ancients. Clay amphorae contained many surprises: marvelous glass beads, an arsenic compound, and a variety of plant seeds. Also recovered was a small personal seal, which might have been used by the merchant to stamp correspondence. A spellbinding encounter with the past, and how lucky we are to have experienced it.

There are eons of drowned cultural history along the Mediterranean. Half a century after Throckmorton's first discoveries, we can hardly begin to estimate the magnitude of what's out there. Imagine the tiny slice of Mediterranean coastline off Israel, an area INA's Shelley Wachsmann calls "a nexus of trade for more than five millennia." Surveys of the region show that on average there is a wrecked ship along every 300 feet of shoreline. Wachsmann's team is excavating a Byzantine site on the shoals of Tuntura Lagoon, a natural harbor near the Bronze Age city of Tel Dor.

A shipwreck properly exhumed is a history book and a museum all in one. It is this remarkable fact that makes sunken treasure in any form such an illuminating cultural resource.

The British Sub-Aqua Club, a group of mostly amateur explorers, has attracted funds from the British government and various individuals in its quest to raise large portions of the 1545 carrack *Mary Rose,* flagship of King Henry VIII. Her recovery off Portsmouth revealed a cross section of Anglo-Saxon society: silver flatware for the officers, crude wooden "trenchers" for the ordinary seamen, gaming boards used by the officers, and arrows, still ready to be launched, proving that Henry insisted that his bowmen use their talents at sea as well as on land.

Whole vessels have been raised intact. In April 1961, salvage experts raised the *Vasa,* a sixty-four-gun Swedish warship that capsized and sank in 1628. Like the *Titanic,* the *Vasa* died on her maiden voyage. She was sailing out of Stockholm Harbor carrying more than fifty crewmen and passengers when her open gun ports flooded. For more than three centuries she lay beneath the deep, preserving anaerobic mud of the harbor. To walk through the *Vasa* today is a true journey back in time. Inside the vessel researchers found sea chests, boots, tools, beer steins, and weapons. Lying among the cannon carriages were partially clad skeletons, one with a sheath knife and a leather money pouch with twenty coins clipped to a belt.

Even more awesome in its state of preservation is HMS *Breadalbane,* a British barque built in Glasgow in 1843. The vessel and its crew were dispatched from England in one of the most daring rescue attempts at sea, as part of a convoy of ships sent to the Arctic in search of two other ships, *Erebus* and *Terror.* In August 1853, *Breadalbane* was at Beechy Island north of Baffin in the Northwest Passage. Ice closed in, shearing away her bottom and sinking her in more than 300 feet of icy water. In 1980, Arctic explorer Joseph McInnis found the vessel in a near-perfect state of preservation.

"Everything is nearly the way it was when she went down," he reported.

How many ships and lost civilizations are waiting to be discovered? Can we make a reasonable estimate of their value?

We're only beginning to answer these questions. Records are limited and those prior to 1900 tend to be unreliable. Advances in technology and computer search methods may give us a better feel for the numbers as the unglamorous grunt work of surveying moves forward. Late in our own century we have begun to piece together a rough outline, a kind of inventory of what's down there.

Prior to the advent of modern navigational equipment at the turn of the century, worldwide ship losses averaged 1,000 to 2,000 annually. Modern electronic gear has cut these losses significantly. However, most of the numbers are based on relatively big vessels, those of 100 tons or more. A 100-ton ship looks like a wooden-hulled World War II torpedo boat or a fifty- to sixty-five-foot motor yacht at your local marina. Most boats are a lot smaller, too small for accurate record keeping.

John Jedrlinic, a U.S. Navy historian, says pre-1900 sinkings were epidemic. Europe destroyed its navies as if they were fodder. In 1822, at a high point in the Napoleonic conflicts, more than 2,000 ships were gunned down and sunk.

"There's no way to get exact totals," Jedrlinic says of nineteenth-century records.

Wars add greatly to the ever-growing marine inventory. Dr. Robert Scheina, official U.S. Coast Guard historian, says during World War I the Allies lost 6,000 vessels, and more than twice that number went down in World War II. To place some economic value on these losses, Scheina suggests that if we could salvage all the oil tankers sunk during World War II, we would have had more than enough reserves to overcome the 1973–1974 Arab oil embargo.

In the United States marine archaeologists have come to a consensus. They estimate there are a minimum of 100,000 pre-1900 wrecks in our coastal waters. Don Kincaid, a photographer who has spent more than three decades photographing and searching for treasure with Mel Fisher's team, believes there is a shipwreck along every quarter-mile of coastline. "Wrecks on top of wrecks," he says. "Every marina, every boat yard, every bay and inlet, riverside dock and jetty."

Kincaid has tried to determine which of these ships has historic or monetary value.

"I could spend my whole life working wrecks between Key West and Miami and I probably wouldn't scratch the surface—no pun intended."

Should we continue to search and dig? Or is it more prudent to let technology lead us? Flinders Petrie wrote at the turn of the century that an excavation without full historical knowledge and technical know-how leads to the "most miserable catastrophes." Petrie, whose position has long been the politically correct mantra of academics, believed it was "better to let things lie a few centuries ... if they can be let alone, than repeat the vandalism of past ages without the excuse of being a barbarian." This last word is often associated with the profiteering types.

V

Archaeologists sometimes disagree on how old a site must be before it's considered historically valuable. Robert F. Marx, who has bridged the gap between treasure hunting and historical archaeology, points out that archaeologists working in the Mediterranean insist that a site be at least 500 years old before committing time and resources to an excavation. In Israel some archaeologists say that a Crusader wreck, dated to about A.D. 1200, wasn't actively pursued because it wasn't old enough. In the United States a century is the bottom line. Marx takes the position that any ship that tells us about the past is important, regardless of age.

"People say we can get the plans for most sunken ships," he points out. "But it isn't true. Spain, France, Holland, and other countries have archives, even models. But most date after 1700. In America, most building plans are post-1800. Before this ships were built by what was called 'knack of the eye,' without any plans or sketches."

Of course, *value* depends on whether one is a treasure hunter, an archaeologist, or one of the new breed of "aquatechnologists" who are developing new robot vehicles and "telepresence" to explore the deepest parts of the sea.

Treasure hunters are interested in the bankable value of gold, silver, and gemstones. The figures are astonishing. The dollar amounts used here come from the best and most experienced of the hard-core hunters: Mel Fisher; Robert F. Marx; Rex Cowan, the British sea rover and treasure hunter; and John S. Potter, Jr., author of the classic *The Treasure Diver's Guide* (Bonanza Books, 1960). The following numbers have been updated conservatively to reflect the markets for gold and silver bullion. "Historic value," a multiple of whatever auction and/or collector demands may bring, is not factored into the following:

- Spanish armadas—Peru to Spain via Cape Horn (1500–1820): $320 billion carried, $4 billion lost.
- Peru Merchantmen—Peru to Spain via Cape Horn (1534–1810): $20 billion carried, $5 billion lost.
- Manila galleons—Acapulco to the Philippines (1570–1815): $10 billion carried, $500 million lost.
- The Spice Route—Europe and the Far East (1502–1870): $20 billion carried, $500 million lost.

Marx provides a remarkable inventory in his *Shipwrecks in the Americas* (Bonanza Books, 1983). This impressive reference covers the years from 1492 to 1825. He documents 3,145 losses, from Columbus's flagship *Santa Maria,* wrecked off Cap Haiti, to the 1812 loss off Sable Island, in Canadian waters, of the *Barbados,* with its multibillion-dollar cargo of precious metals.

"There is so much out there that all the marine archaeologists in the world, working full-time, couldn't make a dent in the population," Marx claims.

In this hemisphere alone, at least 3,000 "important" ships (those with historic and treasure value) have perished. And the list continues to expand. One of the first big strikes in the twentieth century came from the *Laurentic,* whose owners, White Star, also lost the *Titanic.* (Over a period of years White Star saw all of its ships go to the bottom.) During World War I, the *Laurentic* struck a mine off Malin Head, Donegal. She went down with 250 tons of gold bars.

Captain G.C.D. Damant of the Royal Navy took charge of the recovery in 1917. After 5,000 hazardous penetrations of the ship, Damant's team recovered all but twenty-five bars of gold.

In 1981, salvager Keith Jessop pulled off what has to be considered a deepwater salvage miracle. Using advanced diving systems, his team recovered five and a half tons of gold from the British cruiser *Edinburgh.* A U-boat attack during World War II sank the cruiser in 900 feet of water in the Barents Sea off the Russian port at Murmansk. Jessop pocketed $30 million as his share of the recovery.

Rex Cowan, who recovered 350,000 silver coins from the Dutch East India ship *Hollandia,* wrecked off Sicily in 1743, admits that the price of any treasure depends on the quality of the finds, rarity, demand, and a dozen other intangibles.

I met Cowan a few years ago in Rhode Island at a meeting of the Atlantic Alliance for Maritime Heritage Conservation. Except for a briefcase filled with old coins, which he was prepared to sell, he was the exact opposite of the laconic Mel Fisher. He was eager to talk about treasure and interjected his views on art, literature, warfare, and what he considered the superiority of feminine sensibilities.

"Women are interested in everything," he informed me. "You know, people say women gossip." He formed the word with a kind of acid sarcasm. "Well, I happen to think gossip is healthy. It shows an interest in people and how they conduct their lives. ..." It was hard to keep him pinned to the subject of treasure.

"Frankly, there is no way to assign absolute value to anything," Cowan went on, returning to the point. "The only fairly good measure is in the precious metals and their 'melt-down' value. This means that conceivably we can melt the coins into a sizable brick and sell it on the bullion market. But depending on your dealer and the conditions of the markets, the worth can be discounted 40 percent or more."

Cowan reached into his pocket and placed a pillar dollar on the table. Minted by the Spanish, it was the first silver dollar to be used in the Americas.

"There are lots of these around," he explained. "Every coin dealer and every museum in the world has scads of them. So it's not rarity we're dealing with. It's just the fact that the coin came up from the sea after a very long time. There's a challenge connected to it. A mystique. You don't destroy such things. If anything, you highlight them for what they are. And they are not, strictly speaking, monetary units."

Treasure often brings out the worst in people. From the most idealistic archaeologist to greediest treasure hunter, the spectacle of a seabed littered with gold has the power to transform the psyche. But Peter Throckmorton was deadly accurate when he said no one acts more badly than governments.

It was at the governmental level that I became actively involved in the treasure wars. As a cofounder of the Atlantic Alliance, a nonprofit organization made up of academics, treasure hunters, and laypersons, I would come to know firsthand the true sting behind Throckmorton's bitter government-bashing.

VI

There's a saying among treasure hunters that the romance of the mother lode ends the moment you find it.

There's more than a little truth in this. Arthur C. Clarke put it best when he said that with the exception of finding a flying saucer in one's backyard, nothing is more disruptive to normal life. One is transported into a strange world of antagonisms, hatred, and the greed of governments.

Treasure is a magnet for publicity. The finder becomes a public figure, and this in itself has its anguish. There are competing interests with vociferous ideas about why you, the finder, should not benefit from your good fortune. The government surrounds the treasure trove with legal razor wire, claiming that anything historic is "public domain." To lay claim to one's finds is to be called a grave robber, this despite the fact that much of sanctioned, classical archaeology *is* grave robbing. Peruvian mummies, Tutankhamen, Jesse James, President Grover Cleveland, Mayan graves, the Chilean Chinchorro, China's Taklimakan mummies, and North American Indian burial mounds have been dug up by academics. The wet list might include the *Vasa* and the *Titanic,* the *Edmund Fitzgerald,* and the lost nuclear submarine *Thresher,* waiting for us in 6,000 feet of water.

The era of the free-ranging treasure hunter came to a halt in the late 1980s. The quest, once an alluring part of the American psyche, has been legislated out of existence. Its practitioners have been driven offshore to work with foreign governments.

The big turning point was the Abandoned Shipwreck Act, passed by Congress in the late 1980s. Introduced by former Florida Congressman Charles E. Bennett, it is based on the concept of "escheateage," a British common law stating that property of a serf reverts to the manor's lord on the death of the serf. Ships and other historic sites covered by the Bennett Act refer to those "substantially buried in the bottom," covered by coral, or listed in the National Register of Historic Places.

Bennett successfully set aside Admiralty law, which allowed individuals to lay claim to an abandoned shipwreck by applying to a federal court. Under Admiralty one could excavate a site and keep most of what came out of it. Bennett's law allows the federal government to assert its right to title over historic sites but passes it on to states where the discoveries are made. The states write their own regulations on how recoveries are to be handled. Nonarchaeologists may petition for a claim if they agree to work with state-appointed archaeologists and conservators. The artifacts are handed over to state officials, who decide which items a salvor may keep. The act covers the twelve-mile limit of state coastal waters and inland sites.

I was still thinking about that brass belt buckle from the *Rhone* when I interviewed Bennett for the *Smithsonian* story. At the time, his proposal was going nowhere, despite nearly unanimous backing by the academic community. A World War II hero who had sustained war wounds and who walked with a limp, the congressman was certainly no admirer of Mel Fisher. Fisher had lost his son and daughter-in-law near the end of his sixteen-year search for the *Atocha,* and I had a feeling that Bennett blamed him, at least in part, for their deaths. (They drowned one night in their bunks when their salvage boat capsized over the *Atocha* site.)

Bennett had been trying to pass his proposal since 1979. Each time it had been summarily lobbied out of existence by Fisher and his supporters. Mel was, after all, the strike-it-rich "little guy," an "every man" who lived through one of the world's most enduring fantasies. Bennett represented the grasping, taxing hand of the federal establishment.

Yet the congressman was extraordinary tough-minded. When he spoke of treasure his tone was clipped, cutting, but never shrill. Below the surface of his composure one could almost smell a volatile mix of frustration and contempt. He was perhaps as persistent as Fisher, and in the end he scored a win big as the *Atocha.*

"We've all heard and read of some treasure salvor locating a historic shipwreck," he said. "'How wonderful!' we say. 'Just think of the knowledge that can be gained.' But nothing guarantees that. No one except the treasure salvagers will gain. You see, in the haste of many salvage operations the shipwreck site may become a shambles, wrecked again if you will."

I told him about the work of the Atlantic Alliance, how we hoped to bring the various disciplines together. As I spoke his eyes bored into me like lasers.

"Well, they're not *all* looters," he shrugged.

Looters is code for pirates and a class of persons separated from grave robbers by the thinnest of boundaries. I pointed out that Fisher had established a treasure museum in Key West for his *Atocha* finds.

Maybe he'd receive no accolades from the INA. Yet the public could see what a Spanish galleon was all about.

Bennett's mouth tightened. It was his "so what!" expression. I reminded him of his own small museum and wondered where his artifacts had come from. He assured me they hadn't been slipped under his door in the dead of night by looters. Unlike Fisher, Bennett's treasures were for display, not for sale.

"I have this belt buckle from the *Rhone,*" I confessed. "What does that make me?"

Bennett stared hard, shrugged, made no comment.

I spoke with Robert Marx, who was on-again, off-again about the Bennett plan. More world-ranging in his work than Fisher, Marx was a lettered archaeologist. He was difficult to track down, and when I finally arranged an interview he was quick to condemn just about everyone engaged in the treasure wars.

"I just don't like guys in three-piece suits telling me how to do archaeology," he growled, a comment straight out of Throckmorton's book of put-downs. "There are so few active archaeologists. All the academics in the world don't have time to do what needs to be done."

During the public hearings on the Bennett bill, Marx was more than a little put out by the posturing of his fellow archaeologists. They were "purists," he insisted. He pointed to an article in *Skin Diver* magazine with a picture of him holding some gold coins.

"They thought I ought to get out of the business because of that," he laughed. "And what do they do besides stir up bloody trouble for themselves? What have they written in the way of research? I see very little in the journals. What I do see is a lot of blasting of each other. Blasting the states for their laws. Blasting treasure hunters."

I asked if he thought it was wrong to sell duplicative artifacts, of which there are many on most archaeological sites.

"I worked in Brazil where artifacts were auctioned. What's wrong with that? You do need money to keep going and the object is to keep going, to get at the history."

Marx believed the Bennett formula had a good side. It might bring order out of chaos. When he testified before Congress in favor of the plan during a 1985 hearing, he attempted to interject reason into the hot, go-nowhere romance associated with the finding of "vast fortunes."

"I'd like to state in the most forceful possible way [that] no one, no matter how lucky or skillful, can ever make a reasonable living from the commercial salvage of ancient shipwrecks. … I have supported my family with money made from my thirty-one books, hundreds of articles, filming and selling documentaries, and lecturing. The only people who make any big money in this field are those who get gullible people to invest in wildly hyped, highly publicized treasure hunt schemes which grossly exaggerate the actual amounts of treasure."

George Bass also weighed in. His round, boyish face and dainty moustaches gave him the appearance of an Edwardian gentleman, a slightly reserved hero out of a Somerset Maugham play. He spoke softly, confident of his reputation and record of accomplishment in INA. He had built a record. He was apparently so certain of his place in history that he began entertaining second thoughts about the rough trade of mucking around under cold, murky seas. After all, it was gritty stuff, suitable grunt work for his youthful disciples. He hinted he might spend the rest of his career in the parlors of academe, where he might stay dry and warm and engage in research.

"Nautical archaeology isn't about diving," he told me. "There's a lot of confusion over that. It's not romantic. And I'm getting older, you know."

Older? He was forty-five at the time of our interview. I was about the same age, and I was still at it, living on the jetwing. It wasn't until my mid-fifties, a defining moment when I found myself being vanquished on the Great Barrier Reef, that I began to notice my own level of vulnerability. This is not to discredit Bass in any way. I mention it merely as an illustration. He had reached a crossroad and was trimming his underwater time in order to broaden his reach.

To Bass, archaeology was a kind of deity, all-encompassing and universal.

"An archaeological site in a jungle, on a mountaintop, in a desert, or underwater is an archaeological site. Underwater sites are protected in Europe, Africa, Asia, and Australia. Why not the United States?"

The kind of organization represented by the Atlantic Alliance just couldn't cut it, he added.

"A salvage group with one or two archaeologists cannot conduct serious archaeology any more than a large hospital with one or two physicians can practice serious medicine."

And as to the notion of using paraprofessionals to go after those tens of thousands of wrecks that lay undetected: "An amateur archaeologist has no more business directing an excavation than an amateur dentist would have practicing dentistry," he declared.

He reluctantly admitted that treasure hunters were correct when they claim American archaeologists don't have a good record in surveying and excavating shipwrecks in the Americas, that most of the work has been accomplished in foreign waters. But, he went on, there were no archaeologists in Greece or Turkey two centuries ago.

"I believe we are fortunate that not all Greek tombs were robbed or that not all Greek temples were burned for lime. We must think of the future," he said. "One day there will be sufficient archaeological expertise in this hemisphere to do the job, if any worthwhile [sites] remain."

Under the Bennett law, academic archaeologists command the high ground. They alone are allowed to recover and evaluate the "goodies."

Questions remain. Should "redundant" artifacts such as Throckmorton's 1702 rupees be sold to raise money for continued research and excavation? Opinion is divided. Marx says yes; Bass disagrees. Classical archaeologists contend that each artifact, no matter how duplicative, must be preserved and studied. New techniques and investigative tools may someday reveal overlooked details. There is merit to this philosophy, which also lies behind the argument that shipwrecks should remain untouched until there is money, time, and sufficient talent available to properly excavate them.

But are historic sites in danger of being lost forever under current policies? Should the state and federal governments make an all-out push to survey and excavate the thousands of sites still out there, untouched? Will the what's-the-hurry approach lead to neglect and loss of historical data?

No one is more passionate about this than former Florida state underwater archaeologist Wilburn A. "Sonny" Cockrell. A man with a fiery temper and a sharply bitter wit, the lanky Cockrell looks like a pirate-turned-prophet. At the zenith of the treasure wars, his presence on Mel Fisher's salvage boats (mandated by the state) loomed like that of a long-haired, bearded, avenging angel. To be in the same room with him was to feel a distinct static charge. Even his peers called him a "purist," a man prepared to scrap his reputation and give his life to preserve history. He was also a man who put his life on the line exploring the water-filled caves of Warm Mineral Springs, a site on the west coast of Florida thought to be Ponce de León's true Fountain of Youth. Cockrell and his team recovered a 10,000-year-old human skull from the cavern, its brain in excellent condition. It was a

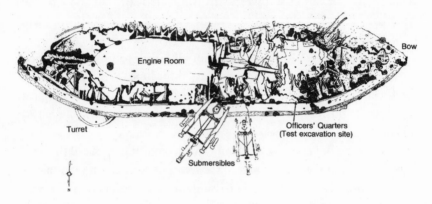

Wreck of the ironclad USS *Monitor* off the coast of North Carolina. The ship is upside down with its gun turret in the sand. *Drawing courtesy National Oceanic and Atmospheric Administration.*

scientific breakthrough far more important than discovering a new pharaoh in the Valley of the Kings.

Cockrell may have been a purist with a quick temper, yet his obsessions were part of the breed. He could spin genuine horror stories. He had seen galleons disappear almost overnight in the Florida Keys, destroyed by treasure hunters and careless sport divers. An incident that truly enraged him was the nearly overnight destruction of an eighteenth-century Spanish galleon. Thought to be the much-prized *San Jose,* the ship was down in very shallow water off Islamorada in the middle Keys.

"The *San Jose* was beautiful," Cockrell recalled. "It could have been an underwater park. I can show you pictures of my son swimming through the eye of a huge anchor. And there were cannons and actual ribbing. It was incredible. And they raped it."

Cockrell believed media visibility and hyping were at least partly to blame for public apathy. Romance, he complained, almost always prevailed over the need to protect and preserve.

On behalf of the state of Florida, Cockrell waged a long, convoluted battle against treasure hunters in general and Mel Fisher in particular. There was costly litigation, much of it against Fisher's Treasure Salvors, Inc. At the outset the state spent $350,000 in legal fees trying to grab Fisher's share of the *Atocha* and her sister ship *Santa*

Margarita, and wound up with nothing to show for it. At one point the state locked away the artifacts in a prison cell in Tallahassee. *The Miami Herald,* in an editorial headlined "Burying Treasure," objected that bureaucrats were "paying a high price for a case of improbable merit."

"People see shipwrecks as something to be 'mined,'" Cockrell fumed. "The myth that treasure hunters are real archaeologists is a lie."

It is curious that late in the twentieth century we are closer to Atlantis than ever before, but the reverberations of the treasure wars are still delaying its discovery. The Bennett legislation has all but eliminated paraprofessional searching in American waters. The cadre of treasure hunters, many of whom might have worked with archaeologists and conservators, have been bum's-rushed. Even the archaeologists appear to have lost their drive.

The sad truth of this may be seen in the fate of one of the most famous ships ever built, the USS *Monitor.* The first true ironclad warship, the little "cheese box on a raft" marked a turning point in the American Civil War when it engaged and sank the Confederate *Merrimack.* Despite its glory in war, the *Monitor* suffered an ignoble fate. Under tow to Charleston, where she was to join a Union blockade, she parted her towing cables around midnight December 31, 1862, sixteen miles southeast of Cape Haterras, North Carolina. Engulfed in a rising storm, she heeled over and sank, with the loss of sixteen hands.

She was rediscovered by a Duke University team in 1974. The boat was upside down, resting on its gun turret below 220 feet of current-swept, shark-infested water. She was exposed and virtually unprotected by covering sediments. While the federal government debated raising the ship, the sea was taking a frightful toll. Investigations showed her hull to be badly worn and corroded and in danger of collapse. Following a decade of debate over how to handle this one-of-a-kind warship, archaeologists recovered one of its anchors and a few artifacts. The bulk of the vessel remains on the bottom, breaking up and becoming less salvagable every day.

Meanwhile, the *Monitor* has been declared a "marine sanctuary" by the National Oceanic and Atmospheric Administration (NOAA), conferring upon it the status of a national park. This is like giving someone a high title and at the same time sentencing him to the gallows. Amateur archaeologists have gone to court seeking permission to salvage some of the artifacts. Their recoveries have been donated to the government, yet the government has done little to display them.

At one point NOAA worked with the National Trust for Historic Preservation to raise money for a salvage attempt. There were discussions, peppered by lively objections from the academic community. The archaeologists were in agreement: The *Monitor* was too fragile to be successfully raised. Better that she take her chances on the bottom. The consensus was to opt for time. Maybe a technological breakthrough would occur allowing a more successful intact recovery. Maybe.

Decades after her discovery, the *Monitor* remains on the bottom, abandoned, ripped by currents and disintegrating in her official hands-off glory. This, more than the attempted escheatment of Mel Fisher's *Atocha* treasure, is what Throckmorton meant by the bad behavior of governments.

The United States isn't the only country attempting to manage its submerged cultural resources. The government of Greece has dropped an opaque curtain around its nautical history. Greece has banished from its waters virtually every team of non-Greek archaeologists. The Americans are at least direct in their policy of just saying no. Greece says no indirectly with a bewildering maze of paperwork, delays, broken promises, and outright deception.

In 1995, I petitioned the Greek government for permission to document and photograph historic objects in their waters. I had seen brochures advertising dive trips. The brochures displayed photographs of amphora and other artifacts. I figured, if they're making history into a tourist trade, surely a journalist will be allowed in. I was wrong.

The tourist operations, I was told by Greek officials, really didn't involve an encounter with cultural artifacts, despite full-color photographs of divers handling amphora. Was this a ruse? Were these artifacts bogus?

Officials at the Embassy of Greece in Washington asked to see these advertisements and promised to return them to me. I never saw the brochures again, despite repeated requests for their return. They simply vanished, and those with whom I dealt claimed they'd never received them.

I had also petitioned the government of Turkey, which was open and cooperative. The Greeks created a monumental flak screen of paperwork. For one entire year they dodged my questions. In frustration, I brought up the example of Turkish cooperation. If Turkey would help me, why not Greece? A highly placed Greek official sneered, "Well, it's not really *their* culture, is it?"

The implication was that artifacts in Turkish waters didn't count because they had come from elsewhere, that Turkey had virtually no indigenous culture to share. It was an arrogant claim. It ignored the simple fact that our most revealing examples of ancient nautical life have been discovered off the Turkish coast, and the discoveries represent many cultures.

The waters around Greece are among the richest on Earth; they may even contain the legendary Atlantis. Its government policies, however, are a tragedy. With so much to share, Greece clings passionately to its status as an archaeological black hole.

With so much at stake, perhaps America's best hope for tracing the footprints of civilization across the ocean floor has come to rest with the technologists. Few events captured the imagination so much as our discovery of the *Titanic*.

The first serious attempt to locate the ship was cobbled together in the 1960s by the Canadian Broadcasting Company. A copy of the CBC's findings was reportedly used by novelist Clive Cussler as background material for his bestseller *Raise the Titanic!*

Dr. Robert Ballard, of Woods Hole, appeared on the scene in the late 1970s with a proposal to use the deep-diving submersible *Alcoa Seaprobe* (a relic of the ill-fated "wet NASA" era) and the smaller submersible *Alvin*. But funding was difficult to find and the project was shelved. In 1978, Ballard tried again, using *Alvin* and a special color television system built by RCA. Once again, funding failed to materialize.

Two years later, Texas oilman Jack Grimm financed his own multi-million-dollar quest. It didn't work. His team used the submersible *Aluminaut* and side-scan sonar to record three possible targets. But foul weather ripped away the magnetometer, making it impossible to distinguish between natural formations and the hull of the ship. The oil tycoon who hoped to make a television special had been blown out. Graciously he made his data available to Ballard and the Woods Hole group. Grimm believes his generosity was partly responsible for the discovery of the ship in September 1985.

The voluble Texan was about to learn just how covetous the tight little world of nautical treasure can be. He was stunned when Woods Hole refused to give him the coordinates of the *Titanic* location. He

Examples of glazed pottery
recovered by archaeologists
working a seventh-century
Byzantine vessel at Yassi Ada,
near Bodrum, Turkey.
Drawing by Kathryn Williams.

had no intention whatsoever of doing salvage: "I just wanted to make a movie," he lamented.

Grimm's data reportedly included a video image of the ship's enormous propeller; it was at Ballard's disposal when the U.S. Navy took an interest in the chase. The Navy gave the Woods Hole group $2.8 million and a five-year contract to develop a new deep-diving robot known as *Argo*. It further permitted Woods Hole to use its research ship *Knorr*, a floating laboratory designed to accommodate *Argo*.

Soon after the *Titanic* discovery was announced, Admiral Bradford Monney, chief of the Office of Naval Research, said the Navy would fund continued probes of the wreck site. There were military lessons to be learned from *Argo* (the John H. Perry principle of exploration at work).

Ballard seldom discusses the Navy's input and avoids mentioning the precise security classification surrounding *Argo*. He keeps discussions of the *Titanic* general and on a high road. His views on the subject, however, suggest the future direction of nautical archaeology. I spoke with him after he had testified before Congress on the future of techno-archaeology. He conveyed an aura of adventure, and yet there was something of the all-suffering professor about him. He listened carefully to my questions, correcting any deviant lines of thought. All the while I sensed something extraordinary in his expression. It was as if the deep had invaded him, had become part of his psyche. His were the eyes of a time traveler, focused on strange images few humans will ever see.

"I'm neither an archaeologist nor a treasure hunter," he said. "I'm a marine scientist and explorer."

He had no real interest in the treasure wars per se. There was something superficial about the shouting, he said, a bit of Faulkner's sound and fury indicating not much of anything. He had told the lawmakers: "I am here to point out that the technological genius most Americans are so proud of has entered the deep in full force and placed before it a new reality."

The "great pyramids of the deep," he continued, "are now accessible. [We] can either plunder them like the grave robbers of Egypt or protect them for the countless generations which will follow ours." Ballard pointed out that unlike the shallows, the deep sea is a highly preserving environment. In the deep sea, shipwrecks enter a world of total darkness. The growth of coral and plant life that overwhelms the shallow wrecks isn't present; it's a desertlike world with an organism here and another one there, the opposite of the complex biotic soup of the shallows. The freezing temperatures inhibit biological activity, as does extreme pressure.

Ballard attacked those who see shipwrecks as "pickles in a barrel." He pointed out that the technology used to find the *Titanic* "is the vanguard of the very technology man will use to find, document, and revisit pieces of history preserved in the deep sea."

He spoke of "telepresence": "The ability to project your thoughts, your eyes, and eventually your hands, is each day becoming an increasing reality."

Clearly, pure exploration of the deep sea isn't the engine driving this technology, though it will benefit from it. Unmanned space probes, the military desire to remove humans from the risks of combat, the commercial world with its proliferation of television coverage, the astonishing leaps made by computer technology—these are the major forces behind telepresence.

Already robotic vehicles have entered the *Titanic*. We have seen its magnificent ballroom, its galleries, its preserved splendor. No salvage operation in the world could duplicate this feat.

The *Titanic* is only one example. Their are galleons down there in the dark, ancient Polynesian outriggers, Egyptian merchant ships, vessels we have only glimpsed on the walls of ancient Mayan ruins. How will we find them? And, more important, what will we do with them? This is the lingering question.

"Will we come to plunder or appreciate?" Ballard asks. "This is a debate which grows louder, not quieter. Technologists, like myself, can only cause the problem and suggest its possible impact."

By mid-1996, a private company was selling coal from the *Titanic*. Was this the start of the plunder? The French partners of the Woods Hole group are salvaging portions of the hull and superstructure, which they hope to put on public display. They have already botched the job and have destroyed portions of the ship.

The vessel rests in international waters, unprotected by any law. How many "grave robbers" will join what appears to be the start of an ongoing plunder? Hollywood's epic romance about the ship and its passengers has become the box-office smash of the century. I have little doubt this alone will excite further commercialization. We may not be too far from the time when the *Titanic* will be turned into a sunken Disneyland with fleets of submersibles ferrying wide-eyed tourists to and from the grave site.

In the next century major portions of the *Titanic* may be on display. But at what price? Without rational preservation, the vessel may be reduced to junk, useless as the treasures being horded in the waters off Greece.

In the new century we'll need a new awareness and a new ethic. As Albert Falco has said, "In the sea everything is moral."

Perhaps we should begin there.

Chapter Five

RINGS OF FIRE

Islands are passing things, created today,
destroyed tomorrow.
                          —Rachel Carson

I

AS I STEAMED THROUGH THE NIGHT off the coast of Australia a new island was taking shape thousands of miles to the north. Far below the surface of the Pacific, the infant "Loihi" was being sculpted by molten rock. The reports came to us in spurts. Weather was in an uproar and our captain wasn't concentrating on distant news. Storms at sea almost always begin their intimidation by roaring at you. This one was in good voice. Loihi was inflicting her birth pains on Hawaii, and the Coral Sea was taking it out on us.

I tried to focus on the faraway scientist in a submersible reporting that Loihi's lava dome had fallen in on itself, creating a pit thousands of feet deep. There was geologic "wreckage" everywhere. It was the first time humans had seen the birth of an island in midcourse. I wished I could be among the witnesses.

But the immediate situation was sufficient. We passed the Queensland offshore buoy and negotiated the maze of the Great Barrier Reef. Waves mounted the walls of coral beneath us. White-streaked seawater spilled over the decks and snaked down the companionways. Our twin screws hissed out of the water and beat against the night air.

Reports of Loihi came in stuttering fragments. At last we received word from Alexander Malahoff, director of the Hawaii Undersea Research Laboratory at the University of Hawaii. He had told a wire service reporter that Loihi was "in the womb going through its birth pains." It would surely be the next island to rise in the Hawaiian chain.

"There's no doubt about it," he said. It might be 50,000 years before its peak rose above the surface, but it was inexorably on its way.

"It's very nerve-wracking trying to find a safe path through the exploded terrain," Malahoff reported. The major action was seventeen miles southeast of the big island. Collapse of the lava dome had occurred over several days. If it had come instantaneously, powerful tidal waves surely would have ravaged Waikiki.

"That's the scary part," Malahoff emphasized, adding that sooner or later a giant tsunami will roar out of the birthing volcanic island.

It was strange reading these reports from the "neighborhood." I felt as if we were part of the unfolding drama. Later I would see films of Loihi's handiwork recorded by the *Pices-V* submersible: towering obelisks of lava, sheer cliff faces falling hundreds of feet into the deep, elephant-sized boulders strewn everywhere. The submersible officer reported the rumbling sounds of volcanic wreckage tumbling into the abyss.

The news came at an auspicious moment. We were heading into the valley of volcanoes, the atoll-rich Coral Sea. Here the Loihis of the past had flamed out and gone silent. Worn down by wind and waves, these muted actors had been reduced to benign rings of coral low against the sea. As the future was being shaped to the north, I was headed into the past. My mission was underwater mountain climbing, exploring the opposite end of the cycle that Loihi had begun.

Night passed. At dawn we scudded along the seaward edge of the Great Barrier Reef. The sun rose higher, colors of the sky spilled into the sea. The tops of the waves were pink and gold against the sky.

Green islets dotted the horizon, a peculiar immobility against the ceaseless motion. The Great Barrier Reef is twice the size of Texas, ranging 1,600 miles from Cape York to Gladstone, a serpentine ecosystem of reefs and islands. At a time when most of the world's coral reefs are being degraded, the Great Barrier Reef remains vigorous, though it, too, must struggle for life.

Graeme Kelleher, chairman of the Great Barrier Reef Marine Park Authority, made sure we knew the reef was inscribed on the World Heritage List. Aussies take this very seriously.

"We have an international obligation," Kelleher told me.

Kelleher's ecological problem, aside from those caused by humans, is the proliferation of the Crown of Thorns starfish. The Crown of Thorns is more than a foot in length and was seldom seen prior to the 1950s, when it began proliferating in ever-increasing numbers near

Green Island, off Cairns. It has sixteen thorny arms and consumes the coral tissue through its suckers. The main predator of the starfish is the trumpet fish. At one time these fish were collected in great numbers by visiting tourists. Good news for the Crown of Thorns, bad news for the reef. Kelleher has attempted, with some success, to put an end to the problem, and the surrounding waters sustain more than 1,500 species of fish.

For the moment my universe was defined by wind and waves and a hull sloshing in a beamy sea. We dropped anchor on the seaward edge of the reef. The plan was to spend the day diving here and try again that night to run eastward toward the Coral Sea. Zodiacs, rubberized inflatable boats the Aussies call "rubber duckies," plopped into the water.

"Good as gold!" exclaimed our reef guide, Lin Sutherland. Her yellow slicker flapped wildly in the breeze, its color imitating her sunstreaked hair. I piled in and adjusted my scuba gear. Lin was steady at the tiller, using the surface current as a guide.

"Go! Go!" she commanded as the duckie pulled beside the coral formations.

I tumbled backward over the gunwales and headed down the face of the reef. One hundred feet below all was still, peaceful.

I drifted like a mote down a sheer wall of color. Red algae coated the surface of the reef, cementing and consolidating the whole and increasing its resistance to erosion. The hard corals, like the plates of an armadillo, overlapped and descended symmetrically into deeper water, shining like Salvador Dali's "beating heart of rubies."

I had to remind myself that this construction was in fact a living creature, a massive animal that we are only now beginning to understand. Its hard exoskeleton is seemingly inanimate, but coral is a miraculous creature, alive as any fish, complex and moody as the torpedo-shaped black-and-white-tipped sharks that persistently patrolled these waters.

One might view the reef as a constantly evolving epidermis capping millions of years of accumulated limestone. Scientists say the Great Barrier is about eighteen million years old; its most visible portion, over which I now cruised, is a relative infant at two million years.

I dove at night to observe how the tissues of the reef-building corals work. In the beams of my artificial light the storm of tiny algae called *zooxanthellae* performed life-giving photosynthesis. Most of the food manufactured by the *zooxanthellae* "leaks" out of the tissues and is available to the coral polyp for its growth. During the day the corals feed from the symbiotic algae. At night they feed themselves, the dark water transformed by clouds of translucent building materials.

As early as 1835, naturalist Charles Darwin sailing aboard the *Beagle* studied the origin of reefs. His categorization of atolls, fringing reefs, and barrier reefs are still fresh. We were studying an example of the latter two. But the atolls, island reefs formed on the rims of extinct volcanoes, were the prize of this trip. These waited for us farther out in the Coral Sea.

But the sea was unrelenting; it would not allow us beyond the Barrier Reef. So we explored and explored, waiting for the weather to break. In the meantime, I spent hours in the ship's library.

In the last century scientists developed competing theories of how islands are built. Darwin knew that coral grows in relatively warm shallow water; its presence in the midocean, he reasoned, could only be explained if it were assumed that corals came to life on the rims of volcanic peaks. When these peaks were sufficiently eroded and dipped below the surface, the coral began to grow. By the time Darwin's *Beagle* pulled into the Sea of the Moon between Tahiti and Moorea, in French Polynesia, his observations had gelled into an observable theory called "subsidence."

In Tahiti Darwin found models to illustrate his theory. The volcanic islands were surrounded by enclosing reefs with a lagoon at the center. As the central portion of the islands eroded and sank into the seabed, all that remained were the rings of coral. To explain the gradual removal of an entire volcano he came up with the notion of "progressive subsidence," the coral keeping pace as the central portion sank into the seabed.

The scientific community resisted Darwin's ideas and came up with alternative models. One of these, known as the "glacial theory," explained coral growth as a product of cyclic fluctuations of the sea level. It was postulated that during the Ice Ages the oceans were too cold to support coral. More recent evidence indicates that during the Pleistocene era ocean temperatures fell forty to forty-four degrees; this would reduce the area where corals might thrive, yet it allowed for growth in a narrow tropic/subtropic belt.

Proof of Darwin's theory had to wait for our century. In 1952, deep corings were made at the Pacific atoll of Eniwetok. The cores revealed a thickness of more than 4,500 feet of coral rock before the base of volcanic basalt was reached. Clearly this was proof of a long, slow subsidence.

As the days wore on and the ocean raged unabated, I found myself wondering how pre-twentieth-century explorers accomplished as much as they did in their wooden sailing vessels. What must it have been like for Cook and Darwin? How did they manage without modern electronics? I imagined them hove to, anxiously waiting until the sun was high, and only then making a guarded passage through the maze of reefs and islands with a lone sailor in the bowsprit calling out warnings as shoals appeared out of nowhere. Those sailors of old truly impressed me.

Three days out of Townsville we finally entered the central Coral Sea about 100 miles east of the Great Barrier Reef. It was an unforgettable moment. In the predawn light the sea shone slate gray and a rising sun tinted the bottoms of the big clouds along the horizon. Sun slanted through the sky and I could see streaks of white water accenting the brightening sea. Thankfully the wind had fallen off and the boat had taken on a more solid feel.

Lin, wrapped in her yellow slicker and holding a huge mug of steaming coffee, came up beside me on deck.

"Made it," she enthused. "Been a right bit rough, eh?"

I told her how my mind had played tricks during a particularly difficult stretch of weather. It was nearly impossible to move around the deck that day, so I held on to a slat-bench and stared unblinkingly at the horizon, the steadiest point in a big confused sea, and the surest way I knew to avoid *mal de mer*. Yet my best methods failed and I experienced the sailors' dreaded madness: wild hallucinations. I imagined the Chesapeake Bay Bridge arching over the horizon and cars streaming toward Annapolis, Maryland. I actually thought we were heading home and that I'd soon be comfortably lounging on the deck of Chart House restaurant half a world away, a cool, soothing beverage in hand.

Lin thought this was highly amusing.

"And you weren't even castaway," she grinned.

She began her chore of filling steel scuba tanks with compressed air and placing them in their racks. There was amazing power in her small, childlike arms.

"Mate says we've had the worst," she chirped. "We'll be at Flinders pretty soon."

Flinders Reef is one of the largest atolls in this sea of drowned volcanoes. It resembles an immense horseshoe canted on its side, its open end pointed north and west. It is one of three island-atolls in the immediate area (Marion and Lihou are the other two). Flinders's central lagoon is spiked by coral pinnacles that the Aussies call "bommies." The bommies soar up from the floor of the caldera like totems. Unlike virtually enclosed atolls we would later explore in French Polynesia, Flinders was virtually wide open. Its northern rim had been vaporized in some long-ago eruption. This volcanic opening allowed a free tidal flow to bathe the lagoon in fresh, clear ocean water.

Lin pointed to a large outcropping resembling a human head set on a long neck of coral. A ring of foam swirled around it.

"First thing Captain Flinders saw," she remarked. "That 'head' out there."

It was a sweet, welcoming sight. We passed into the sheltered lagoon. In less than a minute we had gone from fury to a sea of tranquility. The blue-black depths passed behind us. White water broke over the fringing reef and spilled into the lagoon as gently as a ribbon of foam.

"Like clouds floating below the surface," I said to Lin, commenting on the colors of the bommies that now were clearly visible.

"Rather calming, isn't it?" she replied.

Captain Mathew Flinders, one of the finest chart makers in England, was a twenty-seven-year-old master mariner who circumnavigated Australia and named the Great Barrier Reef. He wrote of the submerged terrain as a "garden but with glowing tints far in excess of the land. … Wheat-sheaves, mushrooms, staghorns, cabbage-leaves, and a host of other imitative forms were quite as various as the forms themselves, and several shades of green, purple, brown, and white were far more vivid than the florist's care and art have ever succeeded in producing. …"

If he was enchanted by the reef, he was shaken by the forces of the Coral Sea: "I have never seen such elemental fury so impetuous."

In 1803, Flinders wrecked out here. He organized a colony of survivors on a small sand cay at the northern tip of the reef. After weeks marooned, he hailed a cutter bound for Sydney, purchased supplies there, and returned to rescue his crew.

With Lin, I later visited that fateful sand cay. I imagined Flinders's distressed crew imprisoned on that desert of sand as the tide rose ominously with its ever-cruising sharks. I pictured the sailors huddled by the hull of their crumbling ship. These images evoked emptiness, a black hole of futility that I have not experienced before or since.

As I wandered over the sand, I allowed my imagination to piece together a rather violent image of the planet. Strip away the water and one would see thousands of volcanoes, with lava spilled across the oceanic basin. One would see fractures, lava tubes, and crevices spewing superheated gases and molten rock—the same processes at work and currently demonstrated by Loihi. Malahoff had described it as a "Mount St. Helens–sized event." A portion of Loihi, Pele's Dome, once thought to be stable, had simply vanished into a pit. Loihi was the alpha, Flinders was the omega.

During the past three decades scientists have concluded that submarine volcanism is the Earth's major island-builder. Nowhere is it more evident than along the Pacific "Ring of Fire." Subduction of the lithospheric plates creates a line of regularly spaced volcanoes along the oceanic trenches. These are the loci of the quakes and tidal waves that sweep the Pacific.

Deep-ocean drilling projects in the 1970s led to W. H. Menard's characterization of this part of the ocean as "the most voluminous midplate volcanism in the available geological record." A founder of the Scripps Institution of Oceanography and a professor of geology, Menard postulated are roughly 300,000 sunken volcanoes worldwide, but only a few thousand on the continents.

And the Pacific steals the show. Its tectonic plate accounts for less than half the world's oceanic floor, yet it supports 25 percent of the active volcanoes, 45 percent of inactive volcanic islands, and 80 percent of guyots and atolls. The sheer volume of volcanic sites lends credence to speculation that Pacific volcanism, not meteoric impact, may have obliterated the dinosaurs. Did this fury produce a "nuclear winter" that altered the food chain and destroyed nature's hardiest long-lived creatures?

"Not your worry," Lin said as we prepared to explore a site called "Trigger Happy."

Lin had been especially attentive after my visit to the sand cay. In her own subtle way she was attempting to fashion an image and feeling for this part of the world that would carry over onto paper. Our explorations were carefully selected, fine-tuned with images layered one on top of the other. She knew when to explain things and when not to, and had an instinct for sites that left me with precise macroscopic impressions of the larger mosaic. Each new exploration was a surprise. And "Trigger Happy," which we explored two days before we returned to Townsville, was a denouement, the Coral Sea reduced to essentials and a metaphor of island birth.

I slid into water clear as air. Directly below the surface the bommies rose straight off the deep bottom to within fifteen feet of the surface. Slowly, slowly, I drifted downward in the warm liquid space, falling as gently as feathers past the towers of coral. I looked around: pinnacles everywhere, as far as I could see, each more massive than the next.

I bottomed out at 130 feet and knelt on the sand. I was stunned by the magnitude of the scene. Lin was beside me. She now seemed even more petite, nearly childlike beside these skyscraper pinnacles. She had mastered the trick of talking through her regulator, enunciating in contrabass, slowly, clearly.

"… A walk in the valley of the volcanoes."

I heard the rumble of her voice as clearly as I heard my own breathing.

We drifted a little higher off the sand. In the canyons between the bommies, narrow passageways edged by soft purple sea fans and feathery gorgonia sloped into deeper water. I saw the other divers from our team. Swimming along the bommies like strange hi-tech boulevardiers, they appeared to stroll, taking in the splendid corals. We had already seen fifteen-foot-high sea fans, red and yellow latticework miracles so overwhelming we had literally bowed down before them in silent praise. Lin called them "super-fans." But this scene was even more evocative.

We swam to a deeper shelf where the seabed vanished in a vertical cliff. A gentle current pushed a ribbon of sand over the edge. We watched it drift featherlike into the blackness. I imagined the whole of the sea floor thousands of feet below. My inner eye roamed over the spreading seascape and across the Pacific where countless volcanic islands reached toward the sky like the bommies at Flinders, galaxies in the universe of the sea, constantly shaping the planet.

II

A few months later, I headed south from Australia to New Zealand, land of the long white cloud.

My agenda was to study the island-building volcanism of the far South Pacific, and New Zealand was as far south as we might reasonably go. A child of the Ring of Fire, its island-building forces are still very much at work. There have been major eruptions in recent years and much of the land surface is still spewing steam and lava. To experience New Zealand is to glimpse the fresh workings of oceanic creation. Late in our century, at a time of exploratory ennui, it is one of those rare places on the map where one can still find that wonderfully rare word, *unexplored.*

There are places that steal your heart, but New Zealand steals it in more ways than any other. Its natural felicity is contrasted with a primal power. The landscape is constantly changing, mixing and matching. I gazed across acres of temperate meadowland, past blue lakes, beyond waterfalls, and into the impenetrable green-black curtain of a tropical rain forest. And rising from the rain forest are the ancient hills, densely verdant, giving way to glaciated mountains banded by clouds. I could not have guessed what surprises awaited me or what events that would reveal a link to my own past.

New Zealand is 2,000 miles below the equator and consists of three main islands: North and South Islands, and Stewart in the extreme south. Beyond Stewart the sea is cold and featureless. Next stop, Antarctica.

My explorations began in the North Island at a place called Tutukaka on the northwestern coast. The night air was so clear I could see twenty miles under a full moon to a maze of pinnacles known as Poor Knights Islands. The primary monoliths, Tawhiti Rahi and Aorangi to the north, and High Peak and Sugarloaf to the south, break the surface out of very deep water.

Captain Cook charted Poor Knights and named them after chess pieces, which to his mind appeared to have toppled over onto the surface of the Pacific. In fact, they are volcanic upthrusts, shafts of stone exploded vertically out of the seabed. They form a twisted maze of natural harbors and caves big enough to shelter ocean-going vessels.

Unlike the warm Pacific waters around the Great Barrier Reef, the ocean here is cold (about sixty-five degrees Fahrenheit) and nutrient poor. But clarity is excellent, and golden kelp grows everywhere. The wounds of volcanism are easy to see in the submerged landscape. The external scars appear to be almost new; it will be a very long time before the kelp softens the appearance of these woundings. It was fascinating to observe the long gashes in the rock. They were unmistakably primal, as if some nameless goddess had dug her nails into the stone in a vain attempt to keep it from breaking free of the ocean bottom. Over time the pinnacles have become something of a paradox. Scared and relatively barren beneath the surface, the upper portions support a prolific wilderness of bright red pohutukawa ("Kiwi Christmas trees"), thousands of birds, and a terrestrial living fossil known locally as the tuatara lizard.

Working in this cold, unforgiving water was a challenge, but it was also rewarding. The exploration at Poor Knights provided a kind of metaphor of prehistory, a Devonian tableau. Once, in fairly shallow water, I was overwhelmed by clouds of medusas, translucent filaments accented by a series of royal blue "eyes." The water was thick with their gelatinous bodies, each the size of a human forearm. They trailed their long tentacles and lit the water with glowing red centers. The red appeared to pulsate in a slow cadence, the sea slowly whitening and pulsing with their presence. They seemed entirely primitive. I felt them covering my body, attaching to my faceplate, soft against my bare palms. For a moment I closed my eyes and I actually believed I could hear them living and dying in a whisper all around me.

A few days later I made my way south to Whakatane, near the Bay of Plenty on the east coast of the island. The landscape was an illustration of island-building volcanism. Everywhere the Earth steamed and bubbled. There were hissing flowerbeds, steaming downspouts, geysers filling the air with hot vapor. The local golf course had superheated mud traps; lose a ball in a Whakatane bunker and it simply melted. The most pervasive aroma was hydrogen sulfide.

My oceanic destination was White Island, an active volcano connected to the mainland by the still-active Taupo Volcanic Zone, which stretches westward from the Pacific to Tongariro National Park, and south to Lake Taupo.

We had run thirty-one miles offshore from the Bay of Plenty before the volcano appeared on the horizon. She was hidden in a shroud of mist and from the mist a shadow spread a wide blue circle on the water.

"There she is," announced my guide, John Baker, who'd been telling me how the sea had changed him. "She's been awfully active. See where the vegetation has burnt off?"

He slowed the boat and drifted into the mist. It must have been like this when Captain Cook sighted the place nearly three centuries ago and named it White Island. Cook noted in his journal: "As such it always appear'd to us."

The virtually barren mass rose out of the sea like a hydra, dark and seething. The Maori natives named it Whakaari, "that which can be made visible, uplifted to view." For them it was a devil's island, where incorrigibles were banished to a nasty fate.

Whakaari is a special gem in New Zealand's oceanic matrix. Fire and ice—glaciers and volcanoes—are at the heart of the South Pacific frontier. And this was a special excitement. The volcano had been visited many times, but the volcanic bottomography, strictly speaking, was new territory.

We had anchored at the southern edge of the Kermadec Trench, which stretches north and south and bottoms at more than 31,000 feet. The landmass of New Zealand sits atop the Lord Howe Rise before dropping into a series of deep basins punctuated by guyots and scarps. Whakaari and the surrounding bottomography are a window in time that would offer a glimpse of the Earth in her youthful violence.

As we prepared to go ashore John Baker gave me a warning.

"She's spitting rocks," he said. "Absolute boulders."

We ran ashore in the dingy. Our plan was to take the pulse of the volcano. Later we'd dive. We hoped by that time we'd be on speaking terms with Whakaari.

Three large cones comprise 800 acres of the White Island wasteland, the issue of a collision of the Pacific and Indo-Australian plates. It was this cataclysm that gave birth to the whole of New Zealand. Everything about the place appeared newly formed, as if the plates had sculpted the landscape only a few days earlier. It gave me a sense of imminent danger.

Everything about Whakaari was violent. We were literally walking across an ongoing explosion. We were insignificant passersby trying to make sense of elemental forces.

It is ironic to recall that it wasn't until the advent of the International Geophysical Year in 1957 that marine geology got its modern lease on life, at last recognizing the 1830 catchphrase of British geologist Charles Lyell, "The present is the key to the past." Climbing the steamy hills of Whakaari, it was hard to believe that a century ago marine geologists believed the oceans had changed hardly at all for billions of year. Whakaari, in fact any oceanic volcano, was sufficient to put static theories on the shelf.

I couldn't help wondering why scientists had failed to extrapolate the idea of violent change following the destruction of Krakatoa in

1883, the largest volcanic explosion in history. An island in the strait between Java and Sumatra, Krakatoa erupted in 1680. For whatever reasons, the event was written off and the volcano was considered "dead." Then in the spring of 1883 smoke and steam reappeared. On August 27, the mountain exploded. Eruptions lasted two days. The entire northern half of the cone was carried away. The ocean rushed in and added fury upon fury. When the lava, steam, and smoke finally settled down, an island that once stood 1,400 feet above sea level had become a crater 1,000 feet below sea level.

The voice of Krakatoa was heard in the Philippines, Australia, and Madagascar. Tens of thousands of people were drowned in a tidal wave that swept through the Indian Ocean, then rounded the Cape into the Atlantic, and continued into the English Channel. For an entire year sunsets all over the world were blood red.

Every volcano is a potential Krakatoa, and I had a feeling that Whakaari would have its day. And it would not be alone. To the northeast volcanoes rose along the Colville Ridge: "Rumbles" I to IV, "Silents" I and II, Clark Island, and Tongroa. Scientists claim "Silents" I and II are extinct. But Taupo Volcanic Zone is unpredictable. Perhaps in the next century, or any day, these "dormant" monoliths may jolt us out of complacency.

Whakaari is clearly unstable. In 1914, when the White Island Sulphur Company operated here, one of the firemen vanished without a trace. A few months later an avalanche obliterated all human presence. The bodies of the ten-man mining crew were never found.

Its tallest peak is 1,053 feet. The crater floor is straight out of Hieronymus Bosch, an anarchy of landslides and exploded rock, lava flows, sulfur-rimmed fumaroles spitting 800-degree superheated gas. There is an unrelenting stench of sulfur. We were compelled to don gas masks.

Whakaari doesn't smile on living things. Vegetation on the seaward walls are sparse and sickly. The ground feels as if it might split open. At one point, wandering about on my own, I stumbled into a patch of quicksand; fortunately, it wasn't superheated. My right leg was instantly sucked in up to my knee. I was shaken by the treachery of it, the man-eating appetite of this innocent-looking "puddle."

It was a relief to finally don our wetsuits and head out to view Whakaari from the bottom up.

The subsea terrain was far more benign. We explored the necklace of stone pinnacles that circled the volcano. Clearly this was a submerged theater of volcanism, with Whakaari and its stone spires "made visible."

The neighboring Volkner Rocks broke the surface out of very deep water. They were forbidding even though the scars of upthrusting had been softened by corals and sponges. I swam away from a vertical drop-off and hung motionless in midwater, examining the rock face. The spire of stone disappeared into emptiness.

"Pretty impressive sights," John Baker remarked after the first dive.

"Paradoxical," I replied.

The transformation of Whakaari below the surface was nearly complete. Time and the sea had transformed a brutal landscape, the sea being more amenable to life than the suffering pit of the crater. Still, these remote South Pacific waters are in no way comparable to the tropical Great Barrier Reef, where all is color and life. In the Coral Sea the volcanoes have subsided and become passive lagoons. But in the waters surrounding Whakaari one sees what the Earth is made of; there is a sense of fickle temper, no peace or safety.

"So now we dive the vents," John announced as we relaxed aboard his boat, sipping coffee from big ceramic mugs. "I believe you'll find it stimulating."

This would be our last dive before resuming our tour of the volcano. John hugged the flanks of the mountain and steered for the heated openings in the shallows. There have been reports of fish "sitting" on the submerged vents enjoying a sort of salty Jacuzzi. But Whakaari is temperamental; water temperatures can change radically. Fishing boat skippers tell stories of "precooked fish" snagged in their nets.

Unlike the monolithic architecture of the island, the thermally heated shallows presented a jumble of garage-sized boulders. The closer we swam to the vents, the warmer the water became.

The boulders were covered by white "mats" formed by heat-loving bacteria. It looked as if the rocks were covered in snow. The bacterial mats were soft to the touch, and the fish apparently enjoyed nibbling the mossy growth.

Swimming through the sea of bubbling water, I thought that here in microcosm was the very activity carried on in the deep seabed. It is the same everywhere, from Loihi to the Mid-Ocean Rift. Venting fluids contain rich levels of hydrogen sulfide, and while this gas is toxic to life as we know it on Earth, certain bacteria can metabolize it. These bacteria form "vent community" food chains. Since the discovery of these bacterial colonies in this century along the Galapagos Rift, we have found markedly different kinds of vents. For example, the Galapagos vents are quite different from the tall chimneys—the "black smokers"—seen at the "Hanging Gardens" along the East Pacific Rise.

We have learned that when a vent dies the creatures that depend on it die, too. Still, there is much controversy. In 1979, biologists observed species in the East Pacific that closely resembled those seen at Galapagos, nearly 2,000 miles away. There are indications at Juan de Fuca Ridge, off the coast of Washington and Oregon, that certain creatures may evolve separately and are considered true aliens.

Until the early 1980s, every card-carrying environmentalist assumed oil in the sea equaled death. For whatever reasons—political, economic, emotional—this assumption held, despite evidence that huge amounts of oil seeped naturally out of the seabed. In the 1940s, oil companies found large deposits a few hundred feet down in the Gulf of Mexico. Three decades later, drilling technology allowed oil to be gathered thousands of feet below in astonishing quantities.

In 1984, a Texas A&M research team made a startling discovery. Trawling above the natural oil seeps in the Gulf, far below the reach of sunlight, their nets produced so many healthy mollusks and tube worms they could barely ship them. The researchers concluded the creatures had washed down from coastal waters. So much life could not exist in the oil-rich environment, they reasoned.

We now know that methane and hydrogen sulfide feed bacteria that support patches of mussels and other shellfish at depths below 1,000 feet. Could it be these hearty mussels thrive on methane, consuming a gas thought to be involved in global warming? Are we now so sure that oil in the deep equals death? Is sunlight necessary to all life? Our old assumptions are being overturned with each new discovery.

The University of Hawaii team working at Loihi observed cracks and vents some twenty feet wide. Superheated water gushed into the surrounding sea and a melange of minerals poured out with it. Biological mats similar to those at Whakaari and clouds of free-floating bacteria were feeding on the chemicals rather than on sunlight. So much life poured from the vents that visibility was close to zero.

"There was 'slime' everywhere," according to Malahoff. The biological communities at Loihi spread out in strange patterns. They reminded him of a haunted house. "It's amazing how quickly life takes advantage of a site," he said.

The team's microbiologist, James P. Cowen, was surprised to observe the short-term waxing and waning of the bacterial communities. With each rock slide the "plumbing" of the vents changed and the bacteria adjusted almost instantaneously.

Recalling the lesson of Krakatoa, seismologist Fred Duenebier, working with a university diving group, hopes to establish a permanent underwater geological observation station at Loihi. It will be risky. The situation is unpredictable. Collapse of the lava dome wiped out a network of sensors. A habitat-sensor operation would, at the very least, live on the cusp of a cataclysm-in-the-making.

I was pondering this as I boarded a helicopter for one last tour of Whakaari. I could see everything from this bird's-eye view. We passed over the ruins of the old sulfur mining operation and a long spine of land jutting into the Pacific from the southeast edge of the island. From this vantage point it resembled a knife. At a lower altitude, however, it took on the aspect of a pharaonic sarcophagus.

I spotted the elongated formation on my map and I gasped. There, in unmistakable black and white, was my family name! The site was called Troup Head. Many European members of my family commonly use this same spelling. My British relations have been in metallurgy for generations, and sulfuric acid is used to extract various alloys. Apparently a great-great-uncle, Frank Hugh Troup, bought into this sulfur-mining plant with J. A. Wilson, a judge of the New Zealand Native Land Court.

As we boarded the boat for our journey back to the mainland, I said to John, "Maybe I'm in line to claim my own island."

He was mildly amused. "You'll be filing papers, I suppose."

Alas, my brief dream of inheriting a piece of Whakaari went up in smoke when I discovered that Uncle Frank sold his half share in 1855. It didn't take him long to realize the island would never be tamed, and that any attempts to make peace with it would only end in disaster. Still, my day of "owning" half a volcanic island was a thrill.

It was a chill dusk when John finally pulled up the anchor and headed back to the mainland. Whakaari's fumaroles glowed red and blue against the lowering sky, a final show of power before slipping back into the white mist. It is the same with blood as with oceans: The closer one gets to the past, the more vivid the present becomes.

"True enough," John said. "We're always discovering something, aren't we? That's how the sea changes us."

III

Three months later I landed in equatorial French Polynesia, perhaps the most famous island chain in the world.

Located in the southeastern Pacific midway between Australia and South America, the islands are spread over an oceanic area as large as Europe and serve as archetypes of the island-building forces that continually shape the planet.

But to me there was something more here: romance. This was the true South Pacific, the stuff of legend and lore, land of the mythic Bali Hai', the realization of a dream that began for me as a child.

My earliest knowledge of the Pacific came during World War II. My father was part of an Army Air Force crew stationed at Tinian Island, where the United States was preparing the *Enola Gay* and its atomic cargo for a world-altering mission over Hiroshima. We had no idea where he was, only that he was somewhere on a faraway island. I strained to envision this anonymous speck in the Pacific. I couldn't begin to find it on a map, let alone imagine the feel, the shape, or the substance of the place.

Then one morning in 1945, I awoke to a huge headline across the front page of the Baltimore *Sun:* "A-Bomb Blasts Hiroshima." A few days later the newspaper declared: "A-Bomb Crushes Nagasaki." There were pictures of an ominous mushroom-shaped cloud, but as a child I had little idea of what all this actually meant.

Not long after my father returned home I was surprised to find that my visions of the faraway Pacific had intensified. I poured over maps, and there it was, Tinian, the island where my father had been stationed. And not only Tinian, but a whole universe of islands spread out before me. The more I studied the maps the more the Pacific seemed to me a kind of galaxy and the islands like distant stars. The melange of sea and islands spun obsessively through my dreams. I yearned to travel to those exotic landfalls. Years later I concluded that this obsession was seered into my psyche by the bomb and my reading of James Michener's book, *Tales of the South Pacific.* Though I did not understand it at the time, a powerful romance had slipped into the mix, a romance that would grow and play out over the decades leading to adulthood.

It all came together in 1994 when I landed in French Polynesia. I had come ostensibly to study island-building and sea life. But on a deeper level I was driven by childhood romance, exotic dreams, and longings.

I will never forget my first glimpse of Tahiti through the port of an Air France 747. The hurried descriptions dashed across the pages of my notebook with the pent-up romance of a lifetime:

> *Dawn. The dark profile of Tahiti rises above the Pacific like an ancient cathedral, its spires canted at impossible angles, its ramparts spiky as a witch's hat. Tahiti's mountains, like the crest of a wave, lift into the clouds. It's as if the island is floating in a sea of clouds until the sun reaches higher and the mist parts and the sea unfolds calm and clear, and the peaks of the volcanoes reach out against the sky and suddenly fall into deep black valleys.*
>
> *Across the narrow passage called The Sea of the Moon, Tahiti's sister, Moorea, looms up like a shark's toothy jaw against a pink, bleeding sky. I have to remind myself that this is real; I'm here, in the shadows of Jack London, Somerset Maugham, Robert Louis Stevenson, captains Cook and Bligh, even Brando.*

British Commander Samuel Wallis first brought white people to these islands in 1767. But Frenchmen gave us the "island of love," *la Nouvelle Cythere*, the earthly paradise. In 1768, Captain Louis-Antoine de Bouganville arrived and told of a bare-breasted *vahine* who paddled her canoe out to his ship. She climbed aboard, dropped the pareo from her hips, and stood naked before the sailors, who hadn't seen a woman in six months. Wrote Captain de Bouganville: "I thought I was transported into the Garden of Eden."

Bouganville found more than unashamed nakedness and "free love." He also discovered a rich mythology in this Tahiti-Nui-I-Te-Vai-Urirau: Great Tahiti of the Colored Waters. He sketched for a jaded Europe a vision practically immune to reality. It wasn't until the middle of our century, with the birth of the Atomic Age, that de Bouganville's romance turned ominous. How ironic that French Polynesia would become islands of anguish at the hands of their romantic French patrons.

The true character of the islands began a precipitous decline almost immediately after the French colonization. By the time the painter

Paul Gauguin arrived in Tahiti in 1894, much of what was wonderous in Polynesia had been skewed by greed and exploitation. Gauguin was enraged. What had happened to the unspoiled, undecadent, un-European beauty he had longed for? Where was the nobility of Tahitian society?

In 1896, he returned to France with his journal of Polynesian life, *Noa Noa* (Fragrant Fragrant), which was considered too racy for publication. The artist had come full circle. Upon his arrival in Tahiti he had come to an "unalterable decision" to live forever in Polynesia, to end his days in peace and freedom, with no thought of tomorrow and "this eternal struggle against idiots." But it took only two years for the "idiots" to drive him back to Europe spewing invective and megalomania: "I am leaving, older by two years, but twenty years younger; more *barbarian* than when I arrived, and yet much wiser."

Like Gauguin, I came seeking a certain purity. And also like Gauguin, I would find bittersweet disenchantment. Yet whatever corruption had dimmed Polynesian society, I was able to take joy in the people I met and find enchantment in the physical reality of the islands. If "free love" and the implications of Bronislaw Malinowski's teasing study, *The Sexual Life of Savages,* had been transformed, the physical marvel of the islands and their overwhelming beauty sustained my romance and held me fast.

French Polynesia is part of the "Polynesian Triangle," the points of which are Hawaii to the north, Easter Island to the southeast, and New Zealand in the southwest. Naturalist/author Jean-Louis Saquet notes that on all three sides of the Triangle we find identical flora, fauna, and climate.

The 118 islands and atolls of "Tahiti-Polynesia" (French territory) between Australia and South America are made up of less than 2,000 miles of dry land, scattered over an area of ocean large enough to drown most of Western Europe. It is a natural theater in which the life and death of the islands are played out in the overall theme of a constantly changing planet. It is this revealing window into the Earth that makes French Polynesia so important and so fragile.

In these archipelagos near the equator we have vivid examples of sea floor spreading, island-building, and the behavior of tectonic plates.

Tahiti, Moorea, and Bora Bora, the best known of the "Society Island" group, are famous for their relatively young volcanic peaks and deep valleys. Bora Bora and Maupiti combine volcanic geology and low coral atolls. Raiatea, about 150 miles northwest of Tahiti, shares a protecting lagoon with its tiny neighbor, Tahaa; it is mountainous, rising more than 1,000 feet above the sea, and has no beaches. There are eight major "passes" gouged out of the encircling reef. North and west of the Societies are the Tuamotus. Spread across more than 600 miles of sea in two parallel northwest-southwest chains, they are the largest collection of atolls in the world: 78 low islands, half of which offer no passage through the circling coral reefs. Powerful currents, sudden storms, and incomplete sailing charts combine to make this area a navigational hazard, the "dangerous archipelago." Aside from the perils of nature, it is stunning to learn that in this exotic setting the French government conducted decades of disastrous nuclear testing that has disturbed, ecologically and politically, all of French Polynesia.

To the west of the Tuamotus are the Gambier Islands. Lying just north of the Tropic of Capricorn, this group is made up of ten rocky landfalls, enclosed by a thirty-mile, semicircular barrier reef. Unlike the mountainous and jungly Marquesas Islands to the north, the Gambiers are covered by tall aeho grass. Of particular interest is Agakauitai, a desolate, rocky island where thirty-five generations of cannibal kings have been mummified and laid to rest.

South of Tahiti are the half-dozen Austral Islands, a 700-mile extension of the submerged volcanic range that makes up the Cook Islands to the north. French Polynesia provides geologists with the so-called "Conveyor Belt Theory," the notion that virtually all islands are volcanic in origin and travel along a "conveyor belt" of submerged tectonic plates. As a crack in the seabed allows volcanic material to escape, the base of a volcano forms. Layer by layer it shoulders its way toward the sun. The events at Loihi confirm this.

The volcanoes actually slide across the face of the ocean. For example, it is now known that the Pacific plate moves northwest at about one-half inch annually. Over many eons the volcano disconnects from the crack where it first emerged and new ones begin life in the southeast, as older islands are conveyed away from the cleft. As this "hot spot" shifts from the direction of the plate, the cycle of island-building is repeated. If it were possible to use time-lapse photography, one would see whole island chains riding across the face of the Pacific.

Coring by late-twentieth-century scientists has generally confirmed Darwin's nineteenth-century island-building theories. In the southeast portion of the Tuamotus the coral formations are about 1,200 feet thick. At Rangiroa, near the northwest quadrant, the coral samples are at least 3,200 feet thick. "Rangi" is obviously older than the Gambiers, where a volcanic mountain still towers some 1,500 feet above sea level.

An amazing island-building "laboratory" exists at the southeast tip of the Australs. Here an active undersea volcano known as MacDonald fumes and boils in its upward path. It is a sister to the emerging Loihi. The mountain is now only 150 feet below the surface. The crack in the sea floor spews out about a cubic mile of lava every century. We are now in a position to watch this growth and document MacDonald's building processes.

IV

Nuclear testing in the islands has affected their geology and vegetation. From 1946 to 1958, the United States exploded more than twenty nuclear devices on target ships anchored in Bikini lagoon, a tiny Micronesian atoll in the Marshall Islands. The largest test came in 1954, with the explosion of a fifteen-megaton hydrogen bomb code-named "Bravo." It sank one whole island, partially vaporized two others, gouged a mile-wide crater in the floor of the lagoon, and sealed Bikini's reputation as hell's own paradise.

The Bikinians, who departed their atoll with U.S. assistance and assurances that they were assisting in God's "great plan," are returning to their homeland after nearly half a century of nuclear nomadism. Bikini is hardly the idllyic setting of its preatomic days. The top sediments of lagoon appear to be virtually free of radiation, but the deeper layers contain plutonium, the world's deadliest substance. The surface soil retains radiation, and it is dangerous to eat coconuts or other indigenous fruits and vegetables. The job of cleaning up the lingering radioactivity will be massive, if not impossible.

Jonathan M. Weisgall, an adjunct professor of law at Georgetown University Law Center in Washington, D.C., has acted as legal counsel for the people of Bikini since 1975. After two decades of litigation he has settled a massive class-action lawsuit against the United States. Weisgall won $75 million in repatriations and $110 million for radiological cleanup. He has written a compelling book on the nuclear testing program and the subsequent dislocation of the islanders. *Operation Crossroads: The Atomic Tests at Bikini Atoll* (Naval Institute Press, 1994) represents a decade of research and the release of documents

once classified as secret. It tells an astonishing tale of arrogance, igno-
rance, and indifference.

I interviewed Weisgall at his spacious, art-adorned home in Maryland. He is perhaps the most determined attorney I have ever known.
He tries hard to see the positive where little of it exists. Among other
things, he helped develop Bikini as a scuba diving destination and was
among the first to test its appeal. He dove 175 feet to the flight deck of
the aircraft carrier USS *Saratoga,* one of the target ships of the early
atomic tests. It stands upright on the bottom near *Nagato,* the flagship
from which Japanese Admiral Yamamoto directed the attack against
the U.S. naval base at Pearl Harbor.

"It was like walking on the moon, only with more history," Weisgall
said of his visit to the *Saratoga.* "The collection of warships at Bikini
rivals those at Truk Lagoon. What happened at Bikini is a turning
point in world history."

Though he is enthusiastic about diving at Bikini, he is quick to
acknowledge the destructive impact of the atomic tests. In his understated manner he described chilling visions of the detonations, "like
seeing the birth and death of a star in an instant."

"Bikini was the Pacific paradise where humans and nature had
coexisted so peacefully," he told me. "Operation Crossroads changed
everything."

The first nuclear blasts turned the coral reefs a deathly white. Thousands of fish floated belly-up in the lagoon. The radioactive isotopes in
other fish created X-ray pictures on photographic plates.

"Bikini," Weisgall continued, "is the story of the arrogance of the
atomic age. It was the world in miniature, a proving ground to alter
nature."

We discussed the Bikinians and their fate. Weisgall was particularly unhappy with the propaganda surrounding evacuation of the original 167 islanders and their leader, King Juda. He spoke of the Navy's
attempts to downplay the dangers of the testing and the future well-
being of the Bikinians.

"They (the military) were dealing with a film studio in Hollywood, putting together a kind of aren't-we-just-great newsreel. It was
ludicrous."

Indeed it was. Newsreels in 1946 explained the purpose of Operation Crossroads in the tone of a lighthearted Disney epic. The narrator
told audiences we needed a protected anchorage six miles in diameter

in an "unpopulated region of the world." The camera panned across the Marshalls and stopped at Bikini. The narrator announced after the fashion of a jolly Amtrak conductor, "Bikini Atoll, a dot on the map of the mid-Pacific, was destined to become a focal point for the eyes of the world!" Faces of the Bikinians appeared on camera: a pretty young female, a toothless man, King Juda standing beside a ranking Navy commander.

"American officials discuss plans with the Bikini natives for the evacuation of the atoll," the narrator continued. "The islanders are a nomadic group, and are well pleased that the Yanks are going to add a little variety to their lives ... ."

"A farce," Weisgall sighed. "An outright lie. The Bikinians aren't nomadic. They've been on that atoll forever."

The Bikinians dreaded their forced evacuation and were frightened by the prospect of being uprooted.

"We started a social blight," Weisgall declared. "We now have the money to help out. But their society is pretty well shot."

As for Bikini lagoon, a half-century of isolation appears to have healed much of the ecological destruction. *National Geographic* photographer Bill Curtsinger, in a photo-essay on gray reef sharks, reported in the magazine's January 1995 edition that he was prepared for a wasteland, but found the reefs swirling with life. The marine systems had been flushed by time and tides, and Bikini's waters had returned to a "rare, undisturbed condition."

With the departure of American nuclear testing in the Pacific in 1958, the French followed up with a new invasion. The Centre d'Experimentations du Pacifique was established in 1963 at the fifteen-mile-long Moruroa atoll, in the southeastern portion of the Tuamotus. Fangataufa, a few miles south of Moruroa, would play a role later on.

This move to the Pacific came after France was forced to abandon its nuclear test sites in the Algerian Sahara following that country's independence. Between 1966 and 1995, more than 175 nuclear blasts, some up to 200 kilotons, were carried out in the Tuamotus. By 1974, more than forty-four atmospheric tests had been conducted, this in defiance of the 1963 Partial Test Ban Treaty signed by the United States, Great Britain, and the former Soviet Union. However, unknown to the other signers, the United States had its eye on the French operations and secretly made a deal to "share" the data.

President Charles de Gaulle flew to Moruroa in September 1966 to witness one of the atmospheric tests, a bomb suspended from a balloon. Unfortunately, weather conditions were poor. Steady winds blew toward the inhabited islands to the west instead of in a southerly course toward Antarctica. De Gaulle grumbled and fumed. He had other business, he complained, and he couldn't afford to waste time in this land of *au sauvage.* He insisted that the test go forward, despite the winds.

As a result, the explosion dropped radioactive fallout across the Cook Islands, Tonga, Samoa, Fiji, and Tuvalu. According to David Stanley, a longtime observer of the nuclear program and author of *Tahiti-Polynesia Handbook* (Moon Publications, 1992), Tahiti was the most directly effected island though the French never acknowledged this fact.

In the early 1970s, the World Court ordered an end to atmospheric testing. The French government balked, claiming the court had no authority to issue the order. In the furor that ensued, former New Zealand Prime Minister Norman Kirk ordered the frigate *Otago* to stand off the test zone and severed diplomatic ties with France. A virtual war had been declared.

To hit back, French special forces boarded the protest vessels *Fri* and the American *Greenpeace III* and arrested their crews. This battle between governments and ocean-focused environmentalists continued for decades. In 1985, the Greenpeace ship *Rainbow Warrior* was bombed in Auckland, New Zealand, by French frogmen. One crewman was killed.

I had inspected the sunken ship in 1994, and what I witnessed in those murky depths symbolized the ongoing destruction of the mid-Pacific. As I rounded the stern of the *Rainbow Warrior* I came upon a jagged hole under the fantail. Obviously the assault had come from the rear, at night, with no purpose other than terror. It seemed a strange irony. France, which had given the world the ability to peacefully enter the undersea world, had used its technology to kill an environmentalist who stood with Cousteau to protect the ecosystem.

Reacting to world outrage, French President Giscard D'Estaing stopped atmospheric testing and switched to a series of underground tests in the Tuamotus. A support base was set up at Hao atoll, north of Moruroa. This allowed the military to fly directly into the test zone without passage through Faaa Airport in Tahiti. It was a cover-up designed to mask an unpleasant reality. D'Estaing apparently believed visions of mushroom clouds might chill the tourist trade.

The nonstop polluting of the mid-Pacific with nuclear waste was sadly obvious to the world's scientific community. An atoll is a fragile creation, its coral porous and open to the flow of pollutants. Even the French recognized the problem. Yet a major investment was in place, an investment shared secretly to some extent by the United States.

Testing was shifted away from the coral outcropping to Moruroa's basaltic core, extending from 1,500 to 3,000 feet below the surface. This was thought to be safe. It was not.

In July 1979, an explosion in one of the bunkers killed two workers and injured many others. Plutonium was scattered everywhere. Then on July 25, 1979, a nuclear device became lodged halfway down a 2,400-foot test shaft. Unable to rescue the device, the scientists detonated it. The explosion ripped away a vast chunk of the atoll's seaward slope. A tidal wave swept across the island and a mile-long fissure split its surface. Two years later a typhoon washed radioactive debris into the ocean. Another storm washed carelessly stored nuclear waste into the lagoon—enough to fill nearly a quarter-million oil drums.

By the end of 1982, the atoll was fractured and sinking. The French switched to underwater testing. But the geologic foundations were compromised. Testing was shifted to Fangataufa atoll.

Not long after the shift a group of scientists was invited to visit Moruroa, albeit with an outlandish caveat: They weren't allowed to sample the northern or western portions of the atoll, where so much testing had taken place, and no sediments were to be taken from the lagoon. The visitors were chagrined and issued a report, which concluded that fracturing accompanied by a test would cause a release of radioactivity to the limestones, thus forcing contaminants to enter the biosphere within five years.

In June 1987, Jacques Cousteau arrived at Moruroa to witness a test. The next day he was allowed to take samples from the lagoon. The samples contained cesium 134, with a half-life of two years. The French shrugged and claimed the isotopes were left over from the atmospheric tests. Cousteau's samples were subsequently studied by Search Technical Services, Davenport, Washington. The firm concluded the cesium had to come from underground testing.

Scientists in New Zealand developed a computer model of Moruroa. They said radioactive groundwater with a half-life of several thousand years was leaking through the atoll at a rate of some 300 feet per year. Professor Manfred Hochstein, head of Auckland University's Geothermal Institute, summed it up chillingly: "In about thirty years, the disaster will hit us."

The United States has paid hundreds of millions of dollars to the Bikinians to compensate for the destruction and human dislocation throughout the Marshall Islands. France, on the other hand, has refused to acknowledge any ill effects of its testing. The rates of thyroid cancer, leukemia, and stillbirths are on the rise. The seafood poisoning in the nearby Gambier Islands is clearly related.

No one can say exactly what the long-range consequences will be. But in the late 1990s, the madness in Oceania took another painful lurch forward.

V

I had been assigned to cover French Polynesia and had traveled through half a dozen islands. By the time I arrived in Rangiroa in late 1994, I was convinced that French Polynesia, and perhaps all of Oceania, was in trouble. Here was a case of split personality, islanders struggling to retain their identity without losing the economic benefits of the French connection. Alex du Prel, editor of *Tahiti Pacific,* admitted the contradiction to me: "We're constantly playing a balancing act. The truth is we want it both ways."

In the impenetrable black night of Rangiroa I sensed a deep unrest. I sat alone listening to the ocean pounding the outer reef. The sound was a deep, troubling rumble, like the Earth falling in on itself. But later, at the Tuamotuan atoll of Manihi, I felt I had at last discovered the South Pacific of my boyhood dreams. Manihi was a ring of gold wrapped in azure sea and silence. I had come full circle and wrote in my notebook:

> *Of all the Pacific islands I have known this is the one that speaks to me, whispers of my past and future. The people here call Manihi "The Edge of the World." It may be true. The remoteness is like a mirage, like a wave far out to sea that rises, crests, and disappears back into the ocean without a trace. It is a pitiless beauty. And at its heart the beauty is forever hiding, just out of reach ... an eternal romance.*

It was hard to imagine that nearby the split personality of French Polynesia was all too real. The sea was under assault. Stories of the Pacific seemed to exhibit two basic emotions: romance and violence, a duality and a built-in duplicity.

The French had called a moratorium on the atomic testing. At Manihi the peace of that moratorium was almost palpable. At other times it seemed as if a manifestation of the chaos would be imitated by nature. In another notebook entry, I described this chaos:

> *The wind rises across the lagoon with sudden anger. The blue mirror of water churns angry white. The air is chilled, whipping through the thatch. The palms toss like waves. The sun is below the bowl of the horizon and the clouds, only a few minutes ago white and puffy, are gray and black, spreading across the lowering sky. ... A boy dashes to the end of the pier to secure his outrigger. He is nearly invisible against the darkness. The wind rises. The lagoon lifts up and races against the shore. The air, like an invisible snake, wraps around me, encloses me.*
>
> *An eerie light accents the gray, like a flash of sunlight slanting across the sea. It is enchanting and violent, a raw streak on the sky. ... The light contains its own destruction. Seeing that strange light I know somehow this is what I have searched for, it belongs inside me, and yet it is ominous, a portent. ...*

A year later President Jacques Chirac resumed nuclear testing. Tahiti exploded in riots. On January 23, 1996, the French government finally acknowledged that its tests had caused leaks of radioactive material, but insisted the levels were too small to pose a threat to the region. The admission sparked new riots. Faaa was burned. The French government, realizing that its cause was too costly, pledged an end to the testing once and for all. And with the end came the contradiction, the split in the personality of French Polynesia.

With the testing ground now a deserted wasteland, would France continue its support of its Pacific colonies? After all, French subsidies and tourism account for more than 70 percent of Tahiti's resources. Departure of the nuclear program seems to have piqued the madness that began in these seas more than two centuries ago. Today we find the majority of islanders fearful of losing their mixed blessings. On my last day in Manihi I sat quietly in my bungalow as a squall kicked up. I wrote:

> *Rain sweeps in from the north, a curtain of gray obscures the motus. You can see the wind before it arrives in the streaks of white water far out in the lagoon. Then the sound of the wind rises slowly, almost imperceptibly, and there are more streaks of white water advancing. The gray lifts; the outlines of the motus reappear. Only a few drops of rain fall. The sky-bound wall of water is carried away to some more distant point of land.*

These waters can tell us a great deal about islands, their birth and death. The lessons of Loihi and Whakaari are powerful ones. So, too, is the human component that has invaded Polynesia. But politics fade. Madness is softened by the sea and sky. Like the squall that never appeared, my romance is carried by the winds to other points of land.

Chapter Six

THE PASHA AND
HIS MAGIC LUNG

I felt strangely reassured about everything.
I sank lower, relaxed and receptive.

—J.-Y. Cousteau

I

I WILL NEVER FORGET THE FIRST TIME I discovered it was possible to live like a fish. I wish I could report it happened in some exotic destination at sea. But it was far more mundane: a swimming pool in Washington, D.C.

My friend Daphne Harden was my first instructor. She set about explaining the basics of scuba. She did her best to be reassuring, yet the more she talked the more apprehensive I became. She patiently described the concept of neutral buoyancy: how I would receive air on demand from this gadget called a regulator. A steel tank filled with compressed air was strapped to my back, a belt with lead weights sagged from my waist, and a horseshoe collar gizmo around my neck called a *buoyancy compensator* would combine to keep me from crashing into the bottom of the pool.

I wanted to know more about the regulator, this black air hose with its shiny mouthpiece attached to a pressure reduction stage at the top of the scuba tank. It seemed to work fine (if noisily) at the surface. But what happened underwater?

The wheezing sound was of no concern, Daphne explained. It was a very old regulator and didn't give up its air without some amount of complaining. It was a U.S. Divers brand regulator, with Jacques Cousteau's endorsement on it. This was some reassurance. But Cousteau's name was no guarantee the air would keep flowing. Fortunately, I had the oversized regulator mouthpiece jammed between my teeth, a rubber gag to keep me from verbalizing my anxiety.

Despite my qualms, a certain logical sense calmed me. I realized the odds were probably on my side. Besides, wasn't it normal to feel a little odd? After all, I was human, a human who was about to betray his natural state as a landlocked, air-breathing mammal.

So, with swim fins on my feet, and what felt like a ton of steel hanging from my body, I waddled to the edge of the pool, pulled the diving mask over my eyes and nose, and took one more *I-can't-believe-I'm-doing-this* look at Daphne.

"Oh," she shouted. "One more thing. *Don't hold your breath.*"

"What do you mean?"

"It's physics," she said. The air in my lungs will be compressed by water pressure at the bottom of the pool. If for some reason I shot to the surface without exhaling the air, it would expand dramatically. She locked two balled-up fists together and flung them open with a sudden explosive burst.

"Boof! Boom! Get it?"

Why I kept going is still something of a mystery. But I did. I stepped over the boundary and splashed into ten feet of chlorinated water.

When the bubbles cleared I was floating face down, a few inches above the bottom. My breathing seemed normal enough. For the first time I experienced weightlessness. I was breathing rapidly. *No breath-holding!* Daphne's words reverberated in my head. Cautiously I moved my swim fins; a single kick, once, then twice. I eased across the bottom, turned, made zigzags, did barrel rolls, stood on my head. I was free to move 360 degrees, effortlessly.

I found myself fascinated by the little nasties endemic to most public swimming pools. The wadded nubs of chewing gum, clumps of hair, bobby pins—somehow these intrigued me; by virtue of their immersion they were like small treasures. What a sensation, what a transformation. And best of all I was alive, free in a way I could never have imagined.

"Well, what'd you think?" Daphne asked when I finally emerged, dripping and grinning. She looked at the little round air gauge attached to the scuba tank. "Sucked up your share, I see."

The air supply was nearly depleted. In my excitement I'd come close to breathing the tank dry. I'd been down only a few minutes, yet it seemed like hours. I was ecstatically exhausted.

"I think I'm in love," I panted.

"Oh, my," Daphne said. "What have I done?"

The answer, though I didn't know it at the time, was that she had opened the door to a new vision that has carrried me forward for more than two decades. I was lucky to know, though vaguely, that my life had changed, that I was on a new path.

II

Thirty years earlier, Captain Jacques-Yves Cousteau had a similar vision, but in a far more romantic and exciting way. The precise moment came in June 1943, when he arrived at the railway station at Bandol on the French Riviera and claimed a large wooden case shipped from Paris.

"In it was a new and promising device, the result of years of struggles and dreams, an automatic compressed air diving lung conceived by Emile Gagnan and myself," Cousteau wrote in his classic work, *The Silent World* (Harper & Row, 1953). If this aqualung worked, diving could be revolutionized.

I read and reread *The Silent World* with the same wonder Cousteau must have felt that day at Bandol. This book about the wondrous invention was important, in many ways transcendent. For the first aqualung was a means to escape our essential nature, to encounter firsthand a world that was barely imaginable, and to do so with relative ease and freedom. It relegated the early diving suits to museum status.

The Silent World had been published in twenty-two languages and had sold more than three million copies in the English language alone. Cousteau's film of the same title had won grand prize at the Cannes International Film Festival in 1956 and a Hollywood Oscar a year later. The whole world, it seemed, was hooked on the Cousteau magic, and I was no exception.

As a journalist I had covered the space program and had been involved in Project Mercury. I wanted to be the first outer space journalist and had taken steps to realize that goal. My heroes were astronauts and rocket scientists. But after my first aqualung experience and my reading of *The Silent World,* my focus shifted from the stars to the underwater domain. I was captivated and headed into territory that seemed every bit as exciting as space, and I was determined to meet my new mentor, the perfectly nicknamed "Pasha." I had no way of knowing it would be easier to roam the floor of the sea than to shake the hand of the man who had so inspired me.

Diving rigs of the early twentieth century consisted of brass helmets, ungainly canvas suits, lead boots, and long, thick hoses plugged into an air compressor coughing and sputtering on the surface. These "hard hat" systems afforded little freedom of movement; the diver was dependent on surface support and the length of his air hose, like a puppet at the end of its strings. The compact and portable Gagnan-Cousteau system was the beginning of the end of "tethered" diving.

In the early 1950s, the aqualung made its way to America. Cousteau licensed the invention to a French company, which founded the U.S. Divers Company in California. Within a few years it was all the rage, a piece of "sporting" equipment nearly as commonplace as a pair of skis, anyone's passage to new worlds. It was also to become one of the most liberating tools of twentieth-century science.

To appreciate its full impact, one has to look to the past and wonder how our view of the planet and our place in it might have been changed by an earlier introduction of the aqualung. Aristotle, probably the first marine biologist, might have solved the mystery of the tides and the origins of the sea in his *Meterologica* three centuries before the birth of Christ. What insights might Plato have given us in his *Phaedo?* In 1690 Edmund Halley descended sixty feet in his little "diving bell"; he sat inside, peeking through a small port, a prisoner in the deep. John Lethbridge reached the same depth in a weird banana-shaped diving suit, though, like Halley, he was tethered to the surface. It is mind-boggling to leap forward to Darwin and imagine what he might have discovered, zooming around as a "man-fish."

One of the most provocative "what-ifs" involves the HMS *Challenger* expedition of 1872. The ship circled the globe in three and one-half years, yet with all its instruments and available scientific talent, there was no diving rig on board. Nearly three decades earlier, Professor Henri Milne-Edwards had accomplished the first "dive for science" in the Straits of Messina off the coast of Sicily. In 1819, the basics of the helmet diving rig were known and used by Augustus Siebe, and soon afterward Benoit Rouquayrol and Auguste Denayrouse developed a crude aqualung. Our view of the world might have been far advanced today if the *Challenger* scientists had made use of these systems.

Given all this, it seems inescapable that the Gagnan-Cousteau aqualung would become a multibillion-dollar business because it was simple, inexpensive, and available. Most important of all, it was given voice—Cousteau's crooning voice, in love with the sea. With the help and editorial skills of adventurers and writers Frédéric Dumas, Phillippe Diolé, James Dugan, and Cousteau's sons Phillipe and Jean-Michel, the Pasha spoke to a postwar generation in a way that pure science never could. Cousteau the romantic tapped into the public imagination, flinging images about like so much confetti. In the ivy towers he was called a "popularizer," though no one before or since has offered a greater enticement to enter the sea.

I set about learning everything I could about him. Probably no single adventurer in our century has seen more newsprint. Soon after publication of his book he began his rise to pop-star status. Everyone it seemed came to recognize the sharply sculpted facial features, the cheerful eyes blazing beneath the ubiquitous red watch cap, the look that seemed the essence of adventure.

I appreciated his poetic stature, because it was this that set him apart from the many scientists who eagerly tossed the dreaded epithet of "popularizer" in his path. "He contributes nothing except to his own glory," one scientist scoffed, typically, when I asked his opinion of Cousteau. "And you think this guy is important. You journalists are a bunch of dupes!"

The remark made me feel a little foolish, but not enough to break my focus. I understood the Pasha's public allure. Yes, he was a popularizer, as was Carl Sagan, another long-standing hero of mine. What the scientists seemed not to understand was the fact that men like Cousteau and Sagan were the engines that made science accessible to the public, piqued its curiosity—curiosity that ultimately translated into funds for further exploration. Indeed, it's the thrill of discovery that makes us feel a little less ordinary, and compels us to support science. It is on this edge of the public's lust for adventure that Cousteau operated with something close to genius.

Cousteau was born in 1910 in St.-André-de-Cubzac, educated in New York, and graduated from the Brest Naval Academy as a gunnery officer. He served as a midshipman onboard the *Jeanne D'Arc* in 1932, and became chief of the French Naval Base in Shanghai a few years later. He trained as a Navy flier until a serious automobile accident ended his ambitions as an aviator; he had broken many bones, punctured a lung, and sat in a wheelchair, paralyzed, for eight months. The doctors said he'd never regain use of his arms.

"It was terrible," he said later. But it did not affect his optimism. "It was a test for me. After such an endeavor, I think you finish stronger than you were before."

Tragedy-turned-success seemed the right beginning for a man who would come to found the Calypso Oceanographic Expeditions in 1957 and assume the direction of the Oceanographic Museum at Monaco for thirty-one years. His work at sea would be supported by the French Ministry of National Education and, in America, by the National Geographic Society.

Yet his personal introduction to the underwater world came quietly, without as much drama as I had experienced at the swimming pool. It was a Sunday morning in 1936 in Le Mourillon, not far from Toulon. He had gone down to the Mediterranean shore with Fernez goggles to practice swimming. He was astounded by what he saw below the surace at Le Mourillon. He spoke of rocks covered with green, brown, and silver forests of algae, schools of fishes unknown to him. He stood up to breathe and saw a trolley car, people, the familiar world of the sun. He put his eyes under again and civilization vanished. He was in a jungle that would enchant him for a lifetime.

From the very beginning, the Pasha grasped the importance of style and communication. It is difficult, at the least, to describe in writing what readers have never seen or experienced. In the 1940s, it might have been easier to describe the surface of Mars—about which a great deal of science fiction existed—than the bottom of the sea. Cousteau overcame the challenge.

His first trial of the aqualung was documented with lyrical narrative. The reader could plainly see the heavily burdened sailor dragging across the sand, accompanied by the concerned wife, Simone, playing the role of *etre partisan*. His description of his transformation from awkward land animal to free-flying "man-fish" is at once vivid and abstract. He said he looked into the sea with "a sense of trespass." A modest canyon opened below him; it was full of dark green weeds, urchins, and white algae. The sand sloped down and the sun struck so brightly he had to squint. He reached the bottom in a "state of transport." He looked up at the shimmering surface and at the center he saw the silhouette of Simone "reduced to a doll." He waved, and the doll waved back at him.

If Cousteau understood literary magic, he was also a keen student of history. He had seen Assyrian bas-reliefs of men attempting to fashion underwater life-support systems out of goatskin bellows. Leonardo da Vinci's sketches of various impractical breathing devices were known to him, as were Elizabethan experiments with leather diving suits. Assessing the seemingly irresistible urge to explore, Cousteau the poet-pragmatist understood why others had failed. There was no popular urge to explore the sea, such as there was on land when the steam locomotive was built or when the Wrights experimented with aircraft.

The presence and/or absence of a "popular economic movement" has been the key to ocean exploration in our century. Cousteau pressed the point for all it was worth, and he did it in his own cock-of-the-walk fashion. From the very beginning it was his belief that we had little choice, that necessity compelled us to move into the sea. He was at times Malthusian: Land resources were being depleted, the sea offered abundance. The same logic applied to the harvesting of mineral and chemical resources. Science was Cousteau's ultimate raison d'etre, but science was also his code word for exploration for its own sake and money to his underwater dream machine.

Microsoft Chairman Bill Gates has his "killer application"—the ultimate can't-live-without-it problem solver. For Gates it has been creation of the digital spreadsheet. Cousteau had the magic lung, but he needed more.

The Pasha, Simone, and their son Phillipe, along with a crew of divers and adventurers, were living at the Villa Barry in occupied territory during the war. Scattered among the aqualungers were various friends whose patience was often stretched thin by endless tales of undersea adventure. They listened, Cousteau confessed, "with maddening boredom." This irritated him; he was, after all, a thinker, a problem solver whose thought processes were as lean and articulated as his physique. The solution was to make photographs; better yet, motion pictures.

Cousteau went bargain hunting, purchased an obsolete Kinamo cinecam for twenty-five dollars, had a new lens ground by a Hungarian refugee, and prevailed upon the machinist to build a submersible camera housing. Because thirty-five-millimeter film wasn't available, Leica film was substituted. The divers spliced together fifty-foot reels. At last the nondiving friends could see what the divers were talking about; Cousteau overcame their "maddening boredom."

There are tales told in the publishing industry that when the first edition of *The Silent World* was published in 1953, its sales were only modest. The book included many photographs, but it was difficult to distinguish facial features underwater; the divers' eyes were particularly hard to see. Cousteau's solution was to shoot additional photographs, instructing divers to stare into the camera and open their eyes as wide as possible. The new photos were inserted and, violà— a best-seller soared to the top of the lists.

"It's strange," one publishing executive noted. "Readers needed open eyes to make a connection."

III

The stage was set for Cousteau's popularity by the 1950 publication of Rachel Carson's *The Sea Around Us* (New American Library, 1950). It was an amazing best-seller, one of the most accessible books ever written on the subject. Its scope was universal and its tone gentle, almost soothing. Her treatment of the emergence of life, its birth and death, and perhaps its resurrection, is equally compelling.

Carson, like Cousteau, was blessed with a certain seductive touch. She wasn't a competitor to the Pasha's derring-do, but rather acted as a kind of foil to make his adventures all the more striking. In the early 1950s, he received permission from the French navy to create a research and exploration arm for the military. Cousteau and company went to work in 1951, and work was the operative word. Anyone who has ever served aboard *Calypso* (except for singers of popular ballads) will testify to hard, nasty, exhausting work. Cousteau enlisted support from the National Geographic Society, the Edo Corporation, and others, and never lost the overriding need for public appeal.

Cousteau did have serious competitors, but for various reasons they didn't measure up. One of Cousteau's early competitors was Austrian Hans Hass. Born in Vienna in 1919, Hass received his D.Sc. degree summa cum laude. He began diving expeditions with his own money in 1939, and a decade later founded the Institute for Underwater Exploration. His work in underwater film technology won him an Oscar in 1951. He dropped off the scene unexpectedly a few years later, and repositioned himself as a terrestrial naturalist, a move that would be imitated much later by the Pasha himself. His American publisher claimed Hass was the "founder of modern underwater research." Indeed, he was a force worthy of recognition.

Though Hass was by no means unknown, he never reached Cousteau's level of popularity. Perhaps he lacked the common touch. For example, his research vessel *Xarifa* was far more elegant than Cousteau's homely *Calypso. Xarifa* was a three-masted beauty with 100-foot masts and a sleek white hull; she had all the good looks of a world-ranging pleasure craft. *Calypso* was a rather lumpy 360-ton minesweeper built in 1942 for the Royal Navy. She was wooden hulled, chunky and businesslike in appearance, and retrofitted with all sorts of inventions to accommodate research diving. Hass gave the impression of a well-to-do adventurer on a lark; Cousteau was tough, a little rough edged, pushy, and engaging.

Hass showed us breathless images of *Xarifa* breezing along under white canvas, sleek and trim. Cousteau gave us a gritty, black-and-white *Calypso,* a no-nonsense workboat pounding into rough head-seas. *Calypso* was outfitted with a bulbous observation chamber beneath its forefoot, like the ram on an ancient Greek war galley; hardly sleek, but practical and pragmatic as the Pasha himself. And there was the insignia of the vessel, the appealing white nymph of Homer's *Odyssey.*

By the time he retired from the French navy in 1957, Cousteau was well ahead of the competition with the aqualung, development of test chambers for deep dives, feature stories about him in *Life,* and offers from Universal Pictures for his short subjects. In 1956, he won an Oscar for best documentary and the *Palme d'Or* award at Cannes for the feature-length *Silent World.* Many would try to catch up, to surpass him; so far, no one has.

Cousteau created the mystique and the mystique spawned generations of "aqua-egos," men and women who are part Nemo, part General Patton. Among those who attempted a Cousteau-esque invasion of the public consciousness, American cinematographer Al Giddings ranks fairly high. I interviewed him in 1979, soon after he took command of a 221-foot minesweeper he named RV *Eagle.* At the time, Giddings had a track record as an active underwater photographer who had captured so much footage that practically any motion picture with underwater sequences had him as its source.

"Our goal is to make *Eagle* the standard-bearer for the United States for responsible ocean conservation policy," he told me, even while making the ship into what amounted to a floating production company. "Since network television programs reach more people ... than other forms of communication, *Eagle*'s 'eyes in the sea' should provide a powerful force in shaping world opinion," he proclaimed with typical modesty.

After dropping a half-dozen or so names during our interview ("Do you realize I have Jackie Onassis waiting in the outer office?"), Giddings flinched at any comparison to Cousteau. To him, the mission of RV *Eagle* was more "direct," more "purposeful," even more ambitious than *Calypso*.

"We're adding a new dimension," he said, "Project 'Ocean Trust,'" an organization that would shape the direction of ocean science and technology. For all his bravado and success as a provider of motion picture material, Giddings never achieved the charisma of the model he wouldn't acknowledge, the viewer-friendly Cousteau.

It was a bit of a shock to the Pasha to realize that his youngest son, Jean-Michel, was also going to compete against him. For a time the soft-spoken Jean-Michel served as executive vice president of the Cousteau Society. He took on a political role while the Pasha roamed the seas. The son wrestled with the implications of the Law of the Sea, which sought to unify global marine interests, a work of almost impossible proportions. It simply wasn't in Jean-Michel's nature to entangle himself in politics. He later quit the Cousteau Society and set out on his own. But, like so many others, he appeared to exist in the shadow of the Pasha.

It is unlikely that Cousteau anticipated the friction that later appeared. I, too, was beginning to see how the Pasha created friction. Despite my admiration for the man, it was clear that his agenda was the only one that mattered. I attempted to set up meetings with him in New York. "He'll be in Paris next week," I was informed by someone at the Cousteau Society in a *who-do-you-think-you-are?* tone of voice. "Perhaps you'll want to reach him there."

I telephoned the Paris office. In my less-than-perfect French I pleaded to speak with their leader. "Oh, *desólé*," came the reply. Captain Cousteau could not be disturbed. He was in a meeting with some head of state. Where was I calling from? Ah, *oui*, Washington, D.C. Well, there was a time difference, and Captain Cousteau was on a very tight schedule. He was committed to appear at this or that place to receive praise, honors, medals. I was asked more than a few times to repeat my name and affiliation, and was at last consigned to wait in the long queue with all the others who were seeking an audience.

Looking for a shortcut, I telephoned Dr. Harold Edgerton, "Papa Flash," the man who had invented stroboscopic light and who sailed with his special cameras aboard the *Calypso* when he wasn't holding forth as a professor at the Massachusetts Institute of Technology.

"Mighty hard man to pin down," Edgerton informed me. "If he needs you, your phone won't quit ringing. Otherwise you won't hear a thing."

I had briefly met Jean-Michel, who was a contributor to a magazine I had helped to develop, but he wasn't terribly forthcoming about his father. A family feud developed, and there was some apparent bitterness over Jean-Michel's departure from the Cousteau Society. It was for me impossible to envision the Pasha through his mild-mannered son, except perhaps as a study in opposites. If J.-Y. Cousteau was keenly strategic in granting audiences, Jean-Michel appeared the very opposite: He was extremely generous and polite and seemed to have time for everyone. Yet I was determined to continue my chase after the Pasha. After all, it was Cousteau who made it obvious that in the chase lay the true thrill.

IV

Calypsonians drank as much as they liked, Cousteau had declared. The average wine consumption per capita was about a pint a day.

This passed for "rapture" at the surface, yet it remained for the billboard-minded Cousteau to make romance out of one of the most notorious dangers faced by underwater explorers. "Rapture of the deep" was his by-now famous phrase. In reality, the rapture is nitrogen narcosis, and a leading cause of the "bends."

In those early days of scuba, everything was trial and error, and not much was known about the physics of diving. Cousteau described the *l'ivresse des grandes profondeurs* as "a state of transport ... a dream." In his night dreams he often had visions of flying by extending his arms as wings. Underwater he flew without wings. He admitted he was receptive to the narcosis, liked it and feared it like doom.

Yet the notion of rapture is still with us. We have invented all sorts of gas mixtures to dull its effects and reduce the possibility of the bends. Yet at 130 feet, hydrostatic pressure on the body is nearly sixty tons, and pressure and nitrogen combine for any number of hazards. Nitrogen is four-fifths of the air we breathe. When the air is compressed, a great deal of nitrogen enters the lungs; instead of being exhaled again, it dissolves in the blood. The deeper one goes, the greater the pressure, and the more nitrogen is absorbed into the body. To avoid nitrogen frothing out of solution (the champagne bottle effect), divers must breathe off a certain quantity of it before rising to the surface, where sea level pressure is less than fifteen pounds per square inch. The process of ridding the body of bubble-forming gas is called "stage decompression." Today this is simple enough to do. We have specific tables to guide us. One rises to the surface in stages, moving upward at decreasing levels of pressure over specific periods of time.

The "rapture" Cousteau talks about is nitrogen as narcotic. Some have called it the "three-martini effect." It may create feelings of well-being, a certain insouciance, though in others it causes confusion, fear, panic, and fatal mistakes.

Cousteau and the early men-fish had to experiment with this rather dicey physiology, and much of what they did fell into the learn-as-you-go category. Yet a decade or so after their hesitant experiments, aqualungs were being rented off trucks along the Riviera.

It's doubtful Cousteau could foresee the future extent of the aqualung's success, though certainly the commercial possibilities were clear enough. By establishing U.S. Divers Company, he anticipated the market. It was helped along in the 1950s when actor Lloyd Bridges scubaed through season after season of underwater dramas in the classic TV show "Sea Hunt." Hollywood produced undersea thrillers, and the market for scuba surged.

Dr. Sylvia Earle, an early star in the twentieth century's galaxy of ocean researchers, was one of many scientists who saw the potential of the lung and developed a lifelong addiction to moving about underwater. In her 1996 best-seller, *Sea Change* (G. P. Putnam's Sons, 1995), she recounted her first impressions and predicted the future importance of the magic lung. After her first experience she was convinced she needed gills "or at least an aqualung!" She said that for marine scientists scuba was comparable in some ways to the microscope. Both provided access, "a way to see things otherwise not visible."

In those early days not a few scientists exposed their conservatism and mocked the invention. Scuba diving, they grumbled, was romance, a lark, more recreation than a tool of fact-finding. But Dr. Earle and others claimed legions of converts.

Again, it was Cousteau who pushed the notion of diving as serious science. However, it should be noted that he did so while retaining his "day job" as a French naval officer. The Pasha took chances in the sea, but business was business, and he had no intention of losing his pension. After the war he turned to his boss, the French navy, with his plans.

V

Cousteau traveled to Paris soon after the German occupation to meet with Admiral André Lemonnier and his staff and showed films of Dumas and Phillipe Tailliez diving on shipwrecks. The admiral was impressed, and the next day Cousteau had his commission to resume diving. Tailliez, who was working as a forest ranger, was delighted to leave a job he considered boring. They made space for the group in the harbormaster's office and put up a sign: *Groupe de Recherches Sous-Marine* (Undersea Research Group). They had only two aqualungs but neglected no opportunity to make themselves known as a powerful bureau.

The French navy was generous, providing men, equipment, and vessels. Most people would have been pleased by such support, but Cousteau was contantly on the move, expanding and glad-handing and reaching for new goals. He set up liaisons with oceanographic units in Great Britain, West Germany, Sweden, and Italy. He discovered Professor J.B.S. Haldane, a scientist who contributed much to the growing science of diving physiology. Haldane was working on ways to neutralize magnetic mines. One of Europe's big problems after World War II was ridding its waters of these floating bombs, and Cousteau sensed an opportunity to underscore the practical side of *plongee sous-marine.*

He later claimed it was Dumas who got them into this "unappetizing game" of demolition because of his interest in underwater effects. Dumas may have brought up the idea of experimenting with underwater blasts, but it was Cousteau who seized the moment. If his team could help rid French waters of mines, it would rebound with honor to the Undersea Research Group.

Thus began a series of daredevil experiments, which, in Haldane's opinion, required "superhuman courage." Dumas tossed hand grenades into the water to kill fish. A few floated to the surface, then Tailliez dove in and brought up many more lying on the bottom. Dumas flung in another grenade; this time, however, it failed to explode. He dove in and found the device leaking tiny bubbles. Without warning the grenade exploded beneath him. The weight of the water supressed the shrapnel, but the shock waves were punishing. Dumas staggered out of the surf, shaken.

This was nasty yet ennobling work for the group. They studied shock-wave tables and set about blasting themselves with one-pound loads of TNT. The idea was to see how close they might come to the blast without sustaining serious injury. The explosions often boxed their ears, smacked their bodies, and, at times, meted out sandbag blows.

At a certain point the blasts became too dangerous and the experiments ended. The group had proven itself and had reached the conclusion that a "naked" diver had better resistance to an explosion than a helmeted diver. The paradox arises from the fact that pressure waves have approximately the same propagation speed in human tissue as in water. The helmeted diver took the blast straight on, the shock waves slamming his suit and meeting no counterpressure. The group concluded (rather impressively) that despite Haldane's tables, a naked man's resistance to shock waves was far greater than anyone had anticipated.

Mine recovery wasn't paramount on the group's to-do list, but going to war after the war proved to the admirals that Cousteau's mission had practical applications.

VI

For Cousteau, a long period of minesweeping ensued after the war, including the discovery of twenty tons of German accoustic explosives in a French harbor. This was all very impressive, yet it was Cousteau the crooner, the man who was imitated by comedians as the explorer who "marvels over zeez tiny shreemp," that dragged the world into the deep and made it entertaining, even glitzy. It seemed as if all of Hollywood paraded across the decks of the *Calypso*. Folk singer John Denver wrote a song about the *Calypso*, which made it briefly to the charts.

"You can't imagine his charisma," says Dr. Eugenie Clark, the famous zoologist "shark lady," who is nearly as popular as the Pasha himself. "I mean, you sit and talk to him, and he is so ..." She hesitates, pondering just the right word. "So damned poetic. You're just drawn into his orbit."

Others have seen the stern, demanding side, pushing his crew to the limits; but when the divers have dragged themselves out of the sea and onto the deck, Cousteau will retire to his cabin, unpack his old-fashioned accordian, and play little French folk melodies to cheer up the exhausted crew. Few appreciate the Pasha's business sense. Immediately after the war, when no money was available from the French navy for undersea research, Cousteau became an entrepreneur. He landed a very generous contract from British Petroleum to explore the Persian Gulf with divers in search of oil. Persistent and lucky as usual, the crew found it off the village of Abu Dhabi. Cousteau didn't ask for any royalties, but it was a good contract and enabled the Pasha to buy new equipment.

His philosophy of money, of wealth building, carried certain spiritual overtones. Everything went into the sea and his various enterprises. On his seventy-fifth birthday in June 1985, Cousteau spelled out his philosophy. He said he felt freer having practically no money of his own, but had no hesitation spending huge amounts on research. Of course, he never defined what having practically no personal wealth meant, but rather explained himself this way: "I don't believe it's an interesting goal to build an estate because, finally, when you die, what's the point? And it's a bad thing to give money to your children. They have to earn it themselves. ... The idea is to own nothing."

Embedded in these remarks are clues to the fate of his family empire.

Cousteau was masterful at finding and using talent. When he met Ed Link, the pilot who invented the famous Link Flight Trainer, he lured him to the sea. Along with U.S. Navy Captain George Bond, a medical doctor known as "Papa Topside," the team took on the challenge of living at great depths. In 1954, Bond had experimented with "saturation diving," a physical state in which the diver's body was saturated with compressed gas so that a balance was achieved between pressure in the body and the surrounding water. Bond worked out decompression tables based on time, depth, and the gases breathed. He got volunteers to live for two weeks at 200 feet, and brought them back safely.

Cousteau and Link leaped ahead of the field. The services of Dr. Joan Membery were enlisted, and experiments began with mice at simulated depths to 1,000 feet. Link decided in 1962 to remain in an underwater station at sixty feet for fourteen hours. Within a month, another experimenter, Robert Stenuit, used the same station for a full day at 200 feet. The point was this: Once the body was saturated at a particular depth, decompression time would be the same no matter how long one stayed down. In Hydro-Lab I, for example, our team was saturated at "storage depth" of fifty feet. We stayed for a week, but it could have been months; either way, decompression time would have been sixteen hours.

Immediately seizing on the possibilities of saturation diving, Cousteau moved to develop several experimental habitats. Soon after Stenuit's dive he introduced "Starfish House," a large living space with a central core and four "arms" radiating outward. The bright yellow habitat accommodated five divers; the arms served as their "apartments," while the center portion was the "living room." It was anchored 400 feet beneath the Red Sea. A year later, Conshelf II used the Starfish dwelling as a kind of central location, with a "Deep Cabin" stationed at ninety feet. The Deep Cabin added a new dimension: The divers locked out and made excursions to 165 feet. Cousteau added to this mix his now-famous Diving Saucer, a submersible capable of ranging long and far over the bottom.

Living under the sea became Cousteau's obsession. In 1965, he placed Conshelf III in the Mediterranean near the coast of France; it was stationed 328 feet down. The divers swam out into the surrounding sea bottom. It was daring yet extremely convenient for searching out undersea oil and natural gas.

In a stroke of Cousteau-esque publicity genius, the Pasha's team Conshelf leader, Andre Leban, conversed with Astronaut Scott Carpenter through a special telephone link. Carpenter was half a world away, 205 feet deep, off the coast of California. And to heighten the symbolic drama, Astronaut Gordon Cooper greeted Carpenter while orbiting the earth in *Gemini V.*

These achievements helped fuel the ill-fated "wet NASA" concept in America. By the mid-1970s, when the "wet NASA" concept was very old news, Cousteau maintained his position. He founded a society in his name, and combined with his television specials and his own eight-year-long television show, "The Undersea World of Jacques Cousteau," he remained the darling of the underwater world.

He was the first to coin the phrase "water planet," and he found ways to make people feel connected to what he was doing.

The Cousteau Society didn't make documentaries, he explained. It made adventure films describing nature as personal adventure. In many ways he was everyone's armchair adventurer guide. "To run around the world, to discover things, look through nature's keyhole—that was my ambition," he said.

On the occasion of the Pasha's eighty-fifth birthday, astronomer Carl Sagan summed up the key to Cousteau's appeal: "[He] epitomizes the fact that science and adventure go hand in hand, as well as the central importance of safeguarding the planetary environment on which all life, in and out of the sea, depends."

Cousteau spoke of underwater cities, colonies in the deep. Yet in the end, his experiments with subsea habitats led him to conclude that long-term underwater habitation was too expensive and too harsh an environment for humans. The same conclusion was reached earlier by other experimenters, but coming from the Pasha it was accepted as the final word.

By the late 1970s, however, something seemed to change. Was the Pasha's luster a bit diminished? The waters turned rough. Cousteau attempted to overcome a growing public apathy to undersea research. He adopted a more holistic approach, positioning himself as the world's most sagacious environmentalist. Off came the red watch cap and on went the various hats of the universal biospherist.

Alas, Cousteau was typecast. The holistic Pasha didn't quite gel. He slipped off the major television networks and into the world of public television. It seemed to be asking too much of audiences to make the leap from Cousteau, champion of the oceans, to Cousteau, champion of all nature.

There was also personal tragedy. In the summer of 1979, his son and heir apparent, Phillipe Cousteau, was killed when his World War II Catalina seaplane developed mechanical trouble and made a forced landing in the Tagus River in Portugal. The Catalina struck a sandbar, flipped over, and sank. Seven French and Portuguese divers who were on assignment with him to film bird migrations escaped with minor injuries, but Phillipe was pinned in the cockpit. It took several days to pull his body from the wreckage.

The fatal accident did not come entirely as a surprise. It was just the sort of thing some observors feared might happen. Some said Phillipe was a natural risk taker. For example, when he was five he nearly drowned on his first aqualung adventure when he took his regulator out of his mouth underwater and tried to talk to his father. At fifteen he was piloting airplanes, and when he joined the crew of the *Calypso* he talked the captain into purchasing a hot-air balloon, which he proceeded to crack up with alarming regularity.

Many in the oceans community understood the closeness of the Pasha and Phillipe, and they feared the loss would destroy the father. But the sixty-nine-year-old patriarch was a hardened survivor. He was determined that the loss of Phillipe would not cloud his future.

His younger son, Jean-Michel, thirty-nine at the time of Phillipe's death, had formed his own operation, the Jean-Michel Cousteau Institute at Hilton Head, South Carolina. He'd hoped to build an independent identity removed from the shadow of his famous father. One of his first moves was to found "Project Ocean Search," a kind of "Outward Bound" program in which students and scientists might conduct research under a nonacademic, independent banner.

The Pasha appeared upset by the loss of the undivided support he had hoped from Jean-Michel. But he was not like his brother. Jean-Michel maintained what some considered a more gentle touch. Where Phillipe was the writer of tough, hard-hitting narrative, the younger brother tended toward poetry. In the 1985 edition of *Calypso Log,* which celebrated the Pasha's seventy-fifth birthday, he wrote:

> *To my boss, my father, my friend,*
> *Only those who have stopped living write their own biographies. So please keep telling us about the future, connections, quality, joie de vivre, hope.*
> *The First Seventy Five Years are like a glimpse of the open sea, the ticking of life, the specks of grass that grow in cracks in the cement, the smile on the face of a starving child. Hope.*
> *You are care, love,*
> *persistence, courage,*
> *tomorrow's heritage.*
> *One earth*
> *One water*
> *One people*
> *Hope*
> *I and millions of friends would like to say we love you.*

By the 1990s, Jean-Michel had jumped ship and the Cousteaus were engaged in a lawsuit over the use of the family name at a resort Jean-Michel had purchased in Fiji. It was a sad affair not only for the Cousteaus but also for the thousands of faithful members of the Society. The friction seemed to skew the empire. For decades the Pasha had searched for practical applications and was ever the savvy marketeer; Phillipe had become the rugged, free-floating visionary. And now this—a legal embroglio! Tragic loss was a challenge of adventure. But energy seemed to pall under the weight of legal briefs, the unseemly feud of the survivors.

It is sad to consider that a larger vision may have been compromised. Before departing to film a series on sharks for David Wolper Productions, Phillipe had written that in an age of efficiency and the law of profitable return, he was leaving with no precise goals, no accounts to render, "free to journey wherever our fancy leads us. Our only task, our profession, was to see …"

He spoke of future generations that would be inspired by his films. He could not deceive this confidence, the need for information, any more than he could have abandoned a blind man crossing a busy street.

Cousteau maintained offices in Paris and the United States until his death in June 1997. No one can dismiss his charisma or his achievements: forty years of world-ranging voyages, forty books, eight sets of filmstrips, four feature films, and more than 100 televsion documentaries. In a recent *Rediscover the World* series produced for television, the *Calypso* and a new research vessel, *Alcyone,* circumnavigated the Earth. The Cousteau Society continues to produce four hours of television yearly.

But as the century ends, Cousteau's contributions are passing into history. The water planet and how we see it has changed. "Telepresence," robots, the discovery of possible oceans on the moon and on Mars have overtaken the public imagination. The thrill of discovery remains, the players are changing, and the horizons have expanded beyond the aqualung.

Throughout his eighties, the Pasha remained active and only slightly less than the heroic figure of old. In a way, he was like a maturing movie idol: He flickered in the mind, a vision not quite whole on the big screen. Clearly he still casts a spell even if his brand of romance, his shining era of discovery, has reached its zenith. What remains bright is the spirit—the thrill of seeing a new world for the first time, the free-ing of oneself from pitiless gravity.

Cousteau's connection to the National Geographic Society often found him in Washinton, D.C. I attended his various appearances at the Society's Explorer's Hall, but getting anywhere near him remained a challenge.

Finally, in the early 1990s, I made my way through a host of ad-mirers who had come to hear him speak on the future of the oceans.

"Captain Cousteau," I said, extending my hand. "I have been try-ing to meet you for many years."

He gave me a quizzical look. He was smaller than I had imagined, pencil-thin, weathered, and his handshake was not the steely grip I had anticipated. He forced a little smile, the face brightening for a moment, the same expression I had recalled over the years: the roman-tic grin, the eyes somehow childlike beneath the racy red watch cap.

"Did you call my office in New York?" he asked with a thick French accent. This, too, surprised me. For some reason I had expected little or no accent at all.

I explained how I had tried reaching him at his offices in New York and Paris, and had left numerous messages. He laughed, a tiny, all-suffering, slightly impatient laugh. Clearly I was just another an-noying journalist looking for a story, and he had more important business.

"Don't stop trying," he said, dropping my hand and melting back into the crowd of admirers.

It wasn't much of an encounter, but it was enough to create a last-ing impression. I wondered what it might be like to sail with this man. In those few moments of meeting him I detected his unrelenting am-bition, his single-mindedness. He had culled out of life just about ev-erything he had ever wanted, and he had done it in style. To have dived with him would have been a supreme honor. He had lodged three-quarters of the planet in the world's imagination. Playwright Eugene O'Neill once said the world drives men to assume characters that are not their own, and I sensed a little of this in Cousteau. But mostly I recall a radiance, a commanding confidence. Yes, gladly I would have sailed with him. He had allowed will to direct his belief, and his belief had transformed our vision of the sea.

At the conclusion of *The Silent World,* Cousteau wrote that inde-pendent diving would advance to the edge of the continental shelves claimed by the statesmen (the 600-foot drop-off line) only when research centers and industrialists decided to make the leap. The aqualung had become primitive and unworthy of contemporary science. Still he believed that the conquerors of the shelf would have to get wet.

He was right. What he may not have imagined at the time was that a new generation of ocean explorers may be wearing spacesuits.

Chapter Seven

BRAVE HEARTS

*The real voyage of discovery consists not in seeking
new landscapes, but in having new eyes.*
—*Marcel Proust*

PART ONE—
CINDY LEE VAN DOVER:
THE "VAN DOVER GLOW"

I

COULD LIFE ON EARTH HAVE COME from the deepest recesses of the sea, far below the sun's rays? Only a few years ago this question was considered absurd. Scientific dogma held that the bottom of the sea was a lifeless void, dark and alien as outer space.

Then there were whispers: Is it possible the seabed is lit up, glowing with eerie thermal illumination? Have life-forms thrived in this otherworldly glow? Did photosynthesis, the basis of life as we know it, begin billions of yeas ago on the sea floor? And did these creatures migrate toward the sun and, finally, crawl out on land?

The whispered questions came from a willowy, soft-spoken woman with quick eyes, amazing intelligence, and the persistence of the ages. And while she may not have all the answers, she is very close to changing the way we view the world.

"Oh, I don't have that kind of gravity," protests Dr. Cindy Lee Van Dover. "I'm fairly simple."

But simple women do not say, "When a ship leaves port and I'm not on it, my heart sinks."

She has spent a life at sea, on it and under it, as a scientist and the only female ever to pilot the legendary *Alvin* submersible. She has roamed the sea floor, discovered the light, and changed our evolutionary paradigm.

Van Dover is always on the move. She is someone you might chance to meet on a high mountain trail, an avian traveler whose lightness of being allows only a brief pause before she vanishes into the wilderness. Though she no longer pilots *Alvin,* she is still looking at the sea floor, cruising the ocean for weeks at a time, roaming the lecture circuit sharing what she calls her "free science," and returning home at last to Alaska, where she lectures as a marine biologist at the university at Fairbanks. Alaska, she complains, is becoming too crowded, its isolation draining away like alluvium, and she would enjoy parting with it.

"Fair Fairbanks" is not exactly a perfect port for someone of Van Dover's kaleidoscopic talents. Her mind is focused on the "extremeophiles," the creatures living in the glow of subsea volcanism. The extremes of cold and isolation of Fairbanks "make me feel exiled," she says—not the most creative situation for someone piecing together the puzzle of life. She is happy at sea, delighting in her discoveries and port stops. If Alaska is too remote, she is nonetheless delighted by Easter Island, the easternmost outpost of Polynesia, and a place some travelers call the loneliest spot on Earth. A strange irony.

"I love Easter," she told me. "It's so incredible." As to the bizarre carved stone faces that are the island's trademark, "They're everywhere. Turned landwards so the tourists won't miss them." Refreshing to hear about the oddities of *Rapa Nui* from a true space drifter.

Among Van Dover's suite of talents is the word. She is a gifted writer, and it was her book, *The Octopus's Garden* (Addison-Wesley, 1996), that first drew me to her. She calls it *"The O's G,"* a memoir of her struggles to become an *Alvin* pilot combined with her ideas about life, evolution, and the glowing ocean bottom. We discussed the book during one of our meetings at the Four Seasons Hotel in Washington, D.C., and I noticed her hands: strong hands, the hands of a hardworking scientist. Courageous hands. Wandering requires courage. The traveler is the perpetual *auslander* who depends upon the good faith of strangers. And to be with Van Dover is to sense the confidence every traveler must have. Hers is a quiet confidence that draws you in.

She wasn't in Washington on my account; there was other business: a meeting of scientists who might add something to her "whisper" that the glow from sunken volcanos may have supported photosynthesis four billion years ago.

"I believe in it, and I will still believe in it even if they say it isn't possible!" she told me.

Van Dover's scenario is built on discoveries made in the late 1970s along the midocean ridges. In a world of molten rock and superheated water rising from chimneylike hydrothermal vents, scientists discovered thriving ecosystems: a snowfall of bacteria, eight-foot tube worms, mollusks, and shrimp. The shrimp are key.

In 1986, while she was at Woods Hole Oceanographic Institution as a graduate student, Van Dover's advisor, Fred Grassle, handed her preserved specimems of *Rimicaris exoculata,* "eyeless fissure shrimp" dredged up from a community surrounding hydrothemal vents. She noticed that each shrimp had bright strips along the front third of its back, and that the strips were tissue joined to a large nerve. She wondered if this strange sense organ could be an eye. Evidence piled up and it became clear the shrimp had been misnamed; the dark strips were organs shaped by evolution into nonimage-forming light detectors. In a stroke, the species was elevated from a "sightless" oddity to a new life-form with profound implications.

"If these shrimp have eyes," she asked, "what are they looking at?"

A typical Van Doverism: a question filled with implications and quiet wit.

I knew it was imperative to meet her after I read *The O'sG.* The book captivated me. It took me on a journey into the unseen world of chemosynthetic creatures, volcanism, superheated water, spreading crust, eerie light radiating from hydrothermal vents, and "phototrophs" rushing in to feed. She had discovered this light and I wanted to share it.

But reluctant celebrities aren't quick to share secrets. "I have this ethic," she said. "I keep my science pure." This is her perpetual dilemma: ducking the media hype she fears may taint her purity, while at the same time accomplishing things that attract even more attention. It took months of cajoling before she mentioned articles about her in *Discover* magazine and *The New York Times,* as if by reading these features my own vision might be tainted. I reread a letter she'd sent me about having been selected to expound on the future by *Esquire* magazine in 1989. At the time, she was receiving considerable attention and had submitted, however tentatively, to the lure. For most of us, a personal quote in a big-time magazine is a personal coup, a tiny smidgen of fame. Yet Van Dover knew her colleagues would not look kindly on such "posturing." *Esquire's* black-tie event in Manhattan gathered rainmakers from the arts, humanities, and science. "I was in the company of people like Lyle Lovett, Michelle Pfeiffer, Spike Lee. Can you imagine?" she asked, genuinely puzzled. Among the glitterati she was one of only three to be chosen for print space. (The others were jazz/fusion saxophonist John Zorn and Millard S. Drexler, president of The Gap.) She came up with her twenty-five words or less and went back to work full-time with the *Alvin* group at Woods Hole Oceanographic Institution. When the magazine's photographer subsequently arrived at Cape Cod she found herself in for a surprise. "So there I am when he shows up, ready for I'm not sure what." Earlier she had carefully blow-dried her hair ("The extent of my daily primping!"), nervously preparing for one of those slightly licentious glamor shots. Instead, the photographer insisted she slip into a bathing suit, head to the beach, plunge into the surf, and spit water. "I never knew how to spit water. Not exactly a girl-thing," she confessed. "So I had to practice. I suppose I love that picture because it expresses the fact that I don't take myself too seriously." The photo conveyed a wet-woman glamor oddly incongruous contrasted with her characteristically understated quote: "There's a whole zone under the crust that's lit up. What it means for humanity, I don't know, but it's a good place to start looking for things. It's better than outer space."

If Ewing convinced us that the ocean bottom is anything but a featureless void, Van Dover added life to his shadowy images, and more. She wasn't the first to confront the now-discredited dogma of a virtually lifeless sea floor, but she took her challenge to another level. Van Dover was talking origin-of-life science, the outer limits of thought, a new look at evolution. And this was combined with a novelist's edge, a scholar's fetish for details, and a poetic talent for word-pictures. These same images had for years glowed at the edges of my mind; they became real in *The O'sG*. Van Dover portrayed a sea floor at once prehistoric and brand new. Did life begin here in the glow of hydrothermal heat? In the Pacific alone there are more than a million submerged volcanoes, each contributing to the continuing metamorphosis and emitting an otherworldly light. Van Dover described what they look like, what it *feels* like to be down there. She spoke of pillows of lava with "elephant-hide skin" draping the slopes like "icing run down the side of a cake." During her training she set the submersible on the seabed and shut down the systems, going "dead boat." The silence and darkness are ultimate, and she felt the silence more than heard it.

One expects this imagery from science-fiction writers, not researchers. I couldn't stop turning the pages of the book. Van Dover told of driving the tiny *Alvin* into fissures cut deep into the lava, "deep beyond seeing," and following the fissures until the walls closed in. At one point she admitted fear. On the black, sightless bottom, some 12,000 feet down, she told of finding herself in a perilous situation. She spooked herself with the thought of being buried alive by a "landslide" in a narrow fissure.

Though other submersible pilots share this sense of mortality, Van Dover is the only one I know who will admit it. That she shared her fear made her all the more accessible. She understood that her experiences on the ocean bottom had to be written as a memoir, though she questioned her writing skills.

"I mean, it isn't *me*—not really," she told me, of *The O'sG.* "It's what I've seen, being a pilot and a scientist. It's the substance, isn't it?"

It was unsettling, this shying away, this handing back compliments. I quoted the 100-year-old Indian writer, Nirad Chaudhuri, who, after seventy-one years as a "vocational writer," said of substance and style: "The old proverb says that the style is the man himself. I would say that the style is the subject itself." To believe one can separate them "is to have the stupidity which is dead to matter and the vulgarity which is dead to form."

"Well," she responded. "How old did you say that writer was?"

A typical Van Doverism. I was undeterred.

When I was researching this book, one scientist told me: "This woman *belongs* in your book. If you can get through, gain her trust, you'll learn a lot."

Becoming one of only forty-three people qualified to pilot *Alvin* had been no easy path for Van Dover. She put in a difficult apprenticeship complicated by sexism and jealousy. She suffered at the hands of her fellow *Alvin* pilots-in-training. She explained that training to be an *Alvin* pilot wasn't easy. It was intense and challenging, and sometimes cruel.

Before she arrived, the Alvin group was a man's world and her presence was perceived as a threat. She believed she was made to pay for that threat. Some were quick to blame every mistake on her, ridicule her questions, even give her false information. But because some

The famed research submersible RV *Alvin* begins its descent to the floor of the sea. *Photo courtesy National Oceanic and Atmospheric Administration.*

people wanted her to fail, she pushed all the harder. In the end, compulsion kept her from walking away.

Later I had an opportunity to feel out one of her former instructors. His response: A scientist didn't bring much value to an engineering task. "It was hard," I was told. "You can get an engineer working a lot quicker. The main thing in piloting is ferrying scientists to where they want to go. Cindy is a scientist and you can't do science and run the boat."

During training she was ordered not to speak to scientists, who were then forced to sneak into her stateroom, playing a game of stealth.

I was moved. She'd been in combat and she didn't exactly trust me, but now I had a compulsion to find my way through her defenses.

✳✳✳✳✳

Our initial contacts were e-mails while Van Dover was at sea in late 1996 studying the bizarre biological communities thriving near the hydrothermal vents. Five years had passed since she last piloted *Alvin;* she had turned entirely to science, and now her view of the sea floor came via robotic vehicles.

We corresponded as she cruised the Pacific aboard the RV *Melville*. She was skpectical at first, though over time a certain rapport began to flourish. She was mildly amused by my fascination with her views and ideas, and at times she strategically deflated my enthusiasm. *Gun shy*, I told myself, and with reason. *Alvin* had taken a toll on her, and in the temples of academe she was anomalous, a too-daring thinker who went around whispering that photosynthesis, the origin of life as we know it, began in the deep and not-so-dark basement of the world.

"I can say it now with some humor," she told me later on. "Shrimp with eyes? What a *silly* idea."

With each reading of *The O'sG*, and with each new e-mail, I was drawn deeper into her orbit until at last I knew she had begun to reshape my own beliefs. I knew a meeting was inevitable after an e-mail about "vision" as a creative adjunct to her emperical science. She was baffled by what she perceived as the rarity of vision in science. Why had so many otherwise hardworking scientists failed to master the transcendent power? Vision, the transforming concept; if one has it, and it acquires hard edges and energy, reality emerges. The trick is in knowing that the vision is true and not a mirage. We were in complete agreement.

I wondered how the publication of her book had affected her life.

"Go 'popular' and people don't talk to you," she told me. "It's the world I live in."

Dr. Robert Ballard learned this lesson the hard way after his discovery of the *Titanic*. He was forced to leave his position at Woods Hole and strike out on his own with Project Jason. What happened to Ballard, she said, also dogged the late Carl Sagan, another thinker demeaned for his popular television shows and books. Sagan was the modern Prometheus who gave the sacred magic of the stars to ordinary mortals and was made to suffer for this transgression by "real" scientists.

What irony. Here was Van Dover, sensitive to any form of "hype," working in an edgy frontier environment, roaming through a world in which nearly all the extension and subduction of the Earth's crust takes place, where fresh lava, enough to cover an area four times the size of Alaska, is generated each year by submarine volcanism, yet her attempt to convey this otherworldly image is dismissed by her peers as a kind of intellectual junk food. *The O'sG* gives the reader to understand that fewer than 1 percent of these volcanoes have been charted, "a reflection of the embarrassing fact that less than 1 percent of our planet's sea floor has been mapped!" Van Dover declared. Every process that has formed the Earth's surface is going on now, out of sight, in the deep sea. This is creation, origin-of-life revelation.

"If we're going to understand the geological forces that shape the planet, we have to understand the features expressed on the sea floor," she insists.

And *The O'sG* creates this understanding, often brilliantly. Imagine the magnitude of the environment, the thirteen-story-high "black smokers," volcanic chimneys belching 650-degree-Fahrenheit chemical plumes, the eerie light seen by "sightless" shrimp. Step by step, with gifted and trained insight, Van Dover moves the reader back in time and then races forward to show the Earth in awesome creation. But *The O'sG* is "out" of the academic flow, ignored, and Van Dover can't cover the sting.

"People don't ask me a lot of questions," she sighs. "None of my colleagues has said much about my book, though I know they've read it." Her voice trails off. She needn't say the obvious. The sea is full of little green creatures.

Like many ocean scientists, she has had to learn a whole spectrum of disciplines. One moment she's scrutinizing tiny slivers of protoplasm that have yet to be named; blink again and there's the *Alvin* pilot cruising through fields of six-foot-tall purple tube worms and maneuvering around superheated waters that would melt the submersible. She also has studied chemistry, math, and the Russian language. It was thrilling, she told me: "I'm a naturalist at heart." Like Rachel Carson, Van Dover believes humankind is challenged to prove its maturity, not its mastery of the natural environment; mastery of ourselves is the preservation of wilderness. "I know where to place myself in the larger universe and what I should do there."

Early on I questioned her about her beginnings. She told me of being drawn to sea creatures, the obscure bits of life most of us seldom notice. She had sent me a partial manuscript written long ago for *Peterson's Field Guide,* a series of word-pictures to accompany watercolors by artist Karen Jacobsen (illustrator of *The O'sG*). She was unhappy with the writing: "I never got it to come out right." I read it and had the opposite reaction; I was touched by its graceful understatement:

There is a small tree nursery closeby the house where I grew up (in New Jersey, a few miles from the Atlantic). I used to gather wildflowers from beneath the tall shady pines that line the lanes, from along the banks of the creek rank with jewelweed during the steamy days of summer, and from the unmown, dry grassy aisles between rows of young scotch pine and blue spruce. I recall those hay-scented summer evenings and the sampling of stems brought home to identify. My mother sits at one end of the couch, I am in my father's chair. Between us, the flowers wilt on the lamp table—a fading still life beside my mother's sweating glass of iced tea and the fingered pages of Peterson's Field Guide. *Together we puzzle leaves and stems with illustrations and text. I bring home different sets of flowers each time and it is always my child's wish to discover a flower not in the field guide.*

She lived through a "bug period" and was later fascinated by the peculiar beauty of lichens, their dual existence as algae and fungus. Amphibians were a fleeting fancy, though even now she lingers at the edges of ponds, quietly contemplating a tadpole. She once had a pet chameleon, but reptiles were "too arid."

My interest in birds paralleled my interest in a boy who liked birds, ending abruptly when he moved away ... . In short, I was a fickle naturalist in my youngest years, flitting from one type of organism to another. But by the time I was thirteen years old, I discovered the passion that seizes me to this day, nearly thirty years later—sea creatures.

Growing up close to the New Jersey shore, she and her two brothers visited the beach almost every day in summer. She thrilled to the idea that there were so many kinds of creatures, that they had not just one pair of eyes, but several pair, or none at all; that they might have multiple legs or look like stars or be transparent and quivery like jelly. She wanted to know why they looked that way, "how they made a living."

"I suppose I might just as easily become an entomologist," she recalled. "But my mother despised anything buglike and her fears became mine. Sea life didn't seem as threatening to her as caterpillars and silverfish."

From *The O's G* I learned that she rebelled, albeit quietly and with no small amount of cunning, against her 1950s-style seaside New Jersey childhood. Her brothers had their own small workbenches in the basement, where they labored alongside her father, an electronics technician for the government. Van Dover often sat beside him as he worked, but she had no workbench of her own. This rankled. She had little taste for household chores, and homework became the standard excuse to avoid "woman's work." Household homeliness wasn't a disgrace, though it was too confining and defining, at least in her mind. Once she had invited a college boyfriend home for dinner. When the meal was over, her father piped up, "Come on, son, let me show you my workshop while Cindy and her mother clean up the dishes." Silently she fumed, embarrassed yet cagey enough to hide it.

Just before his death, her father bequeathed to her his special handmade wooden tool kit, a pine artwork of a box that contained his most valued tools. By now Dr. Cindy was in training to become an *Alvin* pilot, and they talked, "manstyle," of resistors, digital voltmeters, how a penetrator should pass through a submarine hull without causing a leak. Fortunately, her father lived long enough to see her qualify as a pilot.

"I think he was prouder of me for this accomplishment than anything else I have done. So am I," she told me.

Once, between voyages, I tried to reach her by phone at her mother's home. She had warned me in advance that of all the people in her life, her mother was perhaps the most ambivalent.

"Now, if I had given her a passle of grandchildren, she'd think me successful. Of course, her instinct is the proper biological one, which makes it all the more irritating to me."

A cheerful, hard-of-hearing woman answered the phone.

"Mrs. Van Dover?"

"Yes?" It was Christmastime and I wished her seasons' greetings.

"What did you say? No-el? No No-el here."

I explained I was looking for Cindy.

"Oh, she's off to the mountains somewhere. Hiking, I think. Adirondacks, I think. Cindy's *very* independent." She said it cheerfully, as if stating a point of pride.

Later Van Dover told me—a bit poignantly—that, yes, she was independent—painfully so. Men had often remarked on it.

"For me it's always been who I'm with, where I am, and what I'm doing. And sometimes I think I *am* too damned independent!"

Slowly, sometimes awkwardly, Dr. Cindy came to appreciate her poetic side. Van Dover the poet didn't enter with high drama, a diva commanding the spotlight; rather she was pointillistic, revealing splashes of color, bright glimmers, abstractions, enigmas. She was a challenge, and I was on notice that few things escaped her scrutiny. She would probably agree with William Butler Yeats when he remarked, "The mystical life is at the center of all that I do and all that I think and all that I write." At other times she was like H. G. Wells, who claimed an unlimited right to think, criticize, discuss, "suggest."

Van Dover began to think about the deep sea when she was in the third grade. Her teacher had the students snip the continents from a paper map and fit them together. This was in the early 1960s, when plate tectonics was beginning to gain acceptability. Her fascination continued at college; the oceans offered the most exciting combination of science, exploration, and discovery. Yet in this vast world she held to her obsession with the small, often unnoticed creatures:

> *The humble sea squirts and sea mosses, sea cucumbers and sea stars, crabs, shrimp, anemones, worms. My curiosity was captured by their oddies and extremes of form and function—multiples of appendages, excesses or paucities of eyes; swimmers, crawlers, gliders, burrowers, predators, grazers, parasites. No wonder, then, that I should have found my way to the deep sea, where the most bizarre animals are found, where there is no* Peterson's Field Guide *and where every dive can yield species or a dozen species ... never before discovered.*

Early on she was certain she didn't want to be a housewife; housewives don't tell their future children tales of adventure. As it turned out, she was too busy adventuring to have children. Adventure—discovery—is her addiction. Even now she cannot pass up a chance to go to sea, if by doing so she gains access to the sea floor.

The theme of her life was developing, and none of it was particularly easy. She knew she wanted to be a biologist before entering high school, and though she was a good student her guidance counselor recommended she not move on to college.

"With a Ph.D. from MIT, I guess I did okay after all."

*****

When she wasn't roaming around the basement of the world in *Alvin,* Van Dover marveled at it through the eyes of robot vehicles and/or other *Alvin* researchers. She needed to know how much thermal radiation might be visible in the deep environment. No one had ever calculated the degree of light, and no one before Van Dover had ever noticed light at thermal vents. She asked geologist John Delany, of the University of Washington, to go down and look during an *Alvin* mission to the Juan de Fuca Ridge off the coast of Oregon.

It was a dangerous assignment, since Delany, a mile and a half below the surface and less than two feet from a furious vent, had to turn off the lights as the sensitive digital camera went to work. Van Dover was on the surface, aboard the mothership, *Atlantis II,* as Delany began his hour-long ascent. Before breaking the surface he radioed a two-word message that forever altered our view of the deep: "VENTS GLOW."

This thermal illumination, the light no one believed existed, became known as the "Van Dover glow."

Now there were new questions. Did the vents produce enough illumination to justify a conclusion that deep-dwelling shrimp, officially tagged as sightless, actually see things? Did they, in fact, possess eyes? There was much skepticism. Perhaps those odd strips of tissue on the backs of the bottom-dwelling shrimp weren't eyes at all; maybe they were listening devices or aroma sensors. But if the sensors were eyes, they were so delicate that the glare of *Alvin's* high-powered lights would permanently blind them, ruling out the possibility of following or plotting their roamings along the vents.

Steven Chamberlain, a neuroscientist who specializes in invertebrate eyes, looked at Van Dover's original samples. Because they had been poorly preserved, he couldn't be certain that what he was looking at was a sight receptor. His initial take was odd. "If you destroyed an eye, this is what it would look like," he said.

A Woods Hole physiologist, Ete Szuts, a pigment expert, tested the sample to determine which frequencies of light, if any, it absorbed.

The "Van Dover glow" issues from a hydrothermal vent off the coast of Washington State. The 660°F water is laden with dissolved and precipitated minerals. *Photo courtesy University of Washington/Woods Hole Oceanographic Institution/ University of Washington.*

He found its pattern of absorption matched a substance known as rhodopsin, a pigment in human and animal eyes that makes it possible to see. Then in 1993, Chamberlain studied a new batch of shrimp; unlike the earlier specimens, these were well preserved. He and his colleagues confirmed Van Dover's hunch: The odd bands of color on the backs of the shrimp were compound light sensors, oversized photoreceptors. What Chamberlain called "icing on the cake" was his group's discovery that the "sightless shrimps'" neurotransmitters were the same as that of other shrimp with eyes. It was a stunning breakthrough, the promise of which could hardly be measured at the time.

Van Dover's "glow" was more than the presence of light; the implications were revolutionary, yet it took time to sink in for me: *She's hinting at the origins of life! If light exists on the seabed, photosynthesis may have begun there; perhaps this is the origin of all we know.* This late-blooming realization was wonderful and a little terrible. I felt simultaneously elated and foolish. Why hadn't I pieced it together earlier? Then I rationalized: *It's because of the way she thinks, her intuitiveness, her ironic "simplicity."* She insisted time and again: "I live a quiet scholarly life. I'm fairly simple." Her compulsive self-effacement created a mist of secrecy, the irresistible lure. Then, while having dinner with friends, I had a small revelation, a kind of billboard of an idea that appeared to suit her: "The incredible hidden world of Dr. Cindy," I said out loud. The woman seated beside me turned, a fork poised in midair. "What are you are talking about?" she wondered. I wanted to reply, to explain the lit-up sea floor, to make her see, but I was restrained by what I took to be the intellectual caution that forms the atmosphere of Dr. Cindy's hidden world.

In 1997, Van Dover was invited to speak at a scientific gathering on the potential for life at hydrothermal vents at the bottom of the Sea of Europa, Jupiter's alleged oceanic moon. I had taken to the concept of a Jovian moon, but she quashed the romantic ideas. It's merely a reflective surface, she informed me; it may be ice, many miles thick, inert and without a trace of heat. The Jovian sea was, as of mid-1997, more poetry than science. "We're trying to get a program to fire a nuclear bullet," she told me. This would, it was hoped, penetrate the ice (if it was ice) and confirm the presence of water. She said this as offhandedly as one might share a receipe for watercress salad. Once again my view of the universe flip-flopped and I realized the concept of "independent" was out of place, inadequate to describe much of anything about her. Clearly Dr. Cindy was light-years away from the tide pools of New Jersey. But "independent"? No. Too commonplace a word. Again I wondered: Just who is Dr. Cindy Lee Van Dover and what makes her tick? A little breathless after months of chasing her nuances, I had yet to find the key.

II

I met Van Dover in person for the first time on a blustery March 1997 evening at Washington's National Airport. She had flown in from California, where she had attended a meeting of NOAA coastal zone administrators. My mind raced. At any moment she'd enter the terminal and I realized I might not recognize her. I had seen only two images: The first was a photograph on the dust jacket of *The O'sG*, posed in front of tall sea oats, her face half hidden in shadow, a certain tension described in a tentative smile, her body obscured beneath an anorak. The second was a photo I had slipped inside the dust jacket. Clipped from the Fairbanks *Daily News-Miner,* dated January 27, 1997, it was part of a lightly written front page "Spotlight" feature headlined, "UAF Researcher Sees Beauty in Ocean." The *News-Miner* photo caption declared: "DEEP THOUGHTS—Cindy Van Dover, a University of Alaska Fairbanks researcher, studies life on the ocean floor." The photo was remarkable. It showed a willowy, youthful woman standing at a table bristling with agar dishes and various sample containers. She wore an oversized man's white dress shirt, and the oval of her face was bright and welcoming, pale eyes vivid even in the dull coloration of newsprint. I studied this photo as the airline attendant opened the gate and passengers filtered into the terminal like sleep-deprived robots.

Again I glanced at the *News-Miner* photo. The tilt of her head, the straight, easy-flowing hair (not curly as in the book jacket photo), the smile of a woman unassuming yet confident of her powers, an expression that appeared to ask, gently, "What are you doing here and why are you photographing *me?*" This newspaper image was very different from the jacket photo in *The O'sG.* In that photo, the younger *Alvin* pilot wore a somewhat anxious look, a rivulet of anxiety seeping through a slightly ironic smile. So much life lay between these images. In the book she is closer to *Alvin,* closer to the acerbic, envious comments of her colleagues. When the camera was employed by the *News-Miner* photographer, Van Dover was (at least in the opening and closing of the shutter) a confident woman at home in her laboratory, in control of her surroundings.

"I'll be holding up your book," I had informed her in advance.

"Holding my book?" She was incredulous. What a silly thing to do, flashing a book at a flight terminal.

"How else will you recognize me?"

Faces passed through the jetway. I inched closer to the gate. By now I was freezing. There was no heat in the terminal, and the wind piped up out of the north, conditions probably inconsequential to Van Dover, who was acclimated to forty below in Alaska. I was miserable and shivering with a virus and woozy with the depressing pall of antibiotics.

There! Yes—it must be! She looked at me, her smile replicating the one I'd observed in the *News-Miner,* the woman who admitted that if she had half a day to kill, she'd spend it sitting at the base of a black smoker, watching it belch chemicals as the "bugs" raced in to feed.

"Dr. Cindy?" I searched, doing my best to sound healthy. Her hand felt light as a bird's wing, ready to lift off at the slightest stirring.

"Philip?"

We dined that evening at La Fourchette in Adams-Morgan, in Washington's Soho district. She sipped wine and nibbled crusts of bread and studied me as if I were one of her new marine life-forms. I had a hard time concentrating in the noisy French cafe, and the wine was turning up my fever. At one point I introduced Van Dover to Jacquie Chauvet, owner of La Fourchette, only to discover, to my embarrassment, that my French wasn't adequate to describe Van Dover's restless searchings. How does one explain edgy origin-of-life science in the French idiom?

"Oh, oui," Jacquie remarked at my stumbling syntax. "Le plongee sous marin?"

Well, not exactly. Van Dover wasn't a scuba diver. What was the French term for submersible? *Submerger, immerger?* It was challenge enough to describe Van Dover's pursuits in simple English. Jacquie motioned to the shark mural on the wall. "*Le requins*—she swims with them?"

"Well, sort of. But in a submarine."

All the while Van Dover's critical inner eye coolly assessed my performance. Was she amused? Bored? Disappointed? She had once tweaked me about my unashamed enthusiasm for *The O'sG;* she believed I was overly fatuous.

"It was good to hear once that you like my writing," she reponded in an e-mail from RV *Melville.* "Twice was okay, too. But now I just ignore that part of your e-mail. I figure you are either 'just being nice' or you are an eccentric. Are you an eccentric?"

She later told me she hadn't meant to be negative; rather, it was reflexive caution. She told of visiting nature writer John Murray. He had exclaimed over *The O'sG,* which was then in manuscript form, but after his burst of enthusiasm he let her down by telling her he enjoyed being supportive of "new writers." Van Dover said she detected faint condescension. My take on it was that she had been oversensitive; after all, what else might Murray have been expected to say to a first-time author? I asked her why she sought him out.

"I envy nature writers," she replied. "They talk about things everyone can relate to: sunrise, sunset, animals, the seashore. I'm trying to write about things outside ordinary experience," she went on. "I've thought about tackling some bits of essay on Alaska. But so much has been written about nature in Alaska. Finding a new take isn't easy. You need a 'trick,' whereas with *The O'sG* 'trick' was the subject itself."

It was clear Van Dover was struggling against late-twentieth-century niche mentality. Her light-at-the-bottom-of-the-sea/origin-of-life science reflected the difficulties of stating the larger picture. Things moved one small step at a time. For example, she had enlisted Alan

Chaves, a marine physicist at Woods Hole, to help her prove her point about the glowing seabed. Chaves invented a new piece of sensing equipment, a high-powered photometer, which he called OPUS— Optical Properties Underwater Sensor: a Lucite rod and four photo-diodes designed to emit current when bombarded by photons. OPUS made a dozen dives and the findings were presented to George Reynolds, a physicist at Princeton.

"So what kind of light does one see on the ocean bottom?" I wondered.

"It's not ordinary light," Van Dover said. "Sometimes it's an aura. Other times you see flickering. Thermal radiation doesn't produce that kind of pattern."

Minerals may be cracking and producing the flickering light storm, or gas bubbles may be imploding. She said Chaves was working on a new camera designed to record actual images; it will be sufficiently sensitive to capture nine different views of the vents and detect and measure a single photon.

"Back in 1988," Van Dover continued, "I was having a drink with a colleague and wondered out loud if there was enough light for photosynthesis. He said, 'What a stupid idea!' This actually encouraged me. It was a hook."

In 1994, University of London paleontologist Euan Nisbet took the "hook." He and Van Dover postulated a radical scenario for the possible origin of photosynthesis. Could it be that ancient microbes fed on the sulfides emitted by hydrothermal vents at a stage of evolution when they were unable to "see" or sense their positions? Perhaps

Elongated and extruded "pillow lavas" ooze from submerged volcanic fissures. *Photo courtesy National Oceanic and Atmospheric Administration.*

later their light-sensing capability evolved, and future generations re-fined their light-sensing capabilities. At this stage, the organisms would be capable of placing themselves at a safe distance from the vents, nei-ther drifting off into the freezing cold nor boiling themselves in the superheated water. These phototaxis-capable microbes, capable of moving via light stimulation, might have drifted into the sunny upper waters, feeding on sulfides from near-surface hot springs. At this stage they would harness light-energy and convert it to fuel—the begin-nings of modern photosynthesis.

"We're simply suggesting a starting step," Nisbet told a reporter. "We're saying the facts are consistent with the hypothesis."

In its simplest terms, the hypothesis is revolutionary: Life as we know it, everything from mammals to giant redwoods, may trace its origins to the base of glowing hydrothermal vents.

I asked Dr. Cindy why this is so important. I could see her bristle at the question, though she was careful to contain it. She sipped her wine, revealing an enigmatic smile. It was important to understand, she said. One of the things that is so extraordinary about deep-sea research in the past twenty years is the paradigm shifts. One by one, the dogmas have crumbled.

As a student during the period when deep-sea exploration was just coming into its own with manned submersibles and other technolo-gies, Van Dover watched as a small number of scientists revolutionized the field. What's remarkable is the fundamental nature of their discov-eries. No more "brick-in-the-wall science," but rather bits of detail added to an already huge body of knowledge, what she calls "night/day, no/yes revelations." Her discovery of light at the vents is among those revelations.

It was a whispered idea at first, she explained. And there was talk that she was irresponsible even to suggest such a notion. Yet the idea, once examined, was compelling enough to address as a testable hyopthesis. "My motivation came from wondering 'What if ... ' What if there is light on the deep-sea floor? What a phenomenal, extraordi-nary thing, even if there was nothing more to it than that simple fact."

"To make the leap from textbook dogma to supposing there might actually be sustained points of illumination was a wonder. The whis-pering about light has ended. It is indisputable, documented, under study. We don't whisper any more about how much light is present," she explained. "We know. Yes, there's enough to support photosynthesis."

But other whisperings go on. What if there are "phototrophs" present at the vents using a geothermal source of light rather than solar energy? Dover is probing, probing.

The decibel level at La Fourchette was in synch with my core temperature; it was rising. Van Dover, seated across from me, framed by the mural of a shark consuming a mermaid, appeared disconcerted. What to do with a feverish dinner partner?

"You shouldn't be out," she said.

No, I shouldn't. But I had to go on. This was a woman in perpetual motion, a wanderer. When a writer has pinned down a wanderer for an interview, the writer doesn't quit; wanderers, after all, are expert at disappearing acts.

"It's okay," I replied. "Really."

"Okay, okay," she said. "We'll keep going."

So why would it matter if there were phototrophs in the deep sea I wondered.

Van Dover said she was confident phototrophs would prove to be important in the economy of nature at a vent. Deep-sea hydrothermal vents have been around since before life originated on the planet. Perhaps the earliest organisms arose at vents as microbes thriving in hot water on chemical energy.

She leaned forward. "Whispers: What if phototrophs evolved at vents from ancestors that were chemotrophs? Suppose the earliest phototrophs used geothermal light and secondarily evolved to occupy solar habitats?"

Van Dover's "phototroph group" of scientists is proposing high-risk/high-reward exploration. They may not find what they're looking for, but if they do we will have established an important truth about the evolution of photosynthesis. If nothing else, if she finds the creatures, they will be living in an extreme environment where a decade ago no one would have imagined them to be.

There's an aspect of phototroph exploration that reveals what Van Dover calls her "scientific ego." Unlike the discovery of hydrothermal vent communities, which geologists stumbled upon, none of her research has been serendipitous. Even finding the shrimp with a novel photodetector wasn't truly serendipitous; it was insight. Others had looked at the same shrimp and called it "eyeless."

"I recognized it for what it was because I was well trained as an invertebrate zoologist and I'm curious. The presence of an eye adapted for detecting a very dim light raised the question of thermal radiation as a light source at the vents. Maybe I make it sound like an idea that evolved over time. But all of the hypotheses came forward at once. As soon as we understood the nature of the shrimp eye there was a cascade of 'what ifs.'"

"I need the big picture and I need freedom," she insisted. "I value details, they are my building blocks. I am an idea person, not a fact person. I move horizontally, not vertically, and I really do think you should be in bed."

III

Van Dover returned to Alaska and our dialogue continued via e-mail and the telephone. We ranged far afield. At one point she lamented the perpetual second-class status of ocean research and the whining of the larger scientific community. She wondered if science had become circular, a kind of literary criticism offering points of view that provoke further points of view, but stop short of proof as the ultimate test.

In his book, *The End of Science* (Addison-Wesley, 1996), John Horgan postulates the notion that we may be facing the limits of knowledge in "the twilight of the scientific age." He starts by assuming that most major truths have been discovered, leaving us with a tradition grown too abundant. Horgan's view is that the major empiricists have left their successors picking over the remains of past research and focusing on what philosopher of science Thomas Kuhn calls mere "puzzles."

Van Dover had little patience with this argument; she thought it self-serving. Horgan writes of finding "the answer"—a truth so potent it tells us everything we ever wanted to know about our place in the universe, including why we're here. He assumes human intelligence is the ultimate wonder. If this is true, then the next logical leap must be creation of "intelligent machines" capable of transforming matter into mind, supercomputers defining existence and prognosticating the future.

Horgan's up-against-the-wall weariness is hardly new; a certain complacency appears to overtake science at the end of nearly every century. It occurred before Socrates, in the time of Thales and Anaximenes, who explained that all natural phenomena might be traced to water and air. The ancient Greeks stopped short of quantitative understanding; it didn't seem important to them, nor was it critical to the "atomists," who claimed matter was composed of tiny "eternal particles."

"Sounds like lethargy," Van Dover exclaimed. "We're discovering new life-forms every day. We're reshaping everything."

Anyone familiar with the sea floor has to wonder about end-of-science theories. Of the nearly fifty major scientific thinkers he interviewed, none has ever visited the ocean bottom, where creation is clearly visible and new life-forms are being discovered.

Horgan says if he were a creationist he would not attack evolution, which is supported by the fossil record. Instead, he would focus on the origin of life, which he calls "the weakest strut in the chassis of modern biology."

Dr. Cindy and I discussed Horgan's views, and she countered, "That's because most origin-of-life researchers work in artificial environments." Tiny *Alvins* and frustrated scientists have only enough money to peek at the most dynamic forces. "I hate it," Van Dover told me. "We're dismissed as dilettantes. We keep saying no to new ideas." She gave a deep sigh, a mix of resignation and pique. "I keep going in my naiveté, and see what I can find."

Van Dover's vision of the sea is not Cousteau's. She isn't convinced that shallow-water science will be rewarded by paradigm-altering discoveries. We had been discussing NOAA's newest undersea habitat, Aquarius, stationed sixty feet below the surface off Key Largo. As a Hydro-Lab veteran I have a soft spot for habitats, and Aquarius is the next generation. Van Dover was not impressed.

"Why don't they put money into *real* research? Do you know how we have to scrimp and scrounge?"

Millions of dollars have been poured into Aquarius, yet the habitat is a relatively limited item, an elaborate stationary living space designed to focus on nearshore phenomena. I had discussed the habitat with Barbara S. P. Moore, Acting Director of the National Undersea Research Program. Moore has managed to break the cycle of official indifference and had managed to persuade the Clinton White House to endorse hands-on undersea research; this was a political coup, the elegance of which was lost on some die-hard researchers. Despite grumbling and infighting among the half-dozen NOAA field stations involved in less "visual" ocean science, Moore had gained presidential approval, ending seventeen years of silence from the Oval Office. Aquarius, Moore told me, would focus public awareness; it might not be the most exotic or far-reaching of projects, but it was a "grabber," a refocusing of public interest and an avenue of funding.

"Aquarius is accessible," Moore said. "You can understand it. It's imaginative. It'll appeal to a new generation."

Moore's political savvy comes from three years as a senior policy analyst in the Office of Science and Technology at the White House, where she provided advice to the president's science advisor. Her mission included international exchanges of data and technology, ocean study models, and Arctic and Antarctic studies. At NOAA she has endured considerable pressure; each day brings pleas to favor funding of this or that project over some other; and because she has tough decisions to make, she is the object of no small amount of grumbling. She is able to endure it because of her own scientific bona fides: a water-quality expert who developed monitoring instrumentation; project engineer at the National Oceanographic Instrumentation Center; physical oceanographer at the Navy's Oceanographic Office, where she handled sensitive submarine fleet issues; chemical engineer at the U.S. Naval Ordanance Office, threading her way through the arcane field of underwater rocketry. She also is one of the corp of Hydro-Lab aquanauts who believed living undersea provides insight into certain elemental principles.

"I guess it (Hydro-Lab) was one of the inspirational times in my career. It cemented my relationship to the oceans," she recalled. "My state-of-being was lifted up. I thought it was going to be boring. I thought, 'So what do I do with my time when I'm not swimming around out there?' I brought along stacks of reading materials—magazines and stuff. I didn't touch any of it. It was so fascinating—just *observing.*"

As the head of NURP, it is Moore's task to excite public support for ocean sciences generally, and Aquarius is the most visible icon. She had helped meld the undersea lab with Robert Ballard's educational Project Jason, which focuses on young people, a big order on a tight budget.

I asked Moore if satellites and ROVs will replace hands-on science.

"Satellite technology can do phenomenal things. It's a very powerful. But it's only a tool, one of a suite of tools, and it only shows you what's happening on the surface, it doesn't show what's happening in the water column. So you're always going to need some kind of tools to get you below the surface."

But remote sensors don't replace eyes and brains, she added. You get more information by putting a person in place than you do by using computers. The machine looks for what you've programmed it to look for; it isn't intelligent, and it possesses no spontaneity.

"I know this is part of a debate that's going on now. I don't know where it's going to come out. I know where I want it to come out. I want a place left for *people*."

We discussed integrative science, the need to transcend the shadow lines separating one code of disciplines from another. Van Dover's work, and her brand of thinking, stood out as a model.

"Cindy Van Dover could probably fly an F-15," Moore said. "But there are more men with those kinds of skills. She's really exceptional." She paused to consider what she would say next. Perhaps there was some trace of self-consciousness in assumptions about male/female mechanical skills. "I want to be clear," she continued after a while. "Cindy may be a fine sub pilot, but she's also an amazing thinker. She makes a case that there should always be a place for people."

Asked to speculate on the future, Moore remarked, "Well, we can speculate, but truth is that we don't really know. This is the nature of discovery, particularly in the ocean. Things are happening so fast. Look at these extreme life-forms. We don't even know what they are. There's just so much out there."

Ultimately what gets discovered often is the result of a struggle for money. Remote sensing is cheaper, more convenient, and often more productive than human invasion of the depths. Why send fallible, frag-ile, *expensive* humans into hostile environments when relatively safe and inexpensive probes might be developed? Nowhere are funds more tightly held than in the ocean sciences, where a few million dollars qualifies as major money. This economy of scale rankles Van Dover.

"We're chasing pennies!" she once growled. "We're involved in the most fundamental issues, yet very few people seem to be aware."

The need for money is disproportionate to its availability; she is miffed by the lack of focus on the deep sea: "It's amazing. We're look-ing in the wrong places."

Just how wrong was apparent in the early 1980s, when a cadre of physicists asked congress to approve $8 billion for a fifty-three-mile-long Superconducting Super Collider in a tunnel south of Dallas, Texas. Thousands of superconducting magnets would guide dual beams of electrically charged protons in opposite directions. The particles would be accelerated far beyond the highest existing energy levels; protons would collide hundreds of millions of times a second.

According to Steven Weinberg, author of *Dreams of a Final Theory* (Pantheon Books, 1992), the rationale behind this supermachine is that particle physics is "stuck," suffocating under the weight of its own discoveries— another casualty of scientific exhaustion.

We are paying a price for our success, he writes. Further progress will require the study of processes at energies beyond the reach of existing experimental facilities.

I ran down the numbers for Van Dover.

"Preposterous!" she fumed. Another example of skewed values, a lack of balance.

We often debated the pragmatic concerns of politics and the fragility of intuitive science. Like most people who cling to the irrational notion that logic must ultimately prevail, Van Dover's energy occasionally slipped. A weary business, this dark search for money, the assembly-line proposal writing, the infuriating (and sometimes acid) rejections. Then, like a prizefighter catching a second wind, she'd charge back, bloodthirsty for the challenges she'd set for herself.

I wondered which part of her clung to the purity of her internalized vision. Was she driven by the tenacious scientist or the writer's muse? Perhaps it was overcompensation, a Jungian revolt against her childhood.

Moore, on the other hand, appeared to be slightly less idealistic. She understood Washington's self-serving insularity. At the time of our interview the federal budget was still confidential, and I had to scrape together information on the proposed $12 million Aquarius budget. When I had secured the rough total, Moore admitted it was an expensive operation, though it allowed the kind of science that couldn't be done any other way. And beyond Aquarius—what? Adaptations of space technology and greater use of cheap, easily maintained submersibles launched by inexpensive mother ships.

"It's all about ways to get there, and ways to work," she said. "And you have to live with the reality, the bottom line."

When I reported this to her, Van Dover murmured, "So true. Still—" She trailed off, perhaps communing with her muse, her silence radiating an enigmatic light.

IV

The O's G rearranged my vision of the deep. Van Dover's descriptions had given verisimilitude to Ewing's tracings. The computer-generated maps that lined my studio seemed to spring to life, and I could walk around the room sailing as a daydream passenger over the great mountains and ridges, past the black smokers, down into lava-filled ravines, and over vast desert plains. A million volcanos below the Pacific! The imagine was haunting, exciting. My ability to imagine these scenes came slowly, as one slides the pieces of a jigsaw puzzle into a discernible picture. My decades in the ocean had provided only hints; Van Dover filled in the missing spaces.

She quickly, almost impatiently, passed over the undersea world in which I had traveled, the zone of sunlight where the corals are rich and colorful.

"I have a severe bias in my coral appreciation standards," she said. The luxuriant corals of the tropical reefs seemed to her "overdone, the floozies of the marine invertebrate world." She was drawn to the austere skeletons of the corals that live ancient lives in the deep sea. She described the canyons with coral fans stretching out from rocky outcrops, branches with slender waving brittle stars.

My romance with these "floozies" now seemed odd, as if I had been an unwitting dandy and was now embarrassed by my overprecious sensibilities. This feeling was exacerbated when I happened across a letter written in 1905 by the French artist Odilon Redon to one of his patrons, Madame Fontaine, whose portrait in pastel he had completed four years earlier. Redon's mysticism appealed to me as a kind of Great Barrier Reef of art. Yet, in reading his letter to Madame Fontaine, I realized something inside me had changed: "I am still wrapped in flowers," he wrote, "underwater dramas, among those beings which might exist."

Redon's obsession was the polar opposite of Van Dover's. The dark, the ancient, the austere—these produced a new aesthetic. Seen through Van Dover's eyes, the slope of the continental canyons were transformed into magnificent stair-step constructions, caverns and fissures staring into the emptiness, the abyssal plain rolling eastward past august seamounts to the volcanic monolith of the mid-Atlantic mountains.

Van Dover offered an evocative toast: "To the Trilobite Factor," she'd say, an exhultation of faith in the unknown. I loved the spirit of it, for in an infinite universe all things are not only possible, but by definition exist. Van Dover's "Trilobite Factor" escalated her science to a level where ideas, art, and reality appeared to coexist.

In the winter of 1996, Van Dover was once again at sea, sailing aboard the RV *Melville,* not as a pilot but as a biologist using the

Argo-II ROV, a near-bottom towed vehicle designed to operate three miles down.

Rachel Haymon and Ken MacDonald of University of California (Santa Barbara) acted as cochief project scientists. Funded by the National Science Foundation, the primary site was in the southern Pacific between Peru and Bolivia, an underwater mountain range known as the East Pacific Rise. The closest inhabited island was Easter, two and a half days away. Van Dover described her position on board as "the token biologist."

Earlier, the French had cruised the site with their *Cyana* submersible. *Alvin* has not dived there, though Van Dover had proposed that it do so.

The mission was classic: RV *Melville* would document cycles of volcanism and tectonism; it was (and is) an extremely "hot" area. Lava erupts constantly, pushing apart the crust. Earthquakes fracture the crust to make room for more lava. Argo would produce a map of individual lava flows. Other surveys would follow and fix dates for each eruption. Van Dover, focused on the hydrothermal flows, was in the infant stages of cataloging the vent communities. To know their natural history may indicate a path to new therapeutic agents or compounds useful in biotechnology.

"It's an exciting place to explore," she informed me. "Jules Verne would be so envious of me."

I wondered if she would share, via e-mail, the day-to-day events. She graciously agreed. What follows is an edited version of her shipboard messages.

V

November 5, 1996: *We just left Papeete this morning and have an eight-day steam ahead of us before we get to our work site.*

November 7: *Our second day on station, after eight days of transit from Tahiti and one day deploying transponders for our long-baseline navigation net ... Why the interest in this line along the sea floor out here close to nowhere? The plate boundary we are studying begins up in the Gulf of California and extends far into the southern Pacific Ocean, then rounds its way over to the Indo-Pacific. The ridge that defines the boundary is called the East Pacific Rise. Nowhere else on the planet does a plate boundary spread apart as rapidly as it does here ... This is a "superfast" spreading ridge segment ... Where we are focusing our work, the magma chamber lies less than 800 meters beneath the sea floor—it is the shallowest depth anywhere, to our knowledge. Because of this magma chamber characteristic, the area is called The Spike. The short story is that here we expect frequent volcanic eruptions and pervasive hydrothermal activity ... Our job is to work out details of the geological and biological characteristics over a much longer stretch of ridge axis than the submersible work* (by the French) *has accomplished so far.*

November 8: *I always feel a tremendous sense of anticipation when we get ready to lower an instrument to the sea floor. I began haunting the Control Van today even before Argo was lowered into the water to watch the engineers prepare for the launch. I admit, there is some nostalgia here for the days when I was the one doing the final bits of maintenance and troubleshooting on* Alvin. *But mostly it is the anticipation of gaining access once more to the sea floor that captures me. I have this sense that if I can just get there often enough, I will understand it so much better. What compels me to need to understand it is another issue altogether, one which I won't answer tonight ...*

I settle into the Van for good this evening just as Argo goes into the water ... The bottom looms up on the monitors at 2,640 meters: a barren pavement of black, lobed lavas highlighted with scattered reflections from remnants of volcanic glass ... We travel only a few tens of meters over this terrain when first the sonar fails, then the video, the lights, the thruster controls until in rapid succession all of the screens in the Van go blank ... Science is on hold for the night ...

November 9: *When Argo failed last night, it failed catastrophically. Five computer control boards were damaged by a high voltage spike ... Three of the boards were repaired, the other two are being replaced. It has meant long hours for Skip Gleason and Bob Elder, two of the guys who maintain the system. I visited the fantail where Argo sits beneath a blue awning, illuminated by floodlights. Even tonight, twenty-four hours after the mishap, the odor of toasted electronics is evident ... This setback in the operation, while a disappointment, is not devastating to the program. We are optimistic that Argo will be back in the water sometime tomorrow and that the lost day will be made up somehow later in the trip ... I take advantage of my unexpected free time to continue working on chapters for a textbook on hydrothermal vents, a project I began on the long transit out here.*

A cluster of tube worms greets travelers in the deepest regions of the sea. *Photo courtesy National Oceanic and Atmospheric Administration.*

November 10: *Heartbreak this morning. Argo was ready to go back in the water just after breakfast. Two hundred meters down, all the bells and whistles were attached to the cable above Argo and the pilot took control of the winch in the Van and started Argo on her way to the sea floor. But he winched in instead of out. The cable with the attached instruments fed back through the block. Six-inch diameter pressure housings don't go through one-inch block. No one caught the mistake until the damage was done— the cable frayed and we had to begin all over again. Skip and Yogi had to reterminate the cable, a repair that took all day. It takes a thick skin to cope with the kind of stress and attention to detail required in a pilot. There is little tolerance for anything but competence and strength. Today's events reminded me of all this. I might as well have made the mistake myself, for all of the empathy I felt for this pilot.*

November 11: *Today I drank my morning cup of tea watching the sea floor pass by in real time. Argo is hard at work and the spark is back in Skip's eye. Comments on the geology and biology are tossed back to the corner* (of the Van), *where a pair of data loggers dutifully note every word, as a code in a digital log on the system computer, and the old-fashioned way—handwritten in a logbook. Six pairs of eyes are trained on all the information coming in. Our down-looking video gives us the best look of the sea floor. During my watch we crossed endless fields of older pillow and*

*lobate lavas, our view punctuated by a solitary anemone or startled star-
fish. The anemones look like flower beds; the serpulids, living in white
serving tubes, look more like the dabblings of some avant-garde artist fond
of spatterings of white on black. Twice, tall, relict chimneys loomed up
beneath us, evidence that once this area supported hot springs where 350-
C fluids were exhaled from the ocean's crust. The chimneys were built up
along the sides of fissures, indicative of the control that penetrating cracks
have on focusing the upflow of thermally buoyant fluids.*

*Sunday is cookout day and we sailors are allotted our proverbial tot of
rum (though in the form of a carefully monitored disbursement of wine in
a plastic cup) with our barbeque. Though didn't sailors used to get this
once a day instead of once a week?*

November 13: *Argo is a fine survey tool, but because it is passively towed,
we cannot pause to look carefully at anything. From the video images alone,
I cannot put names on all of the vent organisms. I keep a careful catalog of
what we pass over, so that I might return to them with* Alvin ... *There are
three former* Alvin *pilots on board—Will Sellers, Skip Gleason, and myself. Together we span a lot of years of Alvin's life and several hundred dives.
I am glad to have had my nearly 100* Alvin *dives—I have a sense of scale
and texture and color of sea floor features that is hard to get from watching
videos. For much of my work, though, there are two big advantages to
using an unmanned vehicle: Bottom time is far longer (twenty-four hours
a day instead of four or five) and the entire science party can be involved in
observation, rather than just two individuals.*

November 15: *We have continued to ply our way up and down the ridge
axis these past two days. This is our fourth pass. There are stretches that are
truly scenic—catacombs of lava tubes that we chance to peer into, standing
rows of tall basalt pillars like ancient ruins. And then there are those endless intervals of numbing sameness and repetition, flatlands less varied than
the plains of Kansas.*

*We have settled on consistent names for many of the animals we can
see but cannot identify. There are fat-head fish, common fish that swim by
whipping their slender tails side-to-side and so look like giant sperm; the
stealth anemone is a species with very transparent tentacles, difficult to see.
Flying stars are delicate orbs with radiating arms that sometimes attend in
squadrons. Serpulid worms turn out to be among the most abundant of vent
organisms we see. I think they make the rocks look like white Brillo pads.*

On my watch this morning, we passed over the only marker the French left during their dives in 1993. They were diving on Christmas Day and placed a small cutout Santa Claus and a Christmas tree on the top of a pillar, beside a black smoker.

November 21: *Argo was brought back to the surface yesterday. We are moving south to a site known as "The Hump"—a portion of the ridge where the axial profile is at its shallowist. By late tonight, the transponders will be set for navigations and Argo will be sent back to work. This time she will carry a plankton net as well as all her cameras and sensors. Those flying stars taunted me each time they passed by the camera and I mean to catch a few so that I can at least identify them to phylum.*

November 25: *There are acres and acres of fresh glassy lava flows evident on the sea floor and eruptive fissures dominate the landscape. The valley itself is defined by steep walls and a dropped central graben 100 to 200 meters wide and 10 to 20 meters deep. Within the graben, faults and fissures slice through the crust, leaving behind talus ramps and jumbled terrain. This is a tectonically controlled landscape. Along the fissure walls we see long sticklike gorgonian corals and sometimes a "Tim's Hair" anemone. "Tim's Hair" is large, platter-sized, with long purple fronds that bend with the sluggish current that passes through the fissures. There is an occasional white octopus, but we had seen none of the large Dumbo (hooded) octopus that delighted us up north ... Now we are off on a "road trip," taking Argo on a single, unnavigated track north along the ridge axis over terrain no one has ever looked at before.*

November 27: *Our road trip north turned up nothing extraordinary. We continued passing over large lava fields varying in shade and shape. Although I am happy with what I have observed on this cruise, it is frustrating not to be able to study the animal communities more closely. There is so much about the natural history of these animals that I want to know. My childhood fancies of discovering a new species are an everyday occurrence. It is precisely the dearth of knowledge that makes the deep sea such a special place for a naturalist.*

November 29: *Thanksgiving passed by quietly. There was of course turkey and ham with all the trimmings and most of us wore our better clothes to dinner, but watches continued round the clock. I get past the holiday by*

*not thinking much about it—best to treat it as just another day with a
particularly good meal.*

*We are all intent on gathering data into useful formats. Maps of all
descriptions fall off the big Hewlett-Packard plotter as fast as data can be
dumped. During some hours it is hard to find a computer station unoccu-
pied. There must be two dozen scattered around the ship and they are
being worked constantly. Last night we had an abrupt change of plans
when we disovered a gap in our coverage of the ridge axis with Argo. Enough
time was left to put Argo back in the water, so we are finishing up today
with one last look at the sea floor.*

VI

Van Dover was back in Washington in early 1997, touching down in
her light, avian way, always seemingly ready to lift off and fly again.
She was dispensing her "free science" (no-fee lectures), jetwinging in
and out of Fairbanks to scientific conferences around the country.

After two decades roaming the ocean bottom, Van Dover now had
a fix on the sky and the possibility of oceans on other planets. It was an
unsurprising paradigm shift: I had always suspected the seasoned sea
traveler was at heart a space cadet. She approached new puzzles.

Was there an Earthlike sea on the Jovian Europa? A passionate
controversy had arisen. Van Dover imagined the moons of Io, Europa,
and Ganymede repeatedly locked and aligned in a three-body LaPlace
resonance: forced eccentricity, deformation, heat. This was the basis
for tidal heating and what she would later call "the putative hydrothermal systems in Europa's conjectural ocean."

"Can you see how magical this stuff is to me?" she said. "When I
was a kid, space seemed so distant, beyond my reach. But we're out
there now."

A few months later, NASA's Mars *Pathfinder* would give the world
strangely familiar visions of extraterrestrial landscapes, images of Mar-
tian sunrises that would become part of our pop culture. Scientists
would speculate about frozen oceans on Rhea, an icy satellite of Sat-
urn; Triton, the largest moon of Neptune; and Pluto's Charon. We
would learn that "ice balls" the size of skyscrapers bombard Earth's
atmosphere daily. So much ice, so much water. Where did it come
from and what does it portend?

It was fascinating to roam Van Dover's personal "Big Bang" cos-
mology. The young woman who had started her explorations at tide

pools was now discussing "cosmic evolution progression"—galactic, stellar, planetary, chemical, biological, cultural, ethical. She had locked forces with the "Trekies" who had emerged as the leading space explorers of the 1990s.

By now she was confident about the shrimp. Yes, they definitely had eyes and they probably used the vent glow for near-field navigation, though it hadn't been demonstrated conclusively. More compelling, she said, was the possibility of photosynthetic organisms (phototrophs) living at the vents; this went directly to her origin-of-life speculations.

She was writing a textbook about the vents and had been invited to ride in a shallow-depth submersible off the coast of Alaska. After years of nonpiloting she was excited by the prospect.

"It isn't *Alvin*," she smiled. "But I'm not a submersible snob."

Meanwhile, John Delany, whose research was important to her earlier work, had proposed recovery of a massive sulfide mound from the sea floor hot springs on the Juan de Fuca Ridge. This is an area where mounds grow to sixty feet in diameter and tower many stories off the bottom, fantasy pillars ornamented by spires and flanges, "like fairy castles," Van Dover explained.

Delany proposed using explosives to bag the mound and float it to the surface. Once on deck, it would be cut in half. The first half would belong to the expedition sponsor, the Museum of Natural History in New York, and the rest would be probed, poked, and dissected by a variety of scientists.

"Think of it," she said. "It's rather like going to Yellowstone and bulldozing up the largest travertine deposit hundreds if not thousands of years old. A sea floor travesty all in the name of science and museum entrance fees. And there I am, near the head of the line, ready to beg for my bit of sulfide."

If Van Dover had changed, so had I. This came to me in a great rush: How different the world seemed. I puzzled over this, hoping to find the moment when my paradigm had begun its shift. For some reason I recalled Van Dover telling me how simple things could bring tears to her eyes. Once, in Sitka, at a performance of the New Archangel Dancers, a troupe that makes up in enthusiasm for what it lacks in professional polish, she was deeply moved. There were the dancers, young and bursting with energy, doing their best. Unbidden, unexpected tears came to her eyes; they were an embarrassment, unwanted.

A "black smoker" volcanic chimney pours forth dissolved minerals, which sustain bacteria and other deep-sea life. *Photo courtesy National Oceanic and Atmospheric Administration.*

She swiped at them and rubbed her eyes as if a dust mote had floated into them, anything to hide the emotion.

"I don't know where it comes from or why it should be there," she confessed. "This extreme sensitivity to what anyone else would likely take to be, if not entirely ordinary, certainly not extraordinary things."

I have yet to pin down my own turning point. Perhaps it isn't important. Besides, I told myself, I have to go on, try out my new lenses. All the while I sensed Van Dover would come up with another surprise, though I wasn't sure what it might be.

Then on the afternoon of June 11, 1997, a message appeared on my computer screen:

A phone call from National Science Foundation was a show-stopper this morning. It would be hopeless for me to try to get work done right now. My mind is spinning in all different directions. I had three proposals left pending (plus one other that's on a different time track) and I learned two were turned down. One will be funded.

I'm to be chief scientist of an expedition that will take us to explore the vents in the Indian Ocean. No one has ever been to a vent there. It is a piece of the biogeographic puzzle that has been missing, and I get to find it and fit into the map.

Sea and sky, universal domains. Sometime later she would praise the space explorers and align even more closely with them. "They are like me," she would say, "privileged children of the sixties, the moon time, who were given dreams and never had to give them up."

PART TWO—
DR. EUGENIE CLARK, THE SHARK LADY

I

DR. EUGENIE CLARK, THE WORLD-FAMOUS "SHARK LADY," the woman who single-handedly met the ocean's most daunting predators and taught them to do her bidding, seemed a kind of chimera, a personality too big and too various to be placed between the pages of a book. One associate warned of her "painfully sharp wit" and occasional temper. "She'll push," I was told. "Not a lot of give." Others portrayed her as docile. "She's easy," a former student informed me. "You'll love her."

I knew she was a Fellow of the Explorers Club, an organization as loopy and ego-driven as the Billionaires Club, and I had received a club mailing inviting members to sail with her out to the Tuamotus, the "Dangerous Archipelago" of French Polynesia. Anyone who visits this Pacific outback will encounter sharks, the big open-ocean variety. I knew the trip would be a hit. Clark. Sharks. Dangerous Archipelago. An irresistible triumverate.

Still, I couldn't put hard edges on the Clark mystique. So it was that I came tentatively to her door in Bethesda, Maryland, on a cold, rain-soaking afternoon in December 1996, tape recorder in hand, not knowing what to expect. I wondered: Would the shark lady bite?

I had seen many images of her bundled in scuba gear and diving through the pages of popular magazines. One image in particular stayed in my mind: The April 1975 cover of *National Geographic* magazine shows her cozied up to a "sleeping" shark at a time when the dogma insisted that sharks never sleep. An entire generation of sharkophiles carries this remarkable vision in their collective consciousness, this unlikely juxtaposition of woman and predator harmoniously convening beneath the sea.

There were more conventional photographs, with no sharks in them, yet they revealed images equally striking. There was the charismatic young researcher of the 1950s, who, with the blessing of the Vanderbilt fortune, had founded Cape Haze (later the Mote Marine) Laboratory on the Gulf Coast of Florida. In an era when shark behavior was steeped in myth, Clark captured and caged man-eating *carchariidea* and cajoled them, Pavlov-style, to obey her commands. These Gulf Coast images reveal a young woman with a high forehead, dark flowing hair, an ironic smile, and the physique of a competitive swimmer. She seems more the charming, self-assured jock than a scientist or shark tamer.

Now in her seventies, Clark remains one of the most popular and celebrated figures in all of Oceanus. With the passing of Jacques Cousteau in June 1997, her stature has grown; she is elder statesperson of the sea, a bridge between the early days of wonder and today's deep-sea revelations. Ocean science is now a welcoming place for women, and Clark may claim much credit for this. She is the ever-searching spirit to whom even her famous hero, William Beebe, had written a fan letter, a letter she has to her regret misplaced.

Aside from debunking myths about shark behavior—this against a wave of terror churned up by her friend Peter Benchley's best-seller, Jaws—she is the discoverer of at least a dozen species and subspecies, and she is still searching.

As professor emeritus at the University of Maryland, she lectures on the subject of "Sea Monsters," and delves freely in the unknown. In the world of academe she an innovator, a what-if theorizer, unbound. Her students emulate her. Underwater videographer Nick Caloyianis, who studied with Clark, was once mauled by a shark off the Yucatan Pennisula, an encounter that only narrowly escaped being fatal. "Well, it wasn't the shark's fault," he says, a line often espoused by his mentor. A shark is a shark; it isn't driven by animus; mostly it bumbles into an object and takes a bite, the way a child reaching into a cookie jar will sample whatever treat is at hand. Unfortunately, Caloyianis, he was the treat.

These thoughts and images passed through my mind as I waited in the rain on Clark's doorstep in Bethesda. I confess I was a bit edgy.

The door opened and I was greeted by a small woman in a thick woolen sweater, black tights, and slate-colored wool-lined boots. I was stunned. At seventy-four, her baby face smiled at me with a playful, what-are-you-doing-out-there-in-the-rain expression.

"Come in, come in. It's messy," she said. "Please." A sea of white terry-cloth towels was spread on the floor of the foyer. "Here, give me your umbrella. Dry your feet."

We shook hands. She had an amazingly firm grip, evidence of life-long athleticism and regular aerobics and weight training. "Don't you just hate squishy handshakes?" she grinned.

An odd beginning. Yet, huddling in the foyer, testing the chill of the big, well-appointed house, a strange thing occurred to me. The larger-than-life aura, the mystique of celebrity, seemed to melt away. There was a sense of familiarity in the wide, impossibly youthful face. I had the odd sensation that I had visited long ago, when I was younger and she was then quite grown up. Now I felt like the grownup in the presence of a confident, teasing young woman, and the précis of her accomplishments flashed through my consciousness: *Dr. Eugenie Clark, ichthyologist, mentored by the century's best scientists ... discoverer of the cross-fertilizing hermaphrodite* Serranus subligarius *... extracted shark repellent toxins in Moses and Peacock soles ... rides with the whale sharks ... a woman who has penetrated more than 10,000 feet below the waves, roaming the bottom in a submersible in search of 'monsters' ... recipient of uncountable honors and awards ... waltzed through twenty-four TV specials ... wrote best-sellers,* Lady with a Spear *and* The Lady and the Sharks *... honored with the Franklin L. Burr Award by the National Geographic Society for making the life of the sea accessible to the high and dry dwellers of the planet.*

It was as if this small woman's life was too heroic, too supercharged to bother with my cold feet.

"It's an old house," she explained. "Big place. I live alone. It's okay. A lot of people visit. We have parties. I love parties." There was the faint sound of feminine voices drifting up from the basement. "Oh," she said, "I have someone living there. It's a tax write-off."

We toured the music room. There were a Steinway and a collection of fine old prints; she was especially animated in showing them off. "I love prints, don't you? No, no. Of course it isn't an original Hogarth!"

The library sheltered volumes about the sea and scuba diving and Japanese art and culture. I searched for Hemingway's *Islands in the Stream,* with its classic scene in which a hammerhead shark charges over the reef toward the hero's sons, who are spearfishing. It is drama straight out of shark mythology: the big dorsal fin slicing the water, a massive, seemingly invincible body, innocents bobbing helplessly in the waves, the hero firing his .256 Mannlicher Shoenauer a touch ahead of the fish and missing. At last, the mate appears on the deck of the hero's boat, slamming away with a machine gun. The shark is hit, rolls over, black holes opening in its "obscenely white belly." It is the type of stuff that Clark has consistently debunked, and I expected to find a collection of such fiction. How strange to discover the only novel to be Peter Benchley's outrageous tale of demonic sharkdom, *Jaws.*

"I read mostly biography," she explained. "I read one about Errol Flynn. He had a job biting the balls off sheep." She thought this was particularly amusing, the outrageous notion of the film idol performing a mutilation while maintaining his screen idol dignity. "He said it was the only way to do it. Just bite 'em off. I admired Flynn."

A strange reference to hand a stranger. Perhaps she was testing. Could it be that Flynn's cavalier attitude, his peculiar talent, was linked in some way to Clark's obsession with shark behavior?

I recalled an earlier profile published in *Sea Technology* in which Clark enthused over diving for its own sake. "I love it so much," she said. "I think I'm a diver first, a scientist second."

This was easy to understand. The freedom, the weightlessness, immersion in total exotica—these are powerfully seductive elements. Love of adventure is basic to Clark, and she has passed this gene to her children: Underwater photography and ichthyology were career choices of two of them; one daughter is a 727 pilot.

One can't help sense the passion for adventure in Clark, even on a cold, gray afternoon. As the tape recorder hummed, I had the feeling the phone might ring and she would excuse herself, dash to the airport, and wing away to the Red Sea, her diving location of choice.

"I've been there forty-five times," she told me. "I could work five lifetimes over there."

The area known as Ras Mohammed was recently named one of the seven underwater wonders of the world, and it has been dedicated as the first Egyptian national park. Clark played a large role in all this, and the place is recognized as a monument to her work.

We settled in around a big wooden table in her 1950s vintage kitchen. The room was welcoming, despite the lingering chill. Clark's face was framed by S-shaped folds of gray hair. I couldn't help feeling there was something playful in this baby face surrounded by silver streaks, the big dark eyes warming the room. She riffled through a pile of notes, glancing at letters and postcards from around the world; an amazingly large pile of paper. I had been told that, like Napoleon, she was capable of holding two independent thoughts, acting on one while contemplating the other.

I made a quick inventory of her kitchen curios: a photo of Clark diving off a boat with her grandson, Niki; a large Sushi poster cheerful with its delicious delights; a crazy-quilt assortment of snapshots tagged to the refrigerator by colorful magnets; a scuba diver embossed on an old auto tag; a tiny shark jaw grinning against a pink plastic mounting above the sink; pictures of tropical fishes; wooden cupboards with iron handles. Homey. Familiar. And Clark spoke of personal matters in a familiar way, as if we were old friends.

"Hey, I'm in my seventies. What have I got to hide?"

She spoke of the father she never knew, an American, an avid waterman. "He'd swim in the ocean off Long Island. He was a powerful swimmer. Then one day he didn't come back." Years later, a psychiatrist friend suggested her romance with diving might be a subliminal search for her father, Charles Clark. "I don't know," she sighed. "Do you think there's something to it?"

I shuffled through my list of questions, but the Shark Lady was voluable and needed little prompting. She went on in an easy, unaffected way, anticipating much of what I would ask. She was used to interviews, had given hundreds of them. *She's a celebrity*, I reminded myself. *Everything she says is elemental to celebrity.*

"I really admired Beebe," she went on. "A great inspiration. You know, I knew what I wanted to do at an early age. My mother, Yumiko, worked at a newspaper stand in the lobby of the Downtown Athletic Club. She'd leave me at the New York Aquarium at Battery Park. I spent hours there. She'd pick me up after work and we'd eat at a Japanese restaurant called Fuji. You see, I learned more about seafood than any of my schoolmates."

Her stepfather, Masatomo Nobu, owned the Fuji and was its chief chef. He taught Genie the delights of Nippon cuisine, and she in turn amazed her classmates with stories of how the family ate with chopsticks, consumed rice and seaweed for breakfast, ate raw fish, urchin eggs, and shark cakes. Her Woodmont, Long Island, classmates, raised on the meat and potatoes menu of the day, viewed her dietary regime with a sense of bewildered fascination. She had no Japanese/American peers to validate her exotica, and though she was the only student of Japanese ancestry, her one-of-a-kind status conferred no negatives. If she was slightly different, what did it matter? She was future-focused, absorbed by her love of sea creatures, and she knew where she was headed.

"I wanted to be an ichthyologist. My mother was great about it. She supported my study of zoology (at Hunter College) though she hardly understood what my dream was all about."

As she spoke I noticed her Mongolian eyefold, a visible clue to her mixed ethnicity. It wasn't immediately discernible; the spell cast by the eyefold came slowly, like a mist rising out of a valley. Such an alluring personality—quirky, nurturing, disarming. She mixed Mandarin contemplation with bright flashes of Western ego. Here was a woman of three distinct worlds: Asia, America, and the sea. And despite the personal critiques of those who knew her ("Genie's very down to earth!") I found her complex, affecting. The folksy exterior masked many levels of knowing, and I was drawn to her as one is drawn to an extraordinary ideal, a notion that colors reality and kicks it into a different orbit. The first-century philosopher Seneca remarked in *Natural Questions* that "nature does not reveal her mysteries once and for all." Indeed, such layers of mystery seemed the essence of the Shark Lady.

Sea-going expeditions are big, expensive events; they engage many talented people, and expectations run high. Clark feels a responsibility to produce.

"I've had such fun in my life. I've published a lot, but there's still a lot to be published. I'm a scientist. I have a responsibility of taking all these trips and having people dive for me. I have to get the data available for everyone to read. We've done some pretty wonderful studies.

"You know, some people don't give a damn that little tile fishes build 'houses' at 200 feet. I have a friend who puts me in my place all the time. Whenever I tell her how exciting this is she says, 'Who cares? Can you eat them?'"

Clark's personal life is as complex as her career. A romantic with four former husbands, she took the plunge a fifth time, marrying a man who had been introduced to her a half-century earlier by her first husband. Friends say she had been in touch with Henry Yoshinobu Kon and his family during her trips to the Pacific. The eighty-three-year-old retired businessman's wife died in 1996, and he and Clark were married at Mote Marine Laboratory the following year.

Her smile evoked images of the teenage Genie hard at work for Hunter College at Douglas Lake, circa 1940, done up properly in a stylish pants suit, hand on one hip, the athletic body full of energy. I recalled a touching photo taken seven years after Douglas Lake: Genie with her first husband, Hideo (Roy) Umaki, in Hawaii. Standing close beside him she seemed so tender and small, but in her smile lurked a hint of lust. "He was a handsome young pilot," she recalled, offhandedly, continuing to work through her papers. "He was overseas most of the time, but we lasted seven years." Without a sigh, without missing a beat, she shrugged. "We were too damned young."

My mental photo album of Clark flashed on and off as we spoke. I recalled a picture with her early mentor, Charles M. Breeder, Jr., former director of the aquarium at Battery Park; it revealed a curious blend of admiration and independence, as if she were clinging to him though waiting for the first opportunity to bolt. Yet another photo, this one with Carl L. Hubbs at the Scripps Institution of Oceanography pier in La Jolla, circa 1946, unveils a suggestion of vampishness. Hubbs loomed large in Clark's life; he was the one who captured a swell shark and gave it to her to study. The swell is one of the rare creatures equipped to "puff" itself up and become a kind of swimming balloon; it can nearly double its normal size as a survival tool. The swell was exactly the type of metamorphosing creature that so fascinated her in her earlier years. Still another photo, snapped two years later, foreshadowed her Shark Lady celebrity. It reveals Clark standing beneath the palms of Bimini holding two large, toothy barracudas. The picture says conquest, daring, predator, with the odd contrast of her embracing femininity, strong swimmer's legs and a willowy pose worthy of a fashion model. A year later, she would be in the sharky waters of Micronesia working for the Pacific Science Board and the U.S. Navy and perfecting her skin-diving skills with a local fisherman named Kiakong.

It is instructive to compare her various personalities. The professional Clark has a bright, confident aspect, an untapped star quality. How peculiar to notice her seeming diminution beside her second husband, a soon-to-be Greek tycoon with the auspicious name of Ilias Themistokles Papakonstantinou. It was 1950 and he was an intern of orthopedic medicine. The photo of the couple was made on the steps of the American Museum of Natural History in 1959, prior to her Ph.D. defense. Ilias towers above her, a large arm burying her small shoulders. There is a trace of anxiety in her eyes, as if she already senses the marriage will end badly.

"He was obsessed by money," she told me. The couple had four children, but money "crowded out everything."

Money lust is as consuming as any other, but it was stunning to Clark. The scale of it might be measured against her early days with the Vanderbilts, whose wealth helped found the Cape Haze Marine Laboratory, which she would eventually head. It was Ilias's drive to emulate his hero, the late Aristotle Onassis, which became fatally off-putting, a poison pill to the marriage. I had meet Onassis in Washington in the 1970s. The subjects of yachts and sharks came up. Onassis mentioned "this woman very brilliant," who knew everything there was to know about sharks. "Stimulating," he said of her experiments. He knew the details of her work, how she had penned the creatures and trained them, Pavlov-style, to perform various tasks. Onassis found this most intriguing but wondered about its value. "What good is a trained shark?" At the time, he was cruising the power lake of Washington with the former First Lady, Mrs. John F. Kennedy. Yet even in the glow of Jackie-O, the aura of the Shark Lady held its place.

If Clark communed with awesome sea creatures, her tastes in men ran a parallel course. While married to Ilias she agreed to sit for an interview with Chandler Brossard, the "grandfather of American existentialism." Brossard, a protégé of Jean-Paul Sartre, hoped to capture an intimate profile of Clark for *Look* magazine. It was explosive chemistry. Clark was captivated, transported away from Ilias's vertical universe of wealth. He was electric, spiky, controversial. She left Ilias and moved in with Brossard.

As it turned out, Brossard the existentialist had not taken full account of the power of science. He navigated his universe using Sartre's *Being and Non-Being* as a spiritual compass. Sartre's dark roaming had fascinated the postwar world, but Marjorie Grene described his quest as a "dreadful freedom," the ultimate inner odyssey. Clark lived in a brighter place, the world of variegated reality. Unlike Brossard, whose inward journey led him away from empiricism, Clark embraced the tools of science, the desire to grasp facts, to measure the heart of the ocean universe. Thus, the chemistry turned corrosive. The marriage flamed out after a few tense years. She said of Brossard that he was a "wild man, an excuse to break up this nice solid marriage I had with my second husband, who became quite wealthy and seemed to lose his feeling for the family." Undaunted, she tried again with Russian neuropathologist Igor Klatzo, of the National Institutes of Health. It was yet another short-lived union.

"That man was so smart," she said of Klatzo. "I mean, really, totally brilliant."

One had the feeling she was speaking of characters in a novel. I had to wonder what life with the Shark Lady might have been like for her former husbands. Fiercely intelligent, dedicated, always on the jetwing, a presence in an exotic field, a media star; neither fame nor wealth nor philosophy could fully encompass her spirit. It occurred to me sometime later that perhaps her sense of adventure stripped these men of the virginity of conventional marriage.

II

Clark reminded me of the late Carl Sagan, another scientist with a talent for communicating complex ideas in simple ways. Soon after the 1953 publication of her first book, *Lady with a Spear,* an autobiographical account of her research in the Pacific and the Red Sea, foreign rights requests poured in; excerpts were inserted in school texts. The book climbed the best-seller lists.

"I realized I had this talent for communicating about the natural world," she told me. "I came to see it would be my life's work."

The book foreshadowed bigger things. She took a post teaching biology at Hunter College, where Ilias had enrolled to complete his medical studies. At about the same time, the American Museum of National History offered her a research associate position. Nepera Corporation came with an offer to conduct pharmacological research. All the while she was in demand on the lecture circuit.

But the true Shark Lady persona had yet to emerge. The first flickerings were seen in 1954 when Anne and William H. Vanderbilt invited her to lecture at Englewood, on the Gulf Coast of Florida. Anne had read *Lady with a Spear,* and the book fascinated her; she urged "Willie" to read it. The subject of marine life, it seemed, was a family obsession. Ten-year-old Bill, Jr., had lined the walls of his bedroom with aquariums, much as Clark had done as a child. The elder Vanderbilts were more than a little intrigued by Bill's hobby; it soon became a passion, and the passion would eventually be reborn as a thoroughgoing research station.

Clark never dreamed she'd found a research laboratory of her own, but that's exactly what the Vanderbilts offered after hearing her lecture. Anne, a bit coy at first, told Clark that, yes, she'd been invited to lecture, but wouldn't it be wonderful if the lab became a reality? Would she accept the challenge?

"I was speechless," Clark recalled. "I mean, it was a big thing."

She paused, her eyes raised from the stack of papers and postcards. In that brief instant of reflection, I imagined the passages of her life flickering through her memory in slow motion. She smiled warmly, returned to the papers, looked up again.

"You're cold," she said. I nodded. "How about a little sherry?" I nodded agreeably. "I have a neat little trick." She poured sherry into sake cups and placed them in the microwave. A few seconds later she placed the steamy little faux Ming cups on the table. The warm, sweet liquid banished the chill of the kitchen. "Pretty good, huh?"

We returned to talk of the early days and the Vanderbilts, who owned large tracts of Gulf Coast property, including 36,000 acres near Placida, south of Englewood on the Cape Haze Peninsula. Anne Vanderbilt was insistent: The peninsula would be perfect for a laboratory. Cape Haze was a wilderness of bush, scrub, and tiny fishing villages, hardly comparable to Manhattan's West End, where Clark and Ilias lived with their children, two-year-old Hera and the newborn Aya. In the presence of big money and bigger ideas, Clark realized she was in for a major life change. Life along the Gulf had its peculiar attractions, not the least of which were its sharky waters. On any given day, "sport" fishermen hooked everything from sand tigers to hammerheads. These were rich, sharky waters, mostly untapped by science. In the end, Clark understood that the Vanderbilts' offer was a once-in-a-lifetime entrée to the watery wilderness that had shaped her destiny.

Cape Haze Marine Laboratory officially opened its doors in January 1955. It was, Clark realized, a dream, but a dream that needed building from the ground up. She was teamed with a colleague, a local fisherman named Beryl Chadwick, who built and maintained the small wooden structure that housed the lab and an adjacent wooden pier. These days, ocean-going expeditions are big, expensive enterprises, sizzling with high-tech. At that time, Clark and Chadwick hunkered down in a cramped fishing boat with minimal equipment, determined to find, catch, cage, and maintain sizable sharks.

Their pursuit struck the locals as slightly offbeat; sharks were deemed either a general nuisance or a serious menace, frightening bathers and gobbling up game fish. It is hard to imagine that these all-pervasive predators would become prey, but today scientists are waving red flags, not to signal the presence of sharks but to warn of their possible extinction. Juan Salalon, a researcher at the National Aquarium in Baltimore, cautions that sharks are far more wary of people than the other way around. In U.S. coastal waters, the number of species has dropped nearly 70 percent in the past two decades. Fame and/or infamy is leading to oblivion.

Perhaps the Vanderbilts anticipated this crisis. Always practical, they had done a bit of sound planning. The day after the lab opened, Clark received a telephone call from John H. Heller, director of the New England Institute for Medical Research. Heller needed fresh shark livers for his research; would it be convenient if he and his wife, Terry, flew down to Cape Haze to join the hunt? By early February, Clark and Heller were busy dissecting specimens. Overnight, Cape Haze aquired a sound, scientific cachet. Stories appeared in the local newspapers exclaiming that a star had risen over the peninsula. In quick succession, the lab had hosted nearly thirty scientists and cadres of schoolchildren, and Beryl was busy constructing a large shark pen. The Vanderbilts had been canny: Cape Haze and Eugenie Clark were a hit.

"I was studying other kinds of fishes, of course," Clark explained. "But there was also a certain fascination for sharks because I'm a swimmer and a diver. I was curious. Were sharks really that dangerous? My introduction wasn't like *Jaws*. I saw them in the aquarium first. They were swimming around and they were quite beautiful. ... I wasn't afraid of them. I wished I could see them in person, out in the open."

The mission of Cape Haze was to study general marine fauna. Clark was using a new aqualung to track a species of fish known as *Serranus subligarius,* which she discovered to be a group of self-fertilizing hermaphrodites. This was amazing—creatures capable of changing sex within seconds—and she made serious studies. At about the same time, however, she had begun training her penned sharks, probing them for memory and discrimination. Embedded in these studies was a soon-to-be-realized sharkomania. In a world hooked on the exotic, sex-morphing fish played a distant, mundane role in the growing drama.

"The sharks got all the attention," Clark sighed.

Cape Haze expanded with funds from the National Science Foundation, the Office of Naval Research, and other science organizations. Foreign researchers arrived in ever-increasing numbers. And why not? Wasn't it worth traveling halfway around the world to mind-meld with the Shark Lady?

Clark struck up a collaboration with Lester Aronson; together they designed the first experiments testing the limits of shark learning skills. Just as these experiments were getting under way she gave birth to her last child, Nikolas Masatomo Konstantinu. She laughed as she recalled the day in October 1958. "I felt like *Lady with a Sphere!*" However, her expanded middle didn't discourage her from scuba diving all day, a rather rigorous series of dives. "It wasn't a problem," she said. "I think my diving made all my births fairly easy ones."

The early experiments were Pavlovian response-reward exercises. Clark proposed to teach sharks to press underwater targets. Press the right target and the shark was rewarded with raw fish. The trick was to discriminate between targets.

She had completed her Ph.D. work on the reproductive mechanisms of freshwater fish. Already she had begun "hard hat" diving outfitted in a helmet and diving suit, and connected to the surface by an air hose and communications line. The advent of scuba freed her of these encumbrances, but at the same time heightened warnings that a free-swimming diver was prey to sharks. She had spent many hours at the New York Aquarium, her face pressed to the glass walls of the shark tanks, fascinated by the beauty of the creatures. She wasn't prepared to believe they were dangerous, but she wanted to be sure.

To conduct proper studies the sharks had to be kept active and healthy. Her offshore Gulf expeditions typically netted specimens in the nine-to-twelve-foot range. Few places kept live sharks; like many big predators, they didn't fare well in confinement. But the Cape Haze pens were roomy and open to the sea, daily tides sweeping in and out, and this nearly natural environment maintained her captives in good shape.

Conditioning experiments began with two lemon sharks in an open pen, seventy by forty feet, with a target at one end. Within days, the sharks learned to press the target, which in turn rang a bell and released food into the water. Visiting scientists were skeptical, claiming the experiments failed to produce learning per se; the sharks were merely showing up at a convenient feeding station. In response, Clark moved the feeding place.

"The sharks had go to the target, push it, ring the bell, turn around, and get their food at some distance away," she explained.

They also had to swim clockwise, and they had only about ten seconds to snatch their food. When the food was moved farther from the target their clockwise movements were too slow to get the reward in time. Canny creatures that they are, the sharks learned to adapt to counterclockwise movements. Clark continued to increase the distance between the target and the food source, and the sharks learned to make the proper movements and swim faster to get at it.

She noticed that the males always went first. But as the food moved further from the target, the females learned that when the bell rang they could get at the bait, and they'd outswim the males. Soon both males and females appeared to be holding back, as if to say: *You go first because I can snatch the food if you ring the bell.* Once again, Clark moved the food source, setting it up so that the shark that rang the bell had the best chance of receiving its reward.

"Later on, I put in two targets to see if they could discriminate," she said. "We found they could chose between any target where they could see a difference."

It became apparent that the sharks were unable to distinguish a square from a circle, but recognized the difference between a square and a diamond pattern. These arrangements were random, and before long the sharks were once again efficiently feeding themselves. One shark was correct all the time, never missing the proper target. Clark made a gift of this clever animal to the Crown Prince (later Emperor) of Japan.

The sharks not only learned, they retained their knowledge for months at a time, even when a target wasn't present. Clark discovered that some sharks have extraordinary vision; the great white fell into that category. In general, they excelled at distinguishing stripes, and could easily discriminate between horizontal and vertical designs.

These experiments were a magnet for funding. The Office of Naval Research invited Clark to a conference in New Orleans and asked her if she needed money to expand her studies. This is hardly typical in the world of ocean science, where the researchers are usually the ones doing the asking. Clark, however, had the right formula; her work had obvious utility. The military, especially the Navy, had long searched for an effective shark repellent. Everything from sonic gadgets to soluble chemicals had been tried, with little success. Yet it was clear that if anyone was on the verge of a breakthrough, it had to be the Shark Lady.

By 1973, she had come upon the toxic Moses sole (*Pardachirus marmoratus*) from the Red Sea, and the Peacock sole (*Pardachirus pavoninus*) from Japan. Both species seemed to promise high potential for a workable chemical repellent. Though it was early in the cycle of study, there was much media coverage on Clark's work, the hype driven by the horrific impact of *Jaws.* Researchers and television reporters stood elbow-to-elbow as her penned predators swam toward the Moses sole giving every indication that a meal was about to be consumed.

One scientist described the scene: "Then, with their jaws still wide open, the sharks jerked away. They thrashed and leaped about the tank, shaking their heads wildly. … All the while, the Moses sole kept swimming as if nothing unusual [had happened]."

So much promise. A great breakthrough shimmering in the public mind, and in more than a few corporate boardrooms. Clark's devotees were ecstatic. Hoping to become the first to market a reliable shark repellent, they proclaimed over the yet-to-be-produced wonder chemical with unembarrassed hyperbolism, comparing it to the Wright brothers' flight at Kitty Hawk. Alas, synthesizing the toxin was impractical and uneconomical. Biographer Eugene Balon was at her College Park, Maryland, office when an excited telephone call came from a drug company asking how the miracle repellent might be marketed. Clark, with a potential gold mine at her feet, told the caller the simple truth: It had taken four decades to synthesize insulin, and insulin had far more application than shark repellent. Besides, there was no gaurantee shark repellent would ever work.

"I was very much impressed by her answer, and even more by her patiently answering such queries day after day," Balon recalled.

As our interview progressed, I continually probed for signs of starstruckness. I had grilled a scattering of Clark's colleagues and friends. A *National Geographic* photographer who had worked with her seemed positively awed that "Someone who gets paid a dollar a word is so down to earth." He was referring to the days when a dollar a word still counted as "Hemingway wages," and heavy wages for magazine duty. I likewise searched for nonprofessional insights. A former neighbor, a musican who had spent five years touring with singer Tony Bennett, recalled musical get-togethers at the Bethesda house, with Clark passing around cocktails and hors d'oeuvres and fading into the background to listen. Clearly she possessed presence, and was proud of her achievements, yet try as I might, I failed to detect shadows of the Ahab-sized ego so commonplace in a life at sea and the laboratories of science.

"Look," she told me. "I was the only woman doing this work. So it gets blown out of proportion. A man doing the same work wouldn't get nearly the same attention. The timing of my best-seller was because there was no other woman doing this kind of thing. Now there are a lot of women in the marine biology field."

Her remark reminded me of anthropologist Margaret Mead, who had gained notoriety for her best-selling memoir, *Coming of Age in*

Samoa. Mead asserted that nurture played a greater role in human development than nature, a theory since vigorously assaulted by the geneticists. Fascinated by the roles of the sexes, she wrote a monthly column for *Redbook* magazine in which she had once declared, "Life in the 20th century is like a parachute jump—you have to get it right the first time." In similar fashion, Clark had broken through the brick wall of science, had transcended Bronislaw Malinowski's flaming prose, and delivered the common touch. Clark, Mead, Cousteau—lively communicators who made it seem easy.

Like many academics who chance into the glare of the limelight, Clark has her share of detractors. Few colleagues dare criticize her science, though they're quick to turn up their noses at her pop status. The Shark Lady does not take this criticism lightly. A former graduate student who worked with her on a number of projects swore that when punched Clark strikes back hard and follows with a few extra jabs.

"She expects the best," another student said. "She's high-strung. If she thinks you're slacking off or not giving it all, she'll murder you."

I heard this from others with whom she'd collaborated. And, of course, I realized the docile interviewee seated in the quaint kitchen wasn't an endless river of patience. There was a palpable sense of restlessness, a Johnsonian talent for the stinging remark; it was vaguely embedded in the quick, sly wit, the dark eyes that fixed the interviewer as one might pin a moth to a mounting board.

A colleague gives us an insightful glimpse at her ego: a few years ago, when the metal chain-mail diving suit designed to protect divers from shark bites was introduced. The suit was first tested by a well-known biologist, and apparently a shark somehow managed to penetrate the steely outfit. When Clark heard of this, she commented somewhat acidly that exotic suits and equipment were first to be tested on "dummies." "The implication was that the biologist was the dummy," the colleague remarked.

Another associate called her an "Einsteinian figure."

"How so?" I asked.

"Well, she's so damned intelligent, so much so that little common-sense things can slip by her." The young woman offering this shread of gossip referred to Einstein's reputation for being at loose ends in the world of mundane reality; it was rumored, for example, that Mrs. Einstein handled all household finances and even counted out the professor's bus fare to and from Princeton.

"Dr. Clark is a little like Herr Professor," the woman continued. "She's focused on ideas and her science—the big picture. Sometimes little ordinary things get overlooked."

Clark may shrug off her star status, but she is nonetheless covetous of it and the power it confers. Notoriety equals visibility, which equals funding. She is often asked who handles her public relations.

"I tell them, 'No one.' It's this thing of a woman studying sharks," she insists. "And I've never been hurt."

This in itself is remarkable. I have worked with sharks in open water and have spent more than a few dicey moments in their company. I once watched helplessly as a gray shark ripped into a woman's calf while we were diving in French Polynesia. The victim was a Frenchwoman, and quite brave. I asked her how it felt, the actual bite.

"Un instant," she said, her blood leaking into the bilge. *"Je vais voir si je la trouve dans ce livre."* ("Wait, I'll see if I can find it in this book.") She flipped through the *Berlitz*.

"Are you in pain?"

"Oh, *no douleur!*" she smiled, offhandedly. ("No pain.")

At first I believed this was a mix of courage, denial, and pride. Later, while browsing an exotic library, I happened to discover Livingstone's African memoirs, in which he tells of being attacked by a lion. Livingstone's account was a spellbinding description of being assaulted by a lion he had shot but failed to kill. The wounded creature sprang from the bush and seized the hunter by the shoulder. "Growling horribly close to my ear, he shook me as a terrier dog does a rat," wrote Livingstone. "The shock produced a stupor similar to that which seems to be felt by a mouse after the first shake of the cat. It caused a sort of dreaminess, in which there was no sense of pain nor feeling of terror, though I was quite conscious of all that was happening. ... " Livingstone believed this reaction was nature's benevolence in the face of death, and perhaps it was this that the Frenchwoman had attempted to describe after the shark attack. For myself, I had no desire to experience anything like this. And Clark, who had spent a lifetime in the company of swarming sharks, had all her body parts intact. Perhaps, I thought, she had a special affinity.

"Well, I don't know," she smiled. "You don't get cozy with sharks."

Clark never bonded with a shark. Her daughter, Hera, had a special bonding with forest animals and engaged instant rapport with dogs everyone else feared. "I don't have that with sharks. I do have a good fundamental understanding of their behavior, and why they can be dangerous. It gives me a more complete feeling around them than most people have."

The Shark Lady continues to take on serious challenges. She dives obsessively and routinely to considerable depths, despite a hip replacement a few years ago, the result of a fall in her home. For a long time she ignored the pain, which she traced to a slight bone fracture compounded by arthritis. Later there was the chilling prospect of a spinal operation, fortunately avoided when a physical therapist spotted the real problem.

"I thought, 'My God! My hip looks like Swiss cheese!' I know enough about anatomy to know what a bone looks like when it's falling apart. So I had the hip replaced. My doctor said I could go back to diving in six months. I said, 'How about five weeks?' He was startled. I told him I was comfortable in the water," she said, the avid diver in her surfacing right there across the kitchen table. Her doctor was skeptical. "He didn't really want to sanction it. He just warned me to be careful getting in and out of the water."

Five weeks later, she was diving in Belize. A few months later, she had flown to Papua New Guinea to make her deepest descent—a dive on ordinary, unmixed air to 270 feet, this despite warnings that nitrogen bubbles might be trapped in her hip prosthesis. Rather then restraining her, the shiny new hip revitalized her. She was proud of her new body part.

"Look," she said, standing up suddenly. She lifted her sweater and displayed the scar. "There. See it?"

The conversation drifted back to her days at Cape Haze and her rapid celebrity. At first she was flattered, though soon enough notoriety transformed into the inevitable overkill. Gone were the honeymoon days when people simply dropped in to chat about the curious goings-on. The star glow gathered its own force field, attracting admirers, researchers, and a stream of journalists looking for a Sunday feature. The Vanderbilts hired a manager whose almost impossible task it was to keep the demands of celebrity from devouring precious research time. Clark settled into a more structured schedule; she scanned appointments, weeded out time wasters, absorbed the frustrations of time management.

"It wasn't easy," she confessed. "You want to do your science. That's the thing—getting it done."

Cape Haze was booming. The world seemed eager and fascinated to learn that sharks aren't "stupid," that they could discriminate between colors and shapes and, ultimately, be trained. While it may seem obvious that a creature that has survived 350 million years of evolution has to possess some intelligence, Clark raised this assumption to another level. Yet even when the fact of shark intelligence became demonstrable, the demon myths persisted. I recall discussing this with a gaggle of sport fishermen at the University Club bar. They boasted of netting billfish and tuna, these were "intelligent" creatures, they insisted, sufficiently canny to outsmart even the most sophisticated fishermen. "The shark's a buffoon," one gentleman proclaimed. "A finny vaccum cleaner." "Now, on the other hand, you take a marlin: There's a smart fish for you," said another. It was futile to insist that a shark might possess cunning, memory, or intelligence.

Time passed, and I chanced to meet these gentlemen again not long after *Jaws* flashed across American consciousness. By now the bathing beach had been morphed into an arena of terror and destruction. "What would your Shark Lady think of *Jaws?*" I was asked. I offered that perhaps Clark would be outraged, and after the outrage she might smile at the notion of attributing to sharks the motive of purposeful malice. "Oh, really?" one of the sport fisherman interjected. "What about Melville's white whale?" Surely Benchley was as knowledgeable as Melville, and the conversation quickly descended into a morass of convoluted opinion, but with a twist: Through fiction, these doubters had elevated the shark from reflexive buffoonery to the status of clever sadism. Clark would have laughed at this speculation; she might have appealed to empiricism or defended the shark in the way a cleric might defend humanity's foibles. Indeed, the semimystical world of Carcharodon *carcharias* never had a more charming or persuasive defender, though she would certainly wink at the right of fiction makers to play to morbid fantasy. Even today Clark seems a bit torn over the mania engendered by *Jaws,* seeing it as science fiction and, at the same time, as the kind of billboard advertising that coincidentally boosted her bona fides.

At a high point of her popularity and accomplishment at Cape Haze, Clark's mother died. The loss took an unexpected toll.

"I lost interest," she admitted. "I felt I couldn't handle a full-time job."

She wanted to resign and stay home with her children and continue to help her stepfather. Her parents had moved their restaurant from New York to Grove City, near Cape Haze. Masatomo hadn't mastered English, and the loss of Yumiko appeared to cast him adrift emotionally. Clark, taking a long, deep breath, dug in and helped him start a new restaurant on Siesta Key, near her new home in Sarasota. With characteristic pride she donned a kimono and acted as hostess.

"People didn't know who I was," she laughed. "I remember one couple sitting down at the table and asking me if I'd heard about this Cape Haze Marine lab down the road, and I said yes. They said there's a woman director there, and I said yes. They wanted to go down and meet her, and I said, well, call up and ask for an appointment. And you know what? I realized how important it is to greet people, to be nice to them, to make them feel good."

She never mentioned that she was the woman they were looking for.

The process of resettling her stepfather lifted the gloom. The realization dawned: Icons are obligated to maintain their position; they do not have an option to sink into obscurity, at least not voluntarily. In the end, the Cape Haze operation was reinvented with new facilities at Sarasota, and Clark's career seemed reinvented as well.

Demands were being made, and budgeting became a problem. The Vanderbilts doubled their contributions. At one point Clark cut her own salary. It was urgent to keep up the pace; important science was flowing from shark research, including the discovery of "restim," a substance that significantly boosts the human immune system and causes regression of some types of cancer. Clark's science was on a high, though other aspects of her life had taken a rather dark turn.

Her marriage to Ilias, which had produced four children, was on a downward spiral. "Still," she reflected, in a melancholy tone, "it was the only true marriage I had. He encouraged me."

After her marriage to Brossard in 1967, she moved back to New York. Perry Gilbert, head of shark research at the American Institute of Biological Sciences, took over at Cape Haze. Later, transportation mogul William Mote became the official angel, and Cape Haze evolved into the present Mote Marine Laboratory.

III

Clark and Cousteau discovered each other in the late 1950s, and the Pasha, the greatest popularizer of ocean science and himself, immediately seized on the marquee potential of a joint venture. Clark was enchanted. She had been visited in 1958 by Cousteau's eldest son,

Phillipe, who was seeking ways to tranquilize sharks in the open ocean. Clark advised the use of alcohol-loaded darts; Cousteau followed her suggestion, though he gave it his own special spin; instead of ordinary alcohol in the dart ampules, he used fine French cognac.

Phillipe, who sat in on Clark's target experiments, noticed a certain reticence among the females. He later wrote: "The fact that the female waited until the male had eaten several times before advancing on the target ... suggests that there may be some means of communication between which is still unknown to us." This notion of interspecies communication was the rage, and a great deal of attention had been given to dolphin communication. Cousteau, a latecomer to the speculation about dolphin-speak, played up the possibility of shark-speak. It didn't work. People-friendly talking dolphins were apparently acceptable, but public opinion weighed against the proposition that primitive fish were possessed of a language.

I wondered about Clark's first impressions of Cousteau.

"He was absolutely captivating," she told me. "You felt a poetic energy coming from him. He was absolutely brilliant."

Their first meeting took place at a seminar sponsored by the Zoological Society of Florida. Seated between Cousteau and genius inventor Edwin Link, Clark seemed to glow. Clearly she had arrived, had become one of the avant-garde of ocean science. And though she didn't know it at the time, Cousteau had already fashioned tentative plans for a series of joint explorations. No one in the ocean world understood the power of celebrity or used it more effectively than Cousteau, and Clark was the perfect star to place in his ever-expanding galaxy.

The Clark-Cousteau connection turned out to be mutually creative. The Pasha need her expertise to highlight his dramatic "shark encounters" (he often played out tales of facing powerful predators), and she wondered if her behavioral experiments would hold true to form in the wild. Thus, in September 1967, she set sail aboard *Calypso* at Djibouti, steaming north to the Suakin Islands off the coast of Sudan. Once on-site she rigged her targets: One was decorated with vertical stripes, and the other bore a horizontal pattern. Only one of these targets was set to produce a reward of fresh fish. Amazingly, the open-ocean sharks responded like their penned cousins, and they appeared to learn more quickly.

Her travels with Cousteau were mutually beneficial. For a time, it appeared that she and the Pasha competed for top billing. Cousteau, if nothing else, was a commanding public figure. At times his energies were diffused by the fickle nature of show business, while Clark, ever the scientist, found satisfaction in simply doing her job. She was invited to join various academic and scientific institutions, and, finally, she found her way in 1968 to the Department of Zoology at the University of Maryland.

It was at Maryland that she wrote *The Lady and the Sharks,* published a year before her divorce from Igor Klatzo in 1970. The book was a best-seller, establishing once and for all her marquee personality. She became a full professor in 1973, and her engaging courses were prestige events. An honors course, "Sea Monsters and Deep Sea Sharks," indicates the tone she set. "Oh," she told me, "isn't everyone fascinated by monsters?"

She retired in 1992, but still teaches as professor emerita. She has developed a research program ranging over twenty countries, a highly charged and productive enterprise, with at least a dozen major discoveries to its credit, each described for a popular audience in *National Geographic.* The magazine has become the prime outlet for what she calls her "naturalist nose."

One of the major discoveries she sniffed out was the "sleeping shark" phenomenon. She had heard from an aquaintance, Ramon Bravo, that the Yucatan was home to many of these sleepers. Popular belief held that sharks, which unlike other fish are without swim bladders, must swim constantly; to stop was death, since water would cease to flow over their gills, depriving them of oxygen and drowning them. Clark and her graduate students, along with photographer David Doubilet, made nearly 100 dives off Isla Mujeres to a submerged cave sixty feet below the surface, and there they found motionless sharks. And more— the sharks were actually docile, allowing Clark and the others to handle them.

If she has been a prolific scientist, Clark's love of scuba is bone-deep. Diving for its own sake is her first passion. She eventually graduated to submersibles, making dives to 12,000 feet. During a 4,000-foot excursion she documented the largest creature ever seen in the deep sea. She was aboard the French submersible Nautile in 1989 when a Pacific sleepwalker shark (*Somniosus pacificus*) crashed into their bait cage, toppling it into the mud. Clark estimates the shark was at least twenty-three feet long. One of the cameramen, Ralph White, described the scene: "We saw a fish bump into a wall, and then the wall moved.

The sub shook. On the shark's second pass we saw the head. Parasites hung from fluttering gills. As it left, we saw enough of the underside to determine it was female. All we could think was, holy mackerel!"

Clark's take was, "Wow! That was fun. A twenty-three footer!"

Came the irresistible question: Are there any undiscovered "monsters" left in the sea? Clark grinned broadly. There are always "mysteries," she said, but most of them are solved by science. She paused, reflected for a long moment, and went on:

"There is one thing that has not been solved—a mysterious, gigantic blob in the deep sea. It comes up to the surface and it's been photographed. My dear friend [photographer] Howard Hall has a twenty-minute-long movie of it and never took a piece of it to preserve it in gin or vodka or anything they had on board. They were a little bit afraid of it. It's this amorphous gelatin and it has little spots. Howard calls it a UFO—underwater floating object." She said three divers in Hall's group went up to the thing, touched it, and backed off. "It has no form," Clark went on. "It's amorphous and gigantic." She made a wide gesture. "Twice the size of this room."

Another monster is what she calls Pirasoma. "Did you see *The Abyss*, the movie? Well, there's this waterspout monster. There is such a thing ... It won't make a face at you, but it's got a mouth end to it, it's almost all water. I collected all the pictures, going back to Hans Hass. These things live in the deep sea. The come up and die at the surface. You see pieces of them. And they're so big and round and hollow you can swim through them and feel the pulsating currents ... It's in the same phylum we're in, and it's not that far from us [biologically] ... Hans Hass went up to it and put his finger through it; it's seawater. He described it in 1934."

She said the creature is bioluminescent and grows to eighty feet. "Can you imagine this thing coming up to the surface, glowing, a mouth at one end? Now there's the origin of a lot of monster tales."

There are people who affectionately call Clark a "wild woman," still leading expeditions, gathering awards, and diving deep. I wondered how she kept a rational mind at such depths, where nitrogen narcosis can be life threatening.

"It doesn't bother me," she replied. Then she quickly backtracked. "Well, I shouldn't say it doesn't *bother* me. I'm quite aware of it [the narcosis], but I can control it. And I don't do anything that requires great acuity at that depth, and I don't stay long." As a life principle,

"You try everything," she added. "You do it. You make mistakes. You go on."

After decades of chasing after sharks, I wondered if she had large lingering questions about them. She replied that she has lately been focused on deep-sea sharks, and she wonders why they seldom if ever descend beyond 6,000 feet. Their relatives, the chimeras, are dominant fish at these depths. After 350 million years of evolution, it seems odd that sharks haven't developed the proper physiology for deep cruising.

Shallow-water types probably have a very different physiology, Clark explained. The shallow varieties store urea, a salt found in urine; the deep-water sharks apparently don't. If they have less urea, how do they get along?

"Storing urea is the regulatory mechanism for staying in osmotic balance with seawater," she added. "Urea is a salt and seawater contains salt. Could it be that deep-water sharks have lower urea content? We really don't know."

She told of using submersibles and baits to lure the deep-water creatures. Clark has made seventy submersible dives in recent years, using eight different vehicles. On one excursion, in the Russian MIR-1, she counted twenty-one sharks: "So many six-gills around that one swam into the mouth of another." A female wriggled out of a male's mouth with small scars on her head, proof that the male had chomped down on her. "They were both about twelve feet long, so it was quite a sight." Some of her colleagues suggested the two were engaged in a battle. "But the truth is there was good bait and good smells, and they had their mouths open, hoping they'd luck into a meal."

What Cousteau did for ocean science generally, Clark has done for sharks. What was once a realm of pure myth is now almost common knowledge. She dispelled the vision of sharks as insensate, reflexive eating machines. Under her tutelage the world came to known them as creatures of memory, individuality, and intelligence, and to acknowledge that these predators aren't as dangerous or malicious as people make them out to be. She blames her friend Peter Benchley for many lingering misconceptions. It was as if he reinvented "Frankenstein or Dracula—something to be fearful of," she said. "People always ask me what they should do if they see a shark. I say, 'If it's forty feet long with white spots (a whale shark) you hop on and take a ride!'"

She has done just that, and it was perhaps the wildest thing she'd ever done in the ocean.

"She was well over forty feet long. Once I got on her, I just couldn't let go. And I went far away from the photographers and the boat. The shark was cruising steadily at three knots, and after a while I thought to myself, 'Why am I still holding on to the shark, getting farther away from the boat?' Finally I let go. But I can tell you this: I did not ever want to let go."

Chapter Eight

MINDS AT SEA

*The immediate effect of Darwin on science
was one of magnificent release ...
The human mind leaped ahead.*
—*Paul B. Sears*

MARINE SCIENCE HAS ESSENTIALLY BEEN INVENTED in our century. A half-century ago, we knew virtually nothing about the sea floor, and what we did know amounted to semifiction. Darwin's *The Origin of Species*, published in 1859, was the first indicator of what was to come, not only in scientific perception but in the effect of ocean science on public awareness. The ailing ecologist dallied twenty-two years before publishing his work (the original title is itself a masterpiece of wordsmithery: *On the Origin of Species by Means of Natural Selection, or the Preservation of Favored Races in the Struggle for Life*—an impossible title in today's wash of political correctness). The reaction was immediate and sensational.

Darwin was at once the "Newton of biology" and "the man who banished God from the universe." The quantum leap from Darwin to late-twentieth-century science, particularly advances in genetics, has reshaped the concepts of natural selection. We seem to long for Darwin's older notions because we live in a world where artificial intelligence, behaviorists, and cloning leave us shaken, chilled by the unemotional calculus of our fragile being.

Big ideas did not die with Darwin. The twentieth century has given us remarkable insights and astonishing accomplishments. We have landed on the moon, made "one giant step for mankind." Thrilling, perhaps, but what it means ultimately has yet to be defined. At the very least the moon landing and certain other accomplishments in space connect us to a quest, to a search that we instinctively desire.

Like love, science offered up with true spirit may be one of life's most satisfying adventures, but also like love, adventures are meant to be shared. Yet in the field of ocean space the leading exponents are hardly generous.

The notion that life may have begun on the sea floor is exciting as evolution, and yet there is no buzz, no awe at the level of everyday perception. One wonders why did Darwin excite the world while today's scientists, with notable exceptions, seem on the surface to be so tame? Could it be that today's scientists disdain the utility of their pursuits? Do they fail to recognize that an ever-widening no-man's-land separates their work from the public?

Darwin's concept of evolution was hardly new. The Greek philosopher Heraclitus had suggested the notion of a constant growth and flux in his *De Rerum Natura*. More than twenty centuries later, Herbert Spencer published *Principles of Psychology*, a bold attempt to relate evolution to other areas of scientific thought. Yet it was Darwin, the sensitive boy who loathed academic dogma, and whose health was compromised during his fateful 1831 voyage on board the HMS *Beagle*, who understood the value of applying science to life, to humanity. Strange that the ecologist who might have been a doctor (had it not been for his fear of blood) had yet the courage of his intellect. Darwin, like Freud after him, understood that ideas are virtually invisible in a vacuum. Ideas need to be taken from the laboratory and aired in public.

The imperative to make knowledge public has rarely existed in the scientific sector, and by now we have seemingly split society into castes. There is "science" and there is the rest of us, whose duty it is to be humble, patient, and willing to pay the bills for research. This split, which has historical precedent, was exacerbated in the mid-1950s after the launch of the Russian *Sputnik* space satellite. American educators, faced with political pressure to correct what was perceived as an "engineering gap" between the United States and the Soviet Union, eagerly placed students into dichotomous categories: those who showed an aptitude for math and science, and the "others," derisively referred to as "sociology types." There was an ancillary movement within academe to fix an alleged "brain drain." This fix operated on the conceit that something like social engineering, a form of intellectual correctness, had to focus the attentions of the best students on science. As the "space race" heated up, the differentiation between the science/math/

engineering "nerds" and the "sociologists" was exacerbated by President John F. Kennedy's 1960 campaign tactics. A "missile gap" between the nations threatened America's security, Kennedy warned. Soon the Soviets would have weapons on the moon and in Earth orbit. As the space race picked up energy, the strategic objectives of the Apollo moon landing program were blurred by a kind of public-spirited Machiavellism: We weren't venturing into space necessarily to gain military advantage, Kennedy argued, but rather because our noble instincts demanded that we spend more than $30 billion to collect moon rocks.

This was an ironic twist of history. President Dwight D. Eisenhower, a republican and the former Allied commander during World War II, warned in the 1950s of the economic and social dangers inherent in the creation of a "military-industrial complex." Once in office in the 1960s, the liberal Democrat Kennedy opted to spend more than $30 billion dollars to land a man on the moon and built the very military-industrial complex that has perplexed us ever since, with its $600 dollar screwdrivers and $1,200 toilet seats.

The so-called race to the moon served further to widen the gulf growing up between scientists and technocrats and the rest of us. Reasonable scientists and military leaders have argued that, after all, in war it is easier to launch weapons from the Earth; positioning lasers in orbit is impractical, and more impractical still is the exercise of building launch platforms on the moon to fire nuclear weapons over one-quarter million miles back to precise targets on Earth. Such arguments were dismissed by much of the scientific community, which had gained leverage to exercise the powers they had gained earlier in the 1940s Manhattan Project, our first all-out weapons race, in which the United States produced the atomic bomb. National security and Kennedy's moon mania elevated science to the level of morality as the drift of science away from the public continued unabated.

In the era of the 1960s, ocean science benefited from the space race. It was all the rage to build "innerspace ships," Nemoesque submersibles capable of transporting large crews of scientists over hundreds of miles of ocean bottom. The brief rise and and precipitous fall of this so-called "wet NASA" left ocean science in the shadows, a stepchild of space exploration.

Today's space program has given us something new: the possibility of seas on distant planets, and with the suggestion of a sea comes the more profound implication of extraterrestrial life. Thus, we have "astrobiology," an emerging concept that uses the discoveries of ocean-ography and ocean-borne technology to gain funding for the National Aeronautics and Space Administration (NASA) projects. And while ocean science has yet to learn the cash value of public relations, NASA is well seasoned in the art of sparking the imagination and budget building. Astrobiology, which so far has found zero life and which is almost entirely dependent on theories focused around earthly hydro-thermal volcanism, has cleverly managed to capture headlines. *The Washington Post* has exclaimed over the "search for alien slime" and the "evolving respectability" of astrobiology. Yet science writer Joel Achenbach wondered if "this is a bold new science of the 21st century or just a passing fad." His hope was that NASA's newest baby isn't just another "flavor of the month."

Unlike the space spin-off of the 1960s, ocean science has yet to benefit from any of this otherworldly speculation. If anything, it has been overshadowed and the communications gap has widened as ocean-ographers withdraw even further, with good cause: They fear a NASA funding coup. Oceanographers have reason to be skeptical when a savvy columnist such as Charles Krauthammer is convinced we must again fire up the Apollo program and send astronauts to the moon prospect-ing for water. "Life, not fossil but real, possibly just two planets away," he enthused in a March 1998 column. "With findings like these, we must go back: to the moon to see if it can sustain a human colony, and to Europa, with probes onto and below the surface [of its alleged sea] to see what lives." The lunar water is merely a dusting of ice, perhaps the residue of comets, spread over many sunless craters at the North and South Poles. There is no proof whatsoever that Jupiter's moon, Europa, actually has a sea.

The possibilities are exciting, but the real challenge is here on Earth, in our seas, where new species are waiting to be discovered at sub-merged hydrothermal vents. Here at home lies the answer to the origin-of-life enigma. How tragic it is to witness oceanography pushed further into the background as NASA again grabs the spotlight. Ocean scien-tists need to come out of the shadows; they need to assert themselves and connect to the larger public.

Not long ago I had a conversation with Tom Smith, a consulting biologist at the Environmental Protection Agency. A tall, gangly young man with a thin beard and the sweet face of an all-forgiving cleric, Smith appeared dismayed by the lack of interaction between entire

A vision of a brave new world of ocean exploration, perhaps in some distant planetary sea. *Drawing courtesy National Oceanic and Atmospheric Administration.*

fields within the scientific community and the public. Yet he did not believe his colleagues were to blame. "The media," he said, had failed to acquaint us with the eloquence of "the scientific method." One begins with a hypothesis and proceeds outward to proof. If we understood how exacting is the process, how self-critical, we would have a better appreciation of science and its superiority to other forms of knowledge seeking, Smith insisted; indeed, we would at last grasp the idea of immutable "truth."

I prodded him. What is truth? Is it necessarily the by-product of the scientific method?

"Oh, definitely," he replied.

I suggested that throughout history much scientific "truth" has been rejected for subsequent truths. Discovery is an ongoing wrecking ball, and what it wrecks are transient facts. The ancient Greeks believed the night sky was formed by an opaque doom with holes punched in it, a vast cosmic fire raged unabated on the other side, and the glimmerings humans saw at night were glimpses of that fire through the holes. Isn't it likely that scientists in another millennium will view today's vision of the cosmos with equal amusement? Isn't it likely the images recorded by today's space-borne telescopes will be construed and misconstrued countless times?

"It's possible," Smith said. "What's important is the search."

Yes, the search, the heart of the matter. In a perfect world ideas drive research; in our world, however, funding is the engine, and funding relies heavily on public encouragement.

Yet the insularity of the field is legendary. Speaking at a symposium to honor the fiftieth anniversary of Woods Hole Oceanographic Institution, James J. Childress, a biologist at the University of California at Santa Barbara, lashed out at marine science as a closed circuit—removed not only from the public but isolated within its own ranks. His paper, "Oceanic Biology: Lost in Space," presented in 1980, went to the core of science as exotica; viewed through the lens of NASA's hyped-up astrobiology, it seems prescient.

"Even within ocean biology one finds intellectual constructs which are profoundly limiting to oceanic studies," he wrote.

As to the rich potential of deep-ocean biology, Childress complained that it has become a "backwater," in which the practitioners often seem unaware of exciting potentials. "I believe that the field and its workers, by and large, lack a vision of oceanic biology." This has led to stagnation, "a stagnation often cultivated by the major oceanographic institutions. In short, we have a field which is ... 'lost in space.'"

The oceanographic institutions dominate the field in major ways. And in this lies a dangerous, self-defeating temptation. There is an inclination for these institutional powers, organizations such as Woods Hole and Scripps, to seek their own goals of growth and economic security. Self-preservation is natural enough, but it may come at the expense of the rest of the ocean science community. Childress says giving in to these temptations is a terrible blow, since much of the creative force in the field comes from its periphery, individuals trained outside oceanography but who are drawn to oceanic science.

"The health of biological oceanography depends upon increasing the access of those outside the core," Childress insists.

Now, nearly two decades after his pointed attack, little has changed. The field remains dominated by competitive individuals who seldom speak to each other and even less frequently to the larger public, which must find reasons to sponsor exploration. It is nonsense to argue that most of what we know about the sea has already been discovered; this is popular myth, compounded tenfold by the mystification that seems to give ocean science a shield against what it perceives to be an indifferent (perhaps hostile) public.

Oceanographers appear to share the notion that science is under attack by what Dr. Jerold M. Lowenstein, a professor of medicine at the University of California at San Francisco, calls "postmodernist sociologists." Lowenstein perceives a growing antagonism of "some left-wing intellectuals to science," even while "political progressives" have usually been allies in the struggle against mysticism, superstition, and "the dead weight of religious and social dogma." The reaction against science, he continues, has much to do with postmodernist resentment of the prestige science now enjoys in society and within universities. What it really comes down to is a squabble over money, with Lowenstein struggling against what he believes to be a siphoning off of funds by the humanities. Yet Lowenstein has skewed history. Art and the humanities have almost always been the children of charity, and a reactionary wildfire has been blazing in the political arena to cut support for the various public endowments for the arts. During the past two decades, the "sociologists" have been waging a losing battle against a political scorched-earth policy.

Still, Lowenstein's view is high currency in academic/scientific circles.

"The antics of the postmodernists would be funny, except for the reality that they have taken over many of the major university departments of English, sociology, social anthropology, and cultural studies," he declares. "Their absurdities have had little or no effect on science departments, which are mostly unaware of their existence."

It is certainly true that the humanities compete with science for funding, and while monies at the federal level for science are in the multibillion-dollar range, Lowenstein's argument does not take into account the shrinking enrollments among future "sociologists," the demeaning catchall term he uses to lump together the arts.

The struggle at universities is waged across economic lines. During the height of funding for science in this century there was little angst about liberal arts; students were encouraged to seek classical humanist training. At the end of the century, however, funds for marine research are dwindling even as the number of trained practitioners grows exponentially. Scientists now guard their backs against perceived enemies in their own camp, competition is fierce, and the focus is placed on narrow focus and quick results. Any diversion from verticalism makes the competitors very uneasy.

Could it be that science is in need of some broader, civilizing culture? I have in amazement listened to respected researchers speculate about a time in the not-so-distant future when science will become increasingly separate from the lay public until ultimately it is "deculturated," voluntarily sequestered in windowless computer colonies fighting each other with equations and jargoned invectives. This may be today's science fiction, yet seen in a broader context it takes on the sonorous tone of prophecy.

It is notable that most of what the public knows and appreciates in the field of marine science has been offered up by the "popularizers," who have managed to bring the laboratory to the light. Certainly not all are scientists, yet often the dividing line is vague. Hans Hass and Cousteau are laymen who gave science a chance to speak to a wider universe. And there are a select few scientists—Sagan, Ballard, Throck-morton, Jastrow—with a need to connect, to share important visions. They have escaped at midnight beyond the ivy tower to chip away at the walls of academe; they have worked to demystify science, and they understand that shared discoveries connect us to the larger quest to understand the universe.

Demystification is a pathway to knowledge and acceptance, and it shapes in many ways how we choose to manage resources and cope with environmental challenges. And at the end of the century, some very critical and practical challenges remain.

One of the more far-reaching is the proposal to dispose of radio-active wastes in the seabed, an idea with serious sociopolitical conse-quences. The legacy of bungled experiments and contamination left behind by the French Centre d'Experimentations du Pacifique intensified the ongoing debate over how to dispose of millions of tons of materials so deadly, so potentially destructive, that a false move may skew the evolution of the planet. Yet this problem has for the most part remained obscured from public view, stuffed into a gloomy Pandora's box and hidden by bureaucrats, academics, and environmentalists.

By late 1996, the White House had fashioned what one political insider described as a "necessary deal": an off-the-record offer to France, Russia, China, and Great Britain to purchase millions of tons of nuclear and chemical wastes and dispose of them in terrestrial sites. The pro-posal is at bottom designed to keep plutonium and other weapons-grade materials out of the hands of rogue nations.

My science advisor, the late Ned Ostenso, former chief scientist of NOAA and previously Sea Grant director, was horrified by the con-cept of terrestrial disposal, since it threatens to contaminate our infini-tesimal store of potable groundwater.

How much waste is out there? The numbers are sobering. At Oak Ridge National Laboratory alone there are 170.2 metric tons of uranium-

235 and 3.1 metric tons of low-enriched uranium. Contamination problems abound.

Virtually all U.S. weapons plants contain high levels of contaminating waste, and it costs $5.5 billion annually to handle ongoing cleanups (the largest cleanup in history) and $400 million a year to prepare terrestrial disposal sites.

"We're spinning out of control," Ostenso told me. "The recent French tests have resurfaced scientists' concern over the global load of nuclear contaminants. Even more salient is the looming mandate to shape some 'final solution' for the storage of existing stockpiles and munitions."

Ostenso and other scientists postulated the notion of using the deep sea as a nuclear repository. They did not seek to blindly dump wastes in the ocean; on the contrary, they merely wished to *study* the idea, believing nuclear material should be kept out of the sea until scientists were certain it was safe to proceed with subsea burial.

The lessons learned from the French, Ostenso believed, illuminated the degree to which the United States and other nations are being hobbled in their wish to study the problem. International treaties and domestic laws against dumping have declared that even a study of seabed disposal cannot be undertaken. The effect of various international treaties extends to the point of thwarting all research into the desirability of ocean, sea floor, or Antarctic ice cap disposal options, thus dooming us to what Ostenso called an "intellectually bankrupt public policy."

"This misguided environmental protectionism has a 'through the looking glass' effect of putting at risk what is most precious, our population and essential groundwater," Ostenso complained. And precious it is. It is estimated that a mere .01 percent of the Earth's water is available for human consumption; the rest is locked up in seas and oceans, polluted streams and rivers, and other contaminated sources.

Yet the gap between science and public awareness has kept this crucial issue almost entirely in the dark. The seabed burial option seldom surfaces into the public domain where it belongs, and instead has remained confined to the scientific establishment. The issue was, and remains, tied in a Gordian knot. Scientists and environmentalists rage among themselves and do little to reach beyond the confines of their disciplines. There are some glimmers of outreach, but not nearly enough to satisfy the public's need to know. The federal establishment, too, has exacerbated the problem. Bureaucrats have spread a curtain of silence and obscurity in an area already dimmed by self-serving politics.

Proposals to study seabed burial options were short-circuited in 1986 when the Department of Energy (DOE) settled on Yucca Mountain, Nevada, as a primary disposal site. DOE spent more than $2 billion to excavate the site, but has yet to demonstrate its geologic soundness. The mountain is close to active seismic faults and a potentially active volcano. Concern exists that groundwater may seep into the repository, which amounts to nothing more than a huge, stony cavern; if this happens, radioactivity will escape and further contaminate an already glowing aquifer beneath the site. It's interesting to speculate on the numbers of citizens who may or may not know anything at all about this disaster in the making.

Congress for its part has played the "great stone face." Congressman Frank Palone, a Democrat from New Jersey, has called for legislation to ban the study of the seabed burial option, claiming it amounts to another form of "dumping." It seems not to have worried his sense of public service that banning study is like burning books!

"The congressman opposes dumping—period!" I was informed by his environmental assistant, Rick Kessler. Asked if he really equated burial with ocean dumping (they are radically different procedures), Kessler replied, "Yes, definitely." He cited America's participation in the London Convention, which outlaws dumping. "Studying this burial idea with federal money is irresponsible," he snapped. "We need to use precious dollars to study health care, social needs ..."

Indeed, health care and social needs are pressing, and this in itself reveals a strange irony in Palone's logic. Focusing on the overall good health of humankind, threatened as it now is by our broadcasting of radioactive waste, it seems ludicrous to legislate off the table the discussion of an issue so critical to global well-being.

Charles D. Hollister, an oceanographer/sedimentologist and vice president of Woods Hole Oceanographic Institution, took the lead in this area in 1973 and subsequently rallied an international team, which attempted to demonstrate the feasibility of isolating high-level radioactive material in the clay sediments below the sea floor. The concept has since been pursued by eight countries as the only other viable option to land burial.

I visited Hollister at his offices in Cape Cod to discuss the ongoing debate. A political and scientific pro, Hollister is an affable man with a kind of Hemingwayesque bluffness, intense eyes, and the insistent handshake that radiates the comfortable vibrations of a professional fund-raiser.

Hollister is quick to admit that the politics of seabed disposal are off-putting, that he's not entirely comfortable fencing with the bureaucrats. "But I know mud," he grinned. "Ask me anything about mud." And it is mud, hundreds of thousands of square miles of it in the North Pacific, that appears to be a stable burial ground. How stable is this area, I wondered?

"There is an unambiguous geological record of total boredom," he replied. "Not a thing has happened there geologically—ever. And I propose that for the next million years nothing much is going to change. Twenty meters down is about as old as the time of the last days of the dinosaurs. And if you go deeper, say a hundred feet or so, you can see that even when the landmasses were formative this mud was very quiet."

He described the mud as "gooey, like Godiva chocolate that's been sitting in the backseat of a car in Manhattan all summer long." The stuff is ultrafine, amazingly clingy, absorbent, and it has a tenacious desire to trap and hold metals such as plutonium. "Given the wasteland nature of the area," he went on, "given that individual grains of this mud are finer than one-millionth of a millimeter, it's the most useless piece of real estate on the planet, devoid of oil or natural gas, and home to very few living organisms. So we're not talking about tampering with environmental riches, just mile after mile of silly putty."

Hollister has fired projectiles into the mud; it appears to swallow them whole, closing behind them like a sticky trapdoor. It's unlikely that "hot materials" would escape, even after thousands of years. Plutonium, the heaviest known substance, would merely sink deeper into the mud.

The technology to bury and recover bullet-shaped canisters of waste already exists. Hollister said seabed geology and the technology needed to monitor burial have been in place for decades. "We can plant the stuff and we can monitor it, and if we need to we can bring it back."

The burial couldn't be more simple. Canisters would be dropped off the fantail of a ship, free-fall through miles of water, hit the mud at fifty miles per hour, and sink into about 100 feet of gooey, clingy mud.

Hollister and other scientists have postulated a study of the Yankee-II Russian ballistic submarine, which in 1986 sank 500 miles east of Bermuda, on the Sohm Abyssal Plain. This cold war disaster provides an opportunity for unambiguous study. The submarine was loaded with two fully fueled nuclear reactors, two nuclear torpedoes, and thirty-two nuclear warheads mounted on sixteen "Serb" missiles.

"We have reason to believe that maybe 100 kilograms or more of weapons-grade plutonium and other radio nuclides were scattered on the bottom," Hollister explained. "This single accident represents the greatest concentration of weapons-grade plutonium exposed to the marine environment. Can we learn anything? Could we validate or refute the ocean option?" He paused to allow the idea to form itself, to take on a what's-to-lose complexion. "I think the answer is clear," he went on. "A careful study of the 'Yankee experiment' would allow for the first time a field verification of the concentration-dispersion pathway models."

This makes good sense, and given the proliferation of deadly wastes, a study appears altogether appropriate. Yet science's cloak of silence, coupled with obfuscation on the political front, has kept the issue hidden from public view.

The rate and concentration of plutonium dispersion through the food chain due to accidental release has been a key uncertainty for all ocean options. Hollister and others have faith that moving forward with the "Yankee experiment" may answer the question unambiguously once and for all.

"The question I'd like to see answered is, 'What happens to plutonium from the nuclear reactor and weapons? Does it get into the food chain or has it stayed put, as we think it should?'"

Hollister's plans remain stuck for money and chained by treaties. It might take $1 million to carry out the "Yankee experiment," but the money will not be forthcoming until the issue is brought to light before the public. The issue has run its course in political and scientific journals and has been turned into jargon at the governmental level, but it remains for the scientists to step forward, to bridge the gap between the laboratory and the rest of us. Until that is done, this most critical challenge will remain unresolved.

Other environmental issues remain hidden. The Sloan Foundation has funded a cataloging of the stars and has considered doing the same for the sea: a census of the water column. How many fishes are in the sea? How many species? And what of the untold numbers of microscopic creatures, and the biota of the hydrothermal vent communities? It may be unrealistic to sample the entire ocean, but the idea is under discussion by a group led by biologist Fred Grassle. The question is how to begin modestly and fashion models sufficiently elegant to reflect the whole. Will this idea gain support? Will the biologists reach over the communications chasm to ignite public interest? It seems unlikely.

We have come to the end of the twentieth century with many basic questions unanswered. Modern ocean science is less than a century old, but space science is far more youthful, and we know more about the moon and Mars than the bottom of the sea, and for good reason. NASA has moved aggressively to capture support. If its bureaucrats know little of actual science, they are expert in hyping the agency's interests.

A survey conducted in late 1996 revealed that nearly 81 percent of U.S. citizens believe the oceans are threatened by human activity. Overfishing, destruction of coastal habitats, rampant development, and pollution ranked high on the list of acknowledged threats. Nearly half of those polled say the oceans are "important" to them personally, and nearly 70 percent of those in coastal communities agreed.

The survey was based on the responses of 1,300 adults nationwide and was commissioned by Seaweb, a multimedia organization that seeks to focus attention on environmental protection. It was found that NOAA, once an obscure agency, is now viewed as an important and trusted public utility. All this is encouraging, and NOAA struggles hard to make an impact with its public outreach programs. Unfortunately, politics have squeezed funding and made the agency's job more difficult, exacerbating the stoicism of the science establishment.

Barbara Moore, NOAA's director of National Undersea Research, was a bit melancholy when I called to discuss the problem of excess data and minimal sense being made of it, both as public information and as raw material for conservation and other programs.

"Right now, it's our biggest problem," she sighed. "We're trying to convince our scientists to analyze their information so we can use it on the outside. All this data isn't helping anyone if it piles up with no particular purpose. It's just data with no place to go."

NOAA has restructured its undersea research program with an eye to greater dissemination of information. A scientific writer has been added to the staff so that public interest details can be gleaned from the often esoteric scientific papers generated by the program. The idea, according to Moore, is to encourage what she calls a "new variety" of scientists whose mission it is to interpret scientific findings in lay terms.

"We've been hit on the head by people responsible for making decisions," Moore told me. "There's this huge information gap. Managers, the people who put together federal programs, need more general input. They need to fill the gap."

The increasing need is for a synthesis of studies, to bridge the gap and bring raw data into forms that are useful. NOAA has been fighting this battle for years, though Moore believes there's been a slow moderation of the lack of connection among ocean scientists, the public, and other sciences.

"We struggle to take data from principal investigators and make it understandable," Moore says. "It's a survival sort of thing. The scientists have to supply the kind of stuff a technical manager can use."

In the century ahead, a new breed of humanist-scientists may evolve, scientists who are not deculturated, who understand that truth is an ongoing, inclusive process. The "lab rat" needs to become the renaissance keeper of the flame. It is well and good to know everything there is to know about clams, sea mounts, vent organisms, and benthic populations; it is useful to grasp the technology, the new physics of the ocean. Yet if this knowledge stands alone, apart from the larger culture and the larger needs of humankind, it is reduced to curiosities poured over by isolated individuals.

Moore says there is a pressing need for synthesizing studies; they need to add up to something the rest of us can appreciate—a kind of "Ah-hah! Factor."

The sea remains a final frontier. Certainly it is no more predictable than our solar system. We have discovered more in the past quarter-century than in all human history. What was compelling at the beginning of our century, the challenge of the unknown, remains the outstanding challenge of the future. It may be argued that a continual mapping of the ocean's seabed is, in Moore's view, "mundane." To simply explore, to invite serendipity, remains the great magnet.

Contemporary marine scientists agree there will never be enough money to fund all that needs doing, which is one reason to define missions and goals more precisely, and to bring the action into the open. Where does serendipity fit into a more definitive undertaking? Moore believes it should be included in virtually all field research as

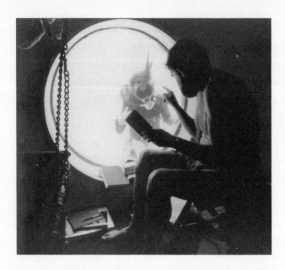

Ocean scientists communicate with each other through Hydro-Lab's view port. Now it's time to communicate to the rest of us. *Photo courtesy National Oceanic and Atmospheric Administration.*

some fraction of the whole. She points out that Americans have visited the Challenger Deep only once, that most of the sea floor is unknown, that satellite technology has given us a surprising new image of the Pacific, beneath which there are 25,000 sea mounts we did not know existed, many of them putatively covered with cobalt crusts. Major geologic features exist, but we have no idea what they look like or how they affect life in the world of sun and sky. It is stunning to realize that a quarter-century ago we had only the vaguest notions of the Mid-Ocean Ridge, the largest chain of mountains on Earth, and even now we are just beginning to comprehend how these features have shaped the planet.

"We can't guarantee a human use for pure exploration," Moore said. "But so much happens by sheer accident. Columbus was looking for a route to the East Indies. Think about it. What I mean is the human benefit can't always be known in advance, which is one justification for pure research. Things just happen! And when they do, we'll find uses we can't predict."

The shape of ocean exploration in the new century will come at the hands of a new force of scientific libertarians. They will storm the academy, raid the laboratories, reinvent protocol. Imagine enlarging the concept of science to incorporate the spirit Walt Whitman expressed in his poetry. The ideal of a humanist/pragmatist science is to discard the concept of status and move forward on the assumption that a populous in touch with the possibilities of science as a social reality will reward its practitioners with a shockproof faith and tenacity. It will be a triumph of sharing over exclusivity.

Science, like art, literature, and education, grows in the light of common experience and can be tested by it. If ocean science is to move forward, it must embrace pragmatic ends. Knowledge standing alone is knowledge in a void. We are speaking here of the largest features of our planet. They cannot be isolated or shrouded in academic robes.

And what might the guiding spirit of this enterprise be? I might start with the words of Confucius: "The Earth, the Universe, belongs to everyone."

BIBLIOGRAPHY

Attenborough, David. *Life on Earth.* Boston: Little, Brown, 1979.

Baldridge, David H. *Shark Attack.* New York: Berkley Publishing, 1974.

Balon, Eugene K. *The Life and Work of Eugenie Clark.* Netherlands: Kluwer Academic Publishers, 1994.

Bass, George F. *Archaeology Under Water.* Middlesex, England: Penguin Books, 1970.

Brewer, Peter G., ed. *Oceanography: The Present and Future.* New York: Springer-Verlag, 1983.

Brown, Theo W. *Sharks.* Boston: Little, Brown, 1973.

Carson, Rachel L. *The Sea Around Us.* New York: New American Library, 1950.

Clark, Eugenie. *The Lady and the Sharks.* New York: Harper & Row, 1969.

———. *Lady with a Spear.* New York: Harper & Brothers, 1953.

Clarke, Arthur C. *The Treasure of the Great Reef.* New York: Ballantine Books, 1974.

Cousteau, J. Y. (with Philippe Cousteau). *The Shark: Splendid Savage of the Sea.* New York: Doubleday, 1970.

Cousteau, J. Y. (with Philippe Diole). *Life and Death in a Coral Sea.* New York: Doubleday, 1971.

Cousteau, J. Y. (with James Dugan). *The Living Sea.* New York: Harper & Row, 1963.

Cousteau, J. Y. (with Frederic Dumas). *The Silent World.* New York: Harper & Row, 1953.

Cropp, Ben. *Shark Hunters.* New York: Macmillian, 1971.

Cross, Wilbur. *Challengers of the Deep.* New York: William Sloane Associates, 1959.

Deacon, Margaret. *Scientists and the Sea: 1650–1900.* London: Academic Press, 1971.

Dinsdale, Tim. *Monster Hunt.* Washington, D.C.: Acropolis Books, 1972.

Earle, Sylvia A. *Sea Change.* New York: G.P. Putnam's Sons, 1995.

Gaskell, T. F. *The Gulf Stream.* New York: New American Library, 1974.

Grissim, John. *The Lost Treasure of the Concepcion.* New York: William Morrow, 1980.

Hass, Hans. *Challenging the Deep.* New York: William Morrow, 1973.

Hickling, C. F., and Peter Lancaster Brown. *The Seas and the Oceans.* New York: Macmillan, 1973.

Horgan, John. *The End of Science.* Reading, Mass.: Addison-Wesley, 1996.

Lyon, Eugene. *The Search for the Atocha.* New York: Harper & Row, 1979.

Mader, Sylvia S. *Inquiry into Life.* Dubuque, Iowa: Wm. C. Brown Publishers, 1979.

Malinowski, Bronislaw. *The Sexual Life of Savages.* Boston: Beacon Press, 1987.

Marx, Robert F. *Shipwrecks in the Americas.* New York: Bonanza Books, 1983.

———. *The Underwater Dig.* New York: Henry Z. Walck, 1975.

Matthews, William H., III. *Fossils.* New York: Barnes & Noble Books, 1962.

Menard, H. W. *Islands.* New York: Scientific American Library, 1986.

Perry, John H., Jr. *Never Say Impossible: The Life and Times of an American Entrepreneur.* Charlottesville, Va.: Thomasson-Grant, 1996.

Ross, David A. *Introduction to Oceanography.* Englewood Cliffs, N.J.: Prentice-Hall, 1982.

———. *Opportunities and Uses of the Ocean.* New York: Springer-Verlag, 1980.

Schmieder, Robert W. *Ecology of an Underwater Island.* San Francisco: Cordell Expeditions, 1990.

Stanley, David. *Tahiti-Polynesia Handbook.* Chico, Calif.: Moon Publications, 1992.

Theis, O. F., trans. *Noa Noa: The Tahiti Journal of Paul Gauguin.* San Francisco: Chronicle Books, 1994.

Trupp, Philip Z. *Diver's Almanac.* Palo Verdes, Calif.: Triton Publishing, 1991.

———. *Tracking Treasure.* Washington, D.C.: Acropolis Books, 1986.

Untermeyer, Louis. *Makers of the Modern World.* New York: Simon & Schuster, 1955.

Van Dover, Cindy Lee. *The Octopus's Garden.* Reading, Mass.: Addison-Wesley, 1996.

Watson, Paul. *Ocean Warrior.* Toronto, Canada: Key Porter Books, 1994.

Weinberg, Steven. *Dreams of a Final Theory.* New York: Pantheon Books, 1992.

Weisgall, Jonathan M. *Operation Crossroads: "The Atomic Tests at Bikini Atoll."* Annapolis, Md.: Naval Institute Press, 1994.

Wertenbaker, William. *The Floor of the Sea.* Boston: Little, Brown, 1974.

INDEX

Note: Italicized page numbers indicate pictures.

ABOUT THE AUTHOR

Phil Trupp uses writing as "wings" to travel the world. He is the author of more than a dozen books, a published poet, and a contributor to major magazines and journals, including *Smithsonian* and *Caribbean Travel & Life*. As the first writer to head a Hydro-Lab mission, Trupp earned the title of NOAA aquanaut. He was among the first journalists reporting from Castro's Cuba and is a Fellow of the Explorers Club. An avid creative nonfictionist, he pursues "the liberation of all things journalistic." His writings range from exploration to music and the arts.